THE
SURVIVORS

THE
SURVIVORS

*A Story of War,
Inheritance, and Healing*

ADAM P.
FRANKEL

HARPER

An Imprint of HarperCollins*Publishers*

HarperCollins books may be purchased for educational, business, or sales promotional use. For information, please email the Special Markets Department at SPsales@harpercollins.com.

FIRST EDITION

Library of Congress Cataloging-in-Publication Data has been applied for.

ISBN 978-0-06-225858-8

19 20 21 22 23   LSC   10 9 8 7 6 5 4 3 2 1

For Soraya and Gabriel

We shall not cease from exploration
And the end of all our exploring
Will be to arrive where we started
And know the place for the first time.

—T. S. ELIOT, *Little Gidding*

AUTHOR'S NOTE

IN KEEPING WITH some of the larger themes in this book—honesty and transparency—I had hoped to use the true names of all the people who play a central role. But, due to the sensitive nature of this story, certain names and details have been changed. I've also modified the spelling of some European family and place names for readability and consistency.

CONTENTS

PART II: INHERITANCE

PART III: HEALING

THIS IS NOT the book I intended to write.

When I left the White House as a speechwriter late in Barack Obama's first term, I wanted to write a book about my mom's parents, Bubbie and Zayde, and my dad's parents, Grandma and Pa.

Bubbie and Zayde were Holocaust survivors, and Pa was a Northwestern student peace activist before serving as a platoon leader in the South Pacific. I'd been inspired by their stories growing up, and I thought others might be, too.

I also thought their stories were important to tell, particularly as fewer members of their generation are alive to share them themselves. Over dinner a few years ago, a German consular official told me it was getting harder to teach young people about the Holocaust because the most compelling instructors—survivors—are all passing away.

A 2018 poll revealed the danger of letting that generation's stories die with them: two-thirds of millennials in the United States could not identify what Auschwitz was, and 22 percent said they hadn't heard of the Holocaust or weren't sure if they'd heard of it. So I started writing this book as a way of keeping that history alive.

I also had another, much more intimate story to tell—about the ways the trauma of the Holocaust has reverberated through the generations of my family. At the time, however, I could not tell that story because I was still living it. And for many years, I wasn't ready—psychologically or emotionally—to tell it. Now, I am.

This book, then, is not only about the Holocaust, not only about

World War II. It's about the lasting scars of that cataclysm. Not only about the past, but about how that past has stayed with us. Not only about the trauma someone, somewhere in our family may have experienced, but about the ways that trauma can continue to play itself out, from one generation to the next. Part I tells the story of my grandparents' experiences during the Holocaust, and parts II and III explore the ways their trauma inflicted pain in my mother's life and, later, my own.

Of course, the traumas that are handed down to us can take different forms. Some of us may be grappling with the cruelty of mental illness or invisible war wounds. Others may be battling the legacy of alcoholism, addiction, abuse, gun violence, racism, or some other scourge.

And yet while the nature of our families' traumas may vary, each of us has in a sense the same choice to make. We can turn away from what we've inherited—in some cases an understandable, perhaps even wise decision. Or we can confront it, in the hopes of conquering that trauma—or at least moving on. That is what I've tried to do, and this book is, in part, about how I've tried to do it.

—Adam P. Frankel
New York City, 2019

THE
SURVIVORS

"FORGIVE HER," MY grandfather told me.

It was just the two of us, sitting across from each other in a booth at Athenian Diner III, a 1950s–style Greek diner on the Boston Post Road; his favorite lunch spot, where he'd always take me on my visits to Connecticut.

The woman he was asking me, *pleading* with me, to forgive was his daughter—my mother. Zayde didn't know what she had done. My mother hadn't told him, and I wouldn't say. I couldn't bring myself to tell him.

But he was uncannily observant, and sensed she'd done something to hurt me, committed some injury I was unable to move beyond.

None of his children were so keenly aware. None, such astute readers of people and situations. Not my uncle. Not my two aunts. They didn't ask why there had been a rupture, instead scolding me for what they saw as my inexplicably cruel treatment of my mother.

Sometimes, I felt like I could hardly blame them. Mom herself not only tolerated the scorn they showed me, the withering judgment, she often seemed to encourage it, portraying herself as an innocent victim of her son's slights, even as she knew they didn't have all the facts.

I looked at my grandfather, the light beating against him, his mushroom omelet half eaten on his plate, the intensity of his stare making his words seem less a request than a command.

I said nothing, and the silence stretched on. One second. Two seconds. Three seconds.

What could I possibly say to this man, who had nearly lost his entire family in the Holocaust, who had been separated from his mother in a concentration camp and never seen her again?

I also wondered: Was the trauma that he and Bubbie endured all those years ago at the root of everything? Had it in some way contributed to the troubles that had plagued my mother all her life? Somehow created the circumstances that were wreaking such havoc in *my* life?

"Whatever she did," he repeated, "forgive her."

PART I

WAR

If we have our own *why* of life,
we shall get along with almost any *how*.

—FRIEDRICH NIETZSCHE, *Twilight of the Idols*

I

The Jewel

Zayde repairing a watch at his bench.

IN THE WINTER of 2012, I received a call from my mother, saying my grandfather needed surgery.

One year earlier, he had fallen on an uneven sidewalk in New Haven. He'd taken quite a spill, and some passersby had called an ambulance. The paramedics insisted on taking my grandfather to the hospital, but he protested. "I'm fine," Zayde said, blood dripping from his forehead. Only after he signed a waiver did they finally let him go.

When news of the fall spread in our family, everyone urged him to see a doctor. "Get checked out," we said. "Make sure nothing is broken." But Abraham Perecman is a stubborn man, and there was nothing we could do.

Not a word was spoken about the incident, not even a whisper of complaint from the man himself, until this call from my mother one year later. Apparently, when my grandfather fell, he had fractured one of the uppermost vertebrae in the neck, the C2. And the break had begun healing awkwardly, putting pressure on his nerves.

Family began to notice him shuffling his feet. Less visible, but more worrisome to Zayde, was the loss of feeling in his fingers. The possibility of being unable to repair watches was unthinkable.

Watches are the man's life, and repairing them, his livelihood. His little shop, Perecman Jewelers, occupies 896½ Whalley Avenue, beneath the shadow of West Rock, a rusty peak overlooking the city. From the outside, The Store, as everyone in the family calls it, looks every one of its nearly sixty years, declaring the name of its proprietor in fat neon tubes. The P stopped working years ago; the E-R-E emit only a dull glow.

"We buy and sell gold and silver," reads a hand-drawn sign in the window, a pull for the occasional walk-in. The avenue's namesake, seventeenth-century English judge Edward Whalley, was a signatory to Charles I's death warrant before fleeing to the New World, the first—but not last—refugee to settle in the neighborhood.

The entire store is a single aisle, ten paces long with a dropped ceiling overhead, brown linoleum tiles underfoot, and a musty smell hanging in the air. On the left are waist-high glass showcases, their tops bare except for a twirling hand-held mirror, a cardboard coin folder for a children's leukemia charity, and a rotating plastic dispenser of Twist-O-Flex watchbands.

Inside the showcases are timepieces, jewelry, and miscellaneous accessories: wristwatches, pocket watches, travel clocks, bracelets, necklaces, brooches, key chains, rings, earrings. Toward the back, where the showcase on the left meets another, straight ahead— forming an inverted L—is a workman's table, a "bench," as it is called in the trade. That's where Zayde himself can be found, hunching over shallow turquoise saucers, brimming with gears, springs, and screws, arranged on a thin sheet of paper.

He is a fixture in the neighborhood, regarded by New Haven's scrappy strivers as one of their own. Once, many years ago, one of my aunts confessed to a customer—a large man in a leather jacket—that she accompanied her father to The Store every day to make sure nothing happened, to protect him.

"Don't worry," replied the man. "We look out for him. Nothing's going to happen to the Jewel."

That might explain why, in all the decades he has been there—decades when violence in New Haven made national headlines—The Store was robbed only once.

In one corner of Zayde's bench is a strange-looking metal contraption: a lathe, used to fabricate watch parts that are now easily ordered online.

"Do you use that anymore?" I ask.

"No," he says.

A glass dish holds watch parts. "What are those?"

"Junk," he replies, squinting one eye around his loupe, his nose barely an inch from the watch he is fixing.

The smallness of the parts accentuates his oversize hands, like those of Michelangelo's David. Rough, callused hands, fingers angling out in odd, unnatural directions. Hands that have toiled, lifted, hauled, and hammered, that bear the scars, the discolorations, the creases of a life of manual labor. Not, in other words, the hands of a watchmaker.

The hands are one of the signs—some subtle, some plain to see—that the man in the shop has a story to tell. The accent is another—some indistinguishable mix of Yiddish, Hebrew, Polish, German, and Russian, all of which he speaks.

And so is the sigh. It comes without warning—long, guttural, melodic, like a verse from some ancient Hebrew blessing. It suggests a sadness otherwise undetectable in the man's disposition, a sadness that has never fully subsided, never fully been eased.

Sometimes, when I am with him, I'll sit in silence as the seconds and minutes tick by, my gaze fixed upon him. At the bushiness of his eyebrows. The pointiness of his ears. The way his skin falls over his cheeks. I'll take it all in—the time-beaten physicality of this man.

And then I'll imagine the loose skin on his face tightening. His thinning hair thickening. And he'll appear—for a fleeting moment—as he was all those lifetimes ago, a young man who outwitted and enchanted his occupiers and captors, Nazi and Soviet alike, when he emerged from the darkness of Dachau to reunite his family across a divided Europe.

I'll squint, stare, and use all my powers of imagination, trying to grasp what enabled this man to overcome the horrors he endured, what qualities of character made him a survivor.

I'll try—and I'll fail. At least for the most part. I did get a glimpse of those qualities once, after Zayde finally relented and got the numbness in his fingers checked out.

Not many people visit a doctor for a C2 fracture. And those who do are typically in far worse shape. But now that he was beginning to present symptoms, the doctor told him, he could expect a rapid decline. Surgery was an option. But there were no guarantees. Survival could not be assured.

The operation would last thirteen hours, the doctor explained, and require detaching his head from his neck to fix the fractured vertebra before flipping him over to complete the procedure. Even if everything went smoothly, the doctor added, his neck might never again bend enough for him to look down at the watches he was fixing.

"That's okay," Zayde responded. He would just place them on some phone books, obviating the need to bend his neck at all.

The surgery was scheduled for December. When the day arrived, the whole family gathered in New Haven. Zayde was outwardly upbeat, reminding us that it was Hanukkah, the festival of miracles. And we tried to be as hopeful as he was.

But an eighty-eight-year-old man undergoing a surgery as serious as this? Who were we kidding?

The surgeon told us the operation required an interdisciplinary team of specialists, and it was often difficult to convene them on short notice around the holidays. But they had pulled it together for Abraham Perecman. Some of them were customers; others had heard stories about the old Holocaust survivor who fixed watches on Whalley Avenue. "One of God's preselected," the surgeon called him.

We got to the hospital early to see him before he went in. Then we waited, playing cards to pass the time, until the surgeon returned in the evening. The operation was a success, he said. Zayde was alive. The surgeon had later gone home and told his family that my grandfather was "indestructible."

A couple of days later, Zayde was finally alert enough for visitors. He was wearing a halo to stabilize his neck and had a trach in his throat. Unable to speak, he was using an alphabet chart on a clipboard to spell—letter by letter—what he wanted to say.

I asked how he was doing. He grabbed the clipboard and slowly moved his index finger from one letter to the next, until it stopped on H.

He dragged his finger down a row and over to the right.

O.

The next letter: P.

Up a row and over to the right, his finger pressed another letter—E—before his hand fell from the chart.

HOPE—a word he first learned thousands of miles from New Haven in a small Eastern European village called Michalishek, where Zayde, the shopkeeper known as Abraham Perecman, was born with a different name, Gershon Gubersky, a secret he—and the rest of my family—would fiercely protect until the day he died.

2

Michalishek

A photograph believed to depict Zayde, second from left,
in Michalishek sometime in the early 1930s.

J UST AS IT was a period of injustice that uprooted my grandparents from their home in Eastern Europe in the twentieth century and brought them to America, it was likely a period of injustice that led their ancestors to settle in Eastern Europe in the first place.

As best I can tell, they arrived sometime in the fourteenth century, making their home in what was then called the Grand Duchy of Lithuania, an expansive swath of earth stretching from the Baltic in the north to the Black Sea in the south; from the Kingdom of Poland in the west to the Grand Duchy of Moscow in the east.

The immediate impetus for their migration is lost, but they might well have had the same reasons as others who sought out the grand duchy at that time: safety and security. While Western

Europe was lapsing into one of its periodic paroxysms of brutality, the grand duchy, ruled by the benevolent pagan Witold the Great, was a haven for Europe's refugees.

Over time, the grand duchy became known simply as Lithuania, or Lita. And many of the refugees who settled there congregated around the city of Vilna—considered, before the decimation of European Jewry, their de facto capital—"The Jerusalem of Lithuania," as it was purportedly called by Napoleon, whose Grand Armée camped there on the fateful expedition to Moscow in 1812.

Zayde visited Vilna only once as a boy, one of the final requests of his mother's ailing father, an Orthodox scholar whose death was mourned by the city's rabbinical elite; family lore holds that they stepped out of their synagogues to bless his casket as it was carried to the grave.

Despite this loose connection to the city, Vilna is the only place anywhere near Zayde's hometown that anyone has actually ever heard of. So whenever people ask where he is from, the family typically answers "Vilna"—the way people who grew up in Long Island say, much to the annoyance of smug Manhattanites, that they're from New York City.

My grandfather's actual birthplace, the village of Michalishek, is situated about forty miles northeast of Vilna, at a bend in the mighty Viliya River, where it arose, like so many other settlements stretching back to the earliest agrarian communities, around a place of worship, in this case a seventeenth-century church.

Unlike the grand buildings and cobblestone thoroughfares of Europe's great nineteenth-century capitals—Paris, Vienna, St. Petersburg—Michalishek was, in the words of one historian, a "dreamy village in slanting wood huts" with streets of mud and sand: white sand and black sand, said to be nutrient-rich, good for growing the potatoes that were staples of every meal.

The abundance of beggars in town gave Michalishek the appearance of "an outlandish rag fair," remembered a traveler who passed through, their bags "filled with crusts of bread, with the skeletons of herrings, with faded onions gnawed by the onion fly, and many other dismal delicacies."

Growing up, I'd sometimes hear about this or that relative who'd lived in Michalishek. One of them was Zayde's cousin Menke Katz, a celebrated Yiddish poet, who immigrated to the United States around World War I. I met Menke only once, at a gathering in a small New York City apartment. But I still remember his long flowing white hair, thin at the top and full around the crown, framing a face set in what seemed a permanent smile. "Bring wine and dance, all who come here," reads the epitaph on his tombstone—a vibrant, irreverent personality, I discerned even then.

The Michalishek of Menke's memory was a magical, mystical place, populated by Talmudists and cabalists, steeped in legend and lore. "I heard stories in the alleys . . . similar to the Anglo-Saxon epic *Beowulf* of the days of yore," he recalled. "Even the various versions of the tales which inspired Shakespeare to write King Lear I heard in myth-loving Michalishek."

On the other side of the Viliya River lay the thick Zaborchi forest. "To get out of the village, we had to shout ourselves hoarse to reach the ears of the barefoot boatman across the river, until we could finally hear the old barge sighing, propelled by tide-worn dragropes," Menke remembered.

The forest of Zaborchi across the river seemed to have no end, with bush and jungle and large powerful beasts with the proud blood of their family, *Ursidae*. The bears moved slowly, awkwardly, when they ate fruit, nuts, berries, acorns, bird's eggs, or honey from ripped beehives, but they could run at awful speed after a stray woman, man, or child. It was said that of the women were left only twisted strands of their braids and the shock of a bear hug; of the men were left only torn beards which fluttered in the wind like broken wings. It was rumored that children were quickly devoured, leaving only the terror of their small footprints.

The forest, a source of nightmares for Michalishek's young children, was a source of considerable wealth for my grandfather's family. His own grandfather—Aaron Velvel (*velvel* means "wolf" in Yiddish) Gubersky—built a successful logging business, floating his products to the port city of Memel, a transit hub on the Baltic, from which they were sold as far as North America. In fact, so-called Memel logs were considered sufficiently durable that they supplied the British Empire's most important construction project: the fleet of the Royal Navy.

What few memories remain for Zayde of Aaron are not fond ones. My grandfather recalls sitting on his own father's shoulders as a boy and coming upon Aaron in the street. "You have feet," barked his grandfather. "Use them." Also lingering in the family annals is the whiff of scandal from the all-too-brief interval that passed between the death of Aaron's first wife and the marriage to his second—a speedy remarriage that may simply have been an imperative for a family that would ultimately grow to ten children.

More illuminating about the man's character is that he expelled one of his grandchildren from his house upon learning that the boy had contracted the dreaded Spanish flu. The child survived, thanks to an aunt who took him in. "If we die," she supposedly said, in a rebuke to her brother Aaron, "we all die together."

Life in Michalishek was fairly comfortable, then, for the Gubersky family in the early years of the twentieth century. And no one had any reason to suspect their circumstances would change. Until they did. During the summer of 1915, Menke recalled, Michalishek, "like hundreds of other villages and little towns, was awakened with horror after ages of calm by German guns." It was, he wrote, a time of "hunger, disease, death." My own grandfather would grow up hearing stories from this time—stories about their German occupiers, remembered a generation later as "the Good Germans."

When it was all over, the people of Michalishek—Aaron among them—discovered that the end of the war had ushered in a new world. Before the war, Aaron had been a subject of the Russian Empire. Now the czar was dead, and the Russian Empire was no more, overthrown during the February Revolution a year earlier. The Guberskys, Aaron learned, were now citizens of a new Polish republic. Before the war, Aaron's lumber business had been buoyed by a stable currency. Now the ruble was worthless, and trade routes he had once relied upon were suddenly blocked, a result of redrawn boundaries and new political realities.

Understanding that his most prosperous days were behind him, Aaron took stock of what remained of his fortune and decided that the best investment he could make, the one that would yield more meaningful, more enduring returns than any other, was an investment in his children—or more precisely, his sons. It was time to bequeath to them the kinds of hard skills—the vocational training—they could fall back upon in a period as volatile as the twentieth century was shaping up to be.

No longer did the Gubersky children need a wealthy father to look after them. What they needed was an occupation. And the occupation Aaron selected for his teenage son Abram, ninth of his ten children—my great grandfather—was horology, or watchmaking.

3

The Watch Doctor

Zayde and his father Abram, in the late 1940s.

THE ART OF manufacturing what would become known as pocket watches—after the introduction of the waistcoat during the reign of England's Charles II provided a convenient place for carrying them—was perfected by eighteenth-century Swiss watchmaker Abraham-Louis Breguet.

Breguet supplied virtually all of the period's European elite, from Napoleon to the foe who would finally defeat him, the Duke of Wellington. The emperor's wife, too, was a Breguet collector. Josephine, it is said, wore a Breguet watch affixed to a gold bracelet—one of the first wristwatches, as such jewelry was starting to be called.

In fact, wristwatches were worn almost exclusively by women

until World War I, when the so-called trench watch—its face guarded by a grid and hands coated with a luminous (and highly carcinogenic) substance—became a fixture of European battlefields, shattering gender stereotypes and paving the way for its continued use after the war by returning veterans.

That, in short, is a history of watches up until the 1920s—around the time Aaron Velvel Gubersky sent his son Abram to apprentice with a master in Vilna. In due time, Abram returned with not only a trade but a wife—Chaya—and a family soon followed. First came my grandfather Gershon in 1924, and then two daughters, Bluma in 1926 and Fruma in 1927, known in my family as Blumke and Frumke, the *ke* (or *le*) ending a term of endearment in Yiddish.

Only a single photograph of my great-grandmother Chaya exists, mailed to relatives in America before family histories were incinerated during World War II. My mother framed the photograph in the entryway of my childhood apartment, alongside other black-and-white stills of our extended family, many of whom perished in the Holocaust—a wall of ancestors like the alcoves in ancient Rome, which held figurines of dead relatives revered as household gods.

In the image, dated 1916, Chaya, all of fifteen years old, stands poised, one arm on a chair, the other on her hip, oval-faced and olive-skinned, her straight black hair cut just below the ears. She appears as I imagine she did when Abram first met her—beautiful, enigmatic, serious, just as her son, my grandfather, would always describe her.

Abram was the more playful of the pair. Every morning, Chaya—very much her orthodox father's daughter—would walk to the front of their house, stand by the window overlooking the square, and pray. And every day, she would expose herself to gentle ribbing by her husband, who would accuse her of choosing the spot so passersby could witness the depth of her devotion.

I once asked my grandfather about those early years when his father taught him how to fix watches. He didn't tell me much. I learned early on the limits of what I could get from my Zayde.

Partly, it was his hearing. You'd need to repeat the question, sometimes three or four times, slowly, loudly, for him to understand. When he did understand, he'd often answer open-ended questions with simple, declarative statements.

"What was your experience like in Dachau?" I'd ask.

"It was so bad. It was unbelievable. You cannot imagine how bad it was."

Getting much beyond that was often frustrating—for me, unsuccessfully trying to elicit more detail, and for him, baffled as to why his initial answer was insufficient—and the conversation would move on. I am forced, therefore, to rely on others for more textured descriptions of what he experienced.

And the best account of Gershon's horology training comes, again, from his cousin Menke Katz, who also studied with Abram. Menke called him "the watch doctor" for the way he treated timepieces as if he were a physician, attributing to them their own unique personalities, ailments, and medical histories.

Watches, Menke recalled Abram saying, are all born differently. Some are born big and some are born small. Some are born healthy and some unwell. When they are fast, it is because they are in a hurry. When they are slow, it is because they are forgetful. And when a watch stops altogether, it is because he has grown tired from running all day. If one of the teeth on a gear had broken off, Abram would put his hand over his mouth, groaning as if he himself had chipped a tooth. And if a watch that had stopped ticking came alive in his hands, he would claim to have resurrected the dead.

Abram began his lessons by teaching his pupils how to use the tools of the trade. Brushes—soft bristles for small parts; tough bristles for large ones. Nippers. Flat-nosed pliers. Hammers. Screwdrivers. Oilers.

Then he would come to the watch itself. When God created Adam, Abram would say, He brought all kinds of living creatures for Adam to name. So, he would say, let's name the parts of the watch. This is the great attic wheel; this, the little attic wheel (possibly because the spokes on the center and third wheels, as they are typically called, resembled the exposed beams of old European attics). This is the escape wheel. The pallet. Stem. Staff. Hairspring. Roller. Hours hand, minutes hand, and seconds hand, ticking and tocking the span of our lives—and on and on into the eternal night.

Outside of watchmaking, there was school—part of a Zionist school network called Tarbut—where Gershon learned Hebrew history, read Hebrew literature, and spoke Hebrew, rather than the Yiddish he used at home. And there was Hashomer Hatzair—Hebrew for "Young Watchman"—one of two popular Jewish youth groups, along with the more militant Betar, both aimed at preparing young Jews to contribute all they could—head, hands, and heart—to the formation of a Jewish state.

Once a year, Gershon and his fellow watchmen would take part in a days-long retreat, full of forest adventures, river outings, and nights singing folk songs around a campfire. It was a "second home," recalled one of Gershon's contemporaries. "We were busy with ourselves. We weren't interested in what was happening around us. I knew that, generally speaking, Jews were hated, but that didn't interest me. Hashomer Hatzair was a different world."

Years later, my grandfather would regret joining Hashomer. "I should have joined Betar," he would say, adding: "Jabotinsky knew what was happening," referring to Ze'ev Jabotinsky, Betar's Russian founder. "He'd go around giving so many speeches."

I'd never heard of Jabotinsky, but I found one of the speeches my grandfather was likely remembering. It was delivered in Warsaw in the late 1930s. "It is already three years that I am calling upon you, Polish Jewry, who are the crown of World Jewry," Jabotinsky pleaded. "I continue to warn you incessantly that a catastrophe is coming closer. . . . Listen to me in this twelfth hour: In the name of God! Let any one of you save himself, as long as there is still time, and time there is very little."

Many survivors remember where they were when they first

realized that things were changing, that the lives of freedom and normalcy they had enjoyed were coming to an end.

My grandmother Rivke would tell me about the day her friends stopped talking to her in the playground. Their parents had told them they were no longer allowed to play with Jews.

For my grandfather, the moment came on a Tuesday during Michalishek's weekly market in the village square, across from their house. It was there, sometime in the late 1930s, that a group of Nazi brownshirts showed up for the first time. They weren't from Michalishek, my grandfather recalled. "I'd never seen them before," he'd say. "They were there to make trouble."

"Don't buy from Jews," they yelled. Graffiti—"Go back to Palestine"—appeared on the front of Zayde's school. And Michalishek's sole synagogue, where he had prayed, studied Torah, and celebrated his bar mitzvah, was burned to the ground.

In 1939 Menke Katz published a book of poetry. The cover, illustrated in black-and-white pencil, depicts a bonfire of books, its flames nipping at a gravestone as the eyes of a Medusa-like creature with serpentine hair glare in the distance. On the gravestone is a short Yiddish verse: "O Michalishek," it reads, "I have seen you in a storm, as one sees a howling thorn."

4

War!

My great-grandmother Chaya in 1916.
She would die on a death march in 1945.

O N JANUARY 10, 2017, Clare Hollingworth passed away at the age of 105. She was, in the words of her *New York Times* obituary, "the undisputed doyenne of war correspondents."

Nearly eighty years earlier, as a twenty-seven-year-old reporter less than one week into a new job at Britain's *Daily Telegraph*, she was in a car speeding down the autobahn from Gleiwitz, along the border with Poland, when dozens of German military motorcycles raced past her. Moments later, some burlap sheets that had been hung along the side of the road parted in the breeze, revealing the valley below. Past the flapping cloth, she later wrote, she could see "large numbers of troops, literally hundreds of tanks, armored cars and field guns."

Her article appeared the following day—August 29, 1939—on the *Telegraph*'s front page. The headline: "1,000 Tanks Massed on Polish Frontier. Ten Divisions Reported Ready for Swift Stroke." "The German military machine," Hollingworth wrote, "is now ready for instant action." It was, the *Guardian* declared in 2015, "probably the greatest scoop of modern times."

Three days later, on September 1, the troops Clare Hollingworth had seen through the sheets—Gerd von Rundstedt's Army Group South—rolled into Poland. World War II had begun.

September 1, 1939, was a Friday. And Gershon's family was preparing for Shabbat dinner when they heard cries of "War!" in the streets. For more than two weeks, they waited for the invading forces to reach them. And when they did—sixteen days later, on September 17—Gershon was startled to find them approaching not from the German border in the west but from the east, from the direction of Minsk—and the Soviet Union. This was not the Wehrmacht. It was the Red Army, executing a secret agreement between Hitler and Stalin to share the Polish spoils—Hitler taking the west; Stalin, the east.

The twenty-one months of Soviet occupation that followed the invasion were as deadly as anything that occurred in the Polish territories occupied by Germany. Yale professor Timothy Snyder has meticulously documented the numbers of Nazi and Soviet victims—in some cases, to the individual life. His grim accounting of Soviet repression in Poland finds "about 315,000 deported, about 110,000 more arrested, and 30,000 executed, and about 25,000 more who died in custody."

The first Polish uprising on either side of the German-Russian boundary took place in Soviet-occupied Czortkow in late January 1940, just a few months after the Russian incursion—and it was led by a group of high school students around the same age as

my Zayde, who was then fifteen years old. Zayde himself did not
lead any uprisings in Michalishek. But he did resist in other ways.
Handed a membership pin for the Young Pioneers, the Communist counterpart to Hashomer, he demurred. "Later," he kept telling
them. "Later."

In truth, my grandfather would tell me, he felt lucky to "have
gotten the Russians," especially after hearing stories about life in
the west from Jews fleeing German-held areas. That is not to say
it was an easy time. Neighbors disappeared at night, never to be
seen again. His Zionist school was shuttered, replaced by a Communist school where he was indoctrinated in the principles of
Marxism-Leninism. And he was instructed to report anyone, even
his own parents, overheard saying anything even faintly counter-
revolutionary.

But he agreed with his neighbor Esther Livingston, then a nine-
year-old girl, who said many years later that for the most part, at
least for Jewish kids like them, the changes that the Soviets brought
to Michalishek were "not bad."

The level of our education at school improved. Many young
people had jobs in different factories surrounding our
town. . . . Others worked on the construction of the new
Russian airfields.

Until the Russian occupation there was a *Gut* (large farm)
about 3 km (2 miles) away from the town, behind a hill, that
belonged to the Turler family. The Russians confiscated the
Gut and turned it into a flight school with an airfield next to
it. More than twenty airplanes were stationed there.

A little farther away the Russians started to build another
airfield—the largest one in the area—close to the town of
Markun, about 6 km (4 miles) away from our town. The Russians called the airfield "Palestine" because of the white sand
in that area.

(Because of the white sand—and, of course, all of the Jews.)

Over the course of the Russian occupation, Michalishkers grew so accustomed to seeing aircraft overhead that on the afternoon of Sunday, June 22, 1941, at first nothing seemed unusual about the formation of planes flying low to the ground.

One boy, gardening in the backyard with his father, would remember waving to the pilots as they flew by. When a few villagers, returning from a funeral, remarked to a Russian soldier that the planes didn't resemble Soviet aircraft, they were quickly dismissed. "Idiots," huffed the soldier. "Of course they're our planes!"

The Russian was wrong. The planes were German—the vanguard of the Luftwaffe. Operation Barbarossa, Hitler's surprise assault on the Soviet Union, had begun. By the time the attack was over, all but a few of the Soviet aircraft had been destroyed, neutralizing the Soviet air forces and clearing the way for the German advance.

Gershon remembers Russian soldiers, stunned and puzzled, desperately trying to reassure frightened Michalishkers. It was no use. "I saw the first trucks with wounded soldiers and workers from the airfield driving into our town," Esther Livingston remembers. "They passed by our house and I could see the blood running from the trucks."

The closest hospital was all the way in Vilna. So the local police station was converted into a triage unit, and the wounded were unloaded on unhinged doors repurposed as gurneys. Injured Polish and Jewish civilians, announced the Russian authorities, could stay and convalesce. Russian forces needed to clear out immediately.

Over the next forty-eight hours, the detachment of Red Army soldiers that had occupied Michalishek evacuated. And the Soviet bureaucracy that had been established over the past couple years—a bureaucracy that had reformed the local economy, reeducated the town's children, and remade the area into a hub of Soviet airfields—was dismantled, office by office, classroom by classroom, barrack by barrack.

The last Soviet soldiers and officials left the village on Tuesday, June 24, 1941. They made it out just in time. Several hours later, German tanks entered Michalishek.

5

The Saints and the Pure

Jews being executed in the Ponar pits in 1941.
Many of Zayde's friends were killed in these pits.

TUESDAY, JUNE 24, 1941, was a bright, beautiful day, and all of Michalishek assembled in the square, across from the Gubersky home, to get their first look at their new occupiers.

Most of the Michalishkers gathered that day kept their distance from the German soldiers. But one of them, an elderly man named Berl Matz, who spoke German and had fond memories of the Good Germans from a generation earlier, figured he would say hello.

It was a kind gesture—the sort that might have been reciprocated a generation earlier—but instead of returning the old man's greeting, the soldier raised his hand and slapped Berl Matz across the face.

"This," Esther Livingston recalled, "was our first encounter with the Nazis."

The Germans swiftly imposed a series of anti-Semitic decrees, requiring them to wear yellow stars at all times and barring them from entering certain parts of town, making them strangers, enemies, in their own neighborhoods.

Around the same time in nearby Worniany, seventeen teenagers, all of them roughly the same age as Gershon—now seventeen—were led into the woods for what they thought was a work assignment. It was a trap. Eight escaped; the rest were killed. The young, the strong, the most likely to fight back—they were always murdered first, Zayde would tell me.

The killings unnerved Michalishek, sending a number of its Jewish residents fleeing into the Zaborchi forest—an act of defiance that inflamed the ferocity of the Germans. Rather than designating fifty houses for the Jewish ghetto that would soon be established, as Nazi administrators had planned, the number was halved. An estimated fifteen hundred people were squeezed into just twenty-five homes—an average of sixty to a house. One of them was the Guberskys'.

The architect of all this—the Nazi overseeing the occupation of Michalishek—was a man Gershon knew only as Gisi. I have tried to identify him. But it is a measure of the commonness of Nazi brutality that despite the terror he exacted upon Michalishek, Gisi himself was sufficiently inconsequential that no documentation survives of his career—a career, it seems, remembered only by the Jews he tormented.

My grandfather first told me of Gisi one evening as we were sitting on the biscuit-colored couch in Zayde's living room, the ranch-style house silent but for the ticking of clocks around us. Most days, my grandfather recounted, Gisi could be seen on a chair by an open window at the large home he had seized—previously the mayor's—shooting stray cats and dogs that had gone meowing and barking for owners who were never coming home. The animals did not die in vain: Gisi had his tanner fashion them into boots.

At some point, said Zayde, Gisi grew tired of shooting small animals and turned to larger forms of prey. First came Fegele, a new mother who had snuck out of the ghetto to get some food for her child. She had nearly made it all the way from her home by the river with food in hand when Gisi spotted her crossing the square. Another victim was sixty-year-old Hirshel, who had helped my Zayde prepare for his bar mitzvah. Hirshel's crime was smuggling a chicken into the ghetto—a chicken Gisi offered as a gift to the widow Hirshel left behind.

My grandfather remained with his family in the ghetto until the summer of 1942, when someone noticed his name on a list of Jews being transferred to nearby labor camps. One of his sisters—Frumke—had already been sent away. "What are you doing?" Zayde's mother Chaya had reportedly shouted at the local police officer who abducted her daughter. "She's just a girl." Cupping the young girl's breasts, the police officer replied: "Feels like a woman to me."

Zayde's parents Chaya and Abram reached out to the one person they thought might be able to help—a wealthy local German who owed them a favor. The man, remembered only by his last name—Brotkopf—had lived in the area since before the war on a sprawling horse farm called Palan that the Nazis allowed him to operate with minimal interference.

During the Soviet occupation, Brotkopf had been jailed. His crime: capitalism. And Gershon's aunt, along with a few others, had intervened on his behalf, persuading the Soviet authorities to let him go. Now it was time to return the favor. If the Nazis were sending Jews to labor camps, Brotkopf wanted as many of them as possible sent to Palan, where he could keep an eye on them.

The Germans granted his request. "He was our Schindler," says my grandfather, who passed the following months milking Brotkopf's cows, farming his land, and shoveling straw and manure, until early one morning in late October. Having spent the previous night in the fields, guarding the horses, Gershon was not in the main farmhouse when German soldiers showed up and, over Brotkopf's pleas and protests, rounded up the farm's Jews—one of several farms they visited that morning, my grandfather would later learn, after liquidating the ghetto in nearby Kamelishek.

Somehow Gershon made his way back into the Michalishek ghetto without attracting notice. But that ghetto, too, would soon be liquidated. During the winter of 1942–43, the Germans declared the border between Lithuania and Byelorussia—a strip that included Michalishek—*Judenrein*, German for "clean of Jews." A senior Nazi commander instructed the heads of nearby labor camps to return workers to their ghettos by March 22, 1943—at which time, it was understood, their liquidation would commence.

In the days preceding Michalishek's liquidation, the Guberskys were told they would be transferred to Schischmaren, a labor camp in Zezmer about eighty miles away—the camp where Gershon's sister Frumke had been working since her abduction. Their destination was not a coincidence; someone at Schischmaren had used his influence to keep Jewish families intact. Gershon's final memory before leaving his house in the ghetto was the sight of their cat, darting around the furniture, agitated by all of the commotion.

His family climbed onto peasant wagons for the bumpy ride to the nearest railroad station in a village called Sol. Several days later, the rest of Michalishek would follow them. But unlike the Guberskys, who boarded a train from Sol to Zezmer, the Jews who came after them boarded a train for the Kovno ghetto.

"The residents of Sol, Oszmiana, and Michalishek have been gathered in Sol and will all be taken to Kovno in 40–50 wagons," wrote Herman Kruk, a diarist in the Vilna ghetto. "The Jewish police will help them as far as Vilna. When I ask why the Jewish police will take the carts of Jews only as far as Vilna, Mr. Gens [Jewish head of the Vilna ghetto] answers that it doesn't matter. He is sure nothing will happen to anybody."

Gens was mistaken. After departing Vilna, the train headed not toward Kovno but in an entirely different direction—toward Ponar, where, months earlier, Russian soldiers had dug up the woods to create emergency fuel storage pits, approximately seventy-five feet wide and twenty-six feet deep in some places. "At dawn," writes historian Yitzhak Arad, the train cars "were opened one after another. The passengers were taken out, marched to the edge of the pits and shot."

When the news reached Vilna, the ghetto diarist Kruk made another entry. "On Monday, April 5, 1943, 29 Adar II, 5703, we received the sad news that the transport to Kovno, along with the entire Jewish community of Sol (about 700 people) and parts of the ghettos in Swieciany, Michalishek, Gudogaje, and Ostrowiec, altogether about 4,000 people, were killed on the Vilna-Kovno road at the Ponar railroad station. May the saints and the pure be bound in life. And may God avenge their blood."

In 2016 Nicholas St. Fleur wrote a story for the *New York Times* describing how a team of archaeologists and mapmakers using radar and resistivity tomography—"Like an M.R.I. for the ground"—had discovered an escape tunnel at the Ponar pits—hand-dug, at times, with spoons found on dead victims. Twelve Jewish prisoners used the tunnel to escape. Twelve lives saved—out of the 100,000, including 70,000 Jews, that scholars estimate died at the pits.

Reflecting on the massacre generations later, Zayde would say simply—his voice cracking—"All my friends were killed at Ponar."

6

The Synagogue Prison

Yad Vashem, Photo Archive, Jerusalem

The wooden synagogue in Zezmer around the time it was
used as a labor camp for Jews, including Zayde and my family.

IN 1999, RESEARCHERS at the US Holocaust Memorial Museum
in Washington, DC, began the painstaking work of documenting the full breadth of the network of ghettos, concentration camps,
labor camps, and myriad other sites of persecution, exploitation,
and execution that the Germans established across occupied Europe
between 1933 and 1945. The project ultimately identified a total
of 42,500 such sites—a number that staggered even scholars of the
genocide.

One of those 42,500 sites was Schischmaren, a wooden synagogue in the village of Zezmer, a choice of confinement that likely
amused the Nazi administrators who came up with the idea. The
synagogue—built in the second half of the nineteenth century for
a Jewish community itself originating several centuries earlier—is

still standing, one of only a dozen or so surviving wooden synagogues in Central and Eastern Europe.

After being adopted in 2015 by the city council in Kaišiadorys, Lithuania, the site was reimagined as a memorial and cultural center, following a long period of disuse when the only indication of its dark heritage was a plaque, identifying it as part of the European Route of Jewish Heritage, along with a penciled note on its western wall. The note had been scrawled, it is said, as a warning from a long-ago prisoner to Hitler's collaborators: "Be sure, Lithuanians," it reads, "your destiny will be the same after the war."

The Nazis had been using the synagogue as a prison for some time before Gershon was transferred there in the spring of 1943. Two years earlier, the last members of the town's Jewish community—precisely twenty men, five hundred and sixty-seven women, and one hundred and ninety-seven children—were ordered to undress, marched from the synagogue into the woods, and shot by Lithuanian police, their clothes later sold in town at a steep discount. Afterward, the forest floor could be seen shifting, alive with the final twitches and clawing of those buried beneath. By the time Gershon's transport arrived in Zezmer, in other words, the area was Judenrein.

Schischmaren was supervised by uniformed members of a German construction firm called Organisation Todt—O.T., for short. I'd never heard my grandfather mention the name O.T., or come across more than a passing reference to it in histories of the war.

And yet this organization—which would play a pivotal role in my grandfather's story—was once the general contractor of the Third Reich, responsible for building everything from the autobahn to the Atlantic Wall fortifications along the European coast. In the final months of the war, O.T. commanded a workforce of approximately one million laborers, including camp inmates. If my grandfather was a slave, and Hitler was his master, O.T. was the overseer.

The O.T. construction project being completed at Schischmaren
was a stretch of highway from Vilna to Kovno. A sympathetic visitor
to the camp around the time of Gershon's arrival, part of a disinfec-
tion delegation after one of its periodic outbreaks of typhus, reported
back on the conditions to the Vilna ghetto underground: "More than
one thousand people are crowded together in the synagogue on dirty
bunks with children. Everyone is terribly hungry. The work brigades
are driven out early in the morning to pave the road. With their
bare hands they drag the stones and put them in place. They conceal
those sick with typhus as they fear the Germans will kill them."

Decades later, my dad's mother would ask Zayde why he had
never tried to escape. To my mother's family, it was the kind of
idiotic question that only someone with no conception of what the
man had gone through would ask. My mom would even repeat
the story from time to time as an example of her mother-in-law's
cluelessness. What my mom did not know—because in those days,
her father spoke less often about the war—was that he had, in fact,
tried to escape.

The details of the plan are hazy. Somehow, my grandfather found
his way into a small ring of plotters, led by a thirty-year-old Polish
army veteran. Their plan was to join the anti-Nazi resistance then
living and fighting, often alongside Soviet partisans, in the surrounding forests. At some point the group learned—from a friendly
Jewish police officer guarding them—of another escape plan being
hatched at a nearby camp, Meligan.

Immediately recognizing that if either group escaped before the
other, there would be a crackdown at both camps, they decided to
coordinate and escape together. From the fragments my grandfather
shared, it seems that planning was nearly complete when he, along
with three others, were dispatched to Meligan to finalize the out-
standing details.

When Zayde's mother Chaya learned about the mission, she
asked her son to do her a favor. For reasons that are still not clear,
locks of her daughter Frumke's hair had wound up in the possession

of a prisoner at Meligan. Chaya wanted them back, believing that leaving the locks of hair at Meligan was a bad omen.

The most plausible explanation I can find for this belief comes from the Zohar, the foundational text of the mystical Jewish teachings of Kabbalah. According to tradition, hair could be used in magical formulae, such as curses, so a lock of hair in the wrong hands was to be avoided at all costs.

Whether or not Chaya's request was rooted in Kabbalah or something else, the story has always reinforced my inability to fully grasp the beliefs that shaped Zayde and his world—yet another reminder of what has felt like an unbridgeable chasm between the myth, magic, and mysticism of 1930s Lithuanian Jewry and the lapsed Judaism that has characterized much of my own life, between a time when a woman could reasonably ask her son to retrieve shorn locks of her daughter's hair, and a time when that woman's great-grandson thinks her request is, well, bizarre.

In my grandfather's telling, the mission to Meligan went smoothly until they were on their way back, and a car pulled up alongside them. The license plate read "GK," short for Gebietskommissar, indicating that the passenger was the Third Reich's regional chief. Rapid questioning followed: "What camp are you from?" "Where are you going?" "Why aren't you wearing your yellow stars?" Apparently satisfied by whatever lies they told, the Gebietskommissar punished them with merely a slap on the face before getting back in his car and driving off.

Upon returning to Schischmaren, the group was summoned to see the head of the camp's Judenrat, a man Gershon remembers only as Ringel. Evidently, after the encounter on the road, the Gebietskommissar had proceeded to Schischmaren, and laid into Ringel for the unauthorized departure.

"At tomorrow's roll call," Ringel informed Zayde and his coconspirators, "you'll each get twenty-five lashes." During an examination the next morning to confirm that the prisoners could withstand what was to come, one of the plotters was diagnosed with typhus.

My grandfather remembers clearly the response of the German charged with carrying out the punishment: "Einhundert müssen rein." One hundred must go in. If one hundred lashes could not be divided evenly, they would be divided unevenly, with the ailing offender receiving half the original allotment, and the difference spread among the remaining three. After that, recalled Zayde, a new rule was issued: If anyone left the camp without permission, their entire family would be killed.

Today, the only evidence of the aborted plot is the 8-millimeter handgun, smuggled into the camp by the group's ringleader, that Zayde buried beneath the earthen steps of its lavatory. There, he insists, the weapon lies to this day, to be discovered, perhaps, by some future visitor to the memorial and cultural center.

During the summer of 1944, construction along the Vilna-to-Kovno highway was completed, and Schischmaren was shut down. Over the coming weeks, Gershon was transported from one camp to another, his movements tracking the Wehrmacht as it beat a retreat from Soviet advances in the east.

Ultimately Gershon would be transferred to Dachau, Germany's original concentration camp, where he would join tens of thousands of slave laborers on an O.T. construction project that was one of the Third Reich's most closely guarded secrets. But first he would be transported to another camp, this one outside Gdansk in modern-day Poland: Stutthof—or, as it was called by one of its more literary prisoners, Planet of Death.

7

Planet of Death

Yad Vashem, Photo Archive, Jerusalem

Red Army soldiers standing on a mountain
of shoes at Stutthof after liberating the camp in 1945.

O F ALL THE camps where my grandfather was held during
the war, the one that would haunt him most—the one he
would call "the worst" more than seventy years later—was Stutthof,
located about twenty miles east of Gdansk along the Baltic coast,
where he spent four nights in July 1944.

I always found this assessment surprising, as if the brevity of
his imprisonment should somehow make its duration any less traumatic, as if the severity of a camp should bear some correlation to
the familiarity of its name. In fact, the causal relationship often
runs in the opposite direction. The least well known sites were often the most deadly, because there were fewer survivors to preserve
their memory.

In the leakage of meaning that always occurs in my conversations with my grandfather—a leakage caused by the elusiveness of memory, his selectivity about what to share, and a language barrier that flattens the complexity of life experience into a string of simple English words—I never fully grasped what made Stutthof so different from any of the others.

The closest I have come to understanding stems not from an oral testimony or a well-researched history, but rather a verse of poetry. "Here," writes Stutthof survivor and poet Franciszek Fenikowski, "the planet of death: Stutthof Camp,

> *In the rain, the dim lamps*
> *Throw a drizzle of light*
> *Onto the absurd landscape.*
> *It was erected by human madness*
> *From the shadows of watchtowers, mist,*
> *The Argus eyes of searchlights,*
> *The striped dress of the prisoners,*
> *Barbed wire, barracks, terror, sadism,*
> *Hunger, blood and mud."*

To the list of Stutthof's defining characteristics, Fenikowski might have added the word *sand*. Whenever Zayde talked about the camp, just two miles inland, he always mentioned the sand. As another poet imprisoned at Stutthof, Balys Sruoga, recalled in his own memoir, *Forest of the Gods*—a title borrowed from the name that locals had called the surrounding woods since ancient times—

On white dunes, sands sifted through the hands of a superior force—pines tall and spindly as yeshiva students . . .

Once, a long, long time ago, this was the bottom of the sea. It looks as if, during a storm, the waves unexpectedly froze and hardened, and the north winds sprinkled their crests with white sands.

The breezy coastal setting was sufficiently serene that it served as the site of a home for the elderly before being repurposed as a forest jail for Polish undesirables in the first month of the war.

After visiting Stutthof a couple of years later, SS chief Heinrich Himmler left convinced it ought to shine more brightly in the emerging constellation of concentration camps. Upon his orders, what had previously been an obscure outpost of the Third Reich was transformed into what one historian has called "the great overflow camp of Eastern Europe," holding, at its peak, roughly sixty thousand prisoners in thirty-nine subcamps spanning almost three hundred acres.

Mother Nature herself may have been conspiring with the Germans, enclosing prisoners with not only barbed wire but riparian barriers—seas, rivers, lagoons later determined to contain unusually high concentrations of salt and iron and unusually low concentrations of lime and chalk, making the surrounding areas inhospitable to assorted forms of life, including our own.

Nonetheless, Gdansk's location, midway between Western and Eastern Europe, made the region a natural transit hub, a rest stop where weary travelers—from the Russian Peter the Great to the Prussian Frederick the Great—could spend the night before going on their way. It was a heritage Stutthof perverted as a "holding camp," in the words of its deputy commandant, Theodor Meyer, where prisoners would spend a few nights or more before going on to work or going on to die.

The railroad station closest to camp was in a nearby village, Tiegenhof. "Tiegenhof! Where was that? We had never heard of it before," recalled a prisoner, William Mishell, who made the journey around the same time as Gershon. The train platform, he says, was spotless; the air, fresh and crisp. The passengers disembarked and boarded small open-air wagonettes for the next leg. Winding their way through a picturesque forest, a sprawling concentration camp—rows of barbed wire, guard towers, a deep moat—emerged from the trees. "Here were beauty and ugliness, life and death, side-by-side," says Mishell.

From the detailed records of the Nazi bureaucracy, we know that Gershon and his family arrived at Stutthof on Monday, July 17, 1944. And from the oral histories of their fellow prisoners, we know that they were immediately led to a large warehouse—as much as four hundred feet long, one hundred and fifty feet wide, and twenty-five feet high, according to one estimate—where they saw, in the words of a survivor, "one huge mountain of thousands and possibly tens of thousands of pairs of shoes. Mixed with the shoes were eyeglasses, wigs, braces, artificial limbs, human hair, dolls, doll dresses, toys, and other items."

A short time later, they were separated, men from women, husbands from wives, brothers from sisters, mothers and fathers from their children. My great-aunt Frumke passed away before I ever had a chance to ask her about that moment. But I did have a chance to ask her sister Blumke. She was bedridden at the time, the result of a botched surgery on her leg, and I joined Zayde on a trip to her home, near his own in Connecticut. Up until she passed away, Zayde would visit her several times a week and check in by phone daily.

After they finished arguing about something or other—their bickering persisted into their nineties—I asked Blumke about the war. I was in my early thirties and felt a visceral need to fill in gaps in my knowledge of my family's story. I started with a question I hoped would elicit a pleasant memory—about the family's reunification. It was a subject that always made Zayde himself emotional. "How many whole families survived?" he would say. "If they would make a movie about such a thing, no one would believe it!"

So I asked Blumke, "How did you learn Zayde was alive after the war?" She had been alerted by a friend, she said, who'd seen him in Berlin after the war, where he'd arrived, clinging to the roof of a packed train car.

"No," Zayde interjected. "That's not how you knew. You knew because you got my letter." Zayde said he'd tracked her down with the help of a relief organization while fixing watches for the Red

Army under a certain "General Marshak"—likely Mendel-Leib Marshak, the head of logistics for Soviet occupation forces, who would later be imprisoned for his secret efforts to help Jews leave Russia.

"Shouldn't I know? You weren't there!" his sister insisted. She glanced over at me. *How can I even argue with this man?* her eyes pleaded.

I moved on to my next question, this one about the separation at Stutthof. Her eyes shifted. "I can't talk about this," she said, cutting me off. "It's too painful. No more questions." Zayde shot me a look. We spent the rest of the visit talking about her grandchildren.

Later, I asked Zayde about the separation. Did he have time to say goodbye? What do you say, I wondered, when you know it may be the last time you see your mother, the last time you see your sisters?

The memory was irretrievable, buried too deep. Zayde would, of course, see his sisters again. But with the exception of a fleeting glance across the camp later that day, that moment in the warehouse was the last time he would see his mother. Soon, he and his father would go on to another camp. But Chaya and her daughters would remain at Stutthof—and Chaya would die before the family reunited.

Gershon's sisters would tell him she had survived until the camp was liberated by the Soviets. She had come down with typhoid, they said, and passed away in the care of Russian physicians. If only she had been liberated by US forces and treated by American doctors, my grandfather would say, his mother would have survived.

In fact, the sisters were lying. Many years ago, my family gathered for a reunion in Lake George, in upstate New York, where some of Zayde's friends from Europe happened to live. One of them had been imprisoned with Chaya, Frumke, and Blumke at Stutthof.

"Isn't it tragic that Chaya died in a Russian hospital?" my mom said to her, echoing her father's oft-repeated sentiment about the cruelty of Chaya's fate.

"Chaya didn't die in a hospital," the friend replied.

She remembered the whole thing vividly: all of Stutthof's women prisoners were in a barn, lying down, resting, dying on a death march, when the Russians found them. When the barn door was opened, all of the women stood up, and Zayde's friend saw Frumke and Blumke stand as their mother collapsed to the ground.

"Did you ever confirm the story?" I asked my mom. Yes, she said, explaining that she hadn't felt comfortable asking her aunts herself, and instead told the story to one of Blumke's granddaughters. "We thought it would be nicer to say she died in the hospital," Blumke later confessed to this granddaughter. It was, Zayde's sisters felt, an important lie, sparing their brother and father the knowledge of the indignity of Chaya's death, and perhaps easing whatever guilt they may have felt about their own survival.

Separated, Gershon was now informed that he was being taken to the showers. Stripped naked, toes clutching the sand, he stood outdoors, breathing in the humid air. Upon a guard's command, he was led inside to an area adjacent to the showers. One prisoner remembers,

> The room was brightly lit, with tiled walls as in a shower, but there were no shower heads.
> Inside the room were a number of gynecological tables. Men were lying on them and screaming bloody murder. A number of capos were holding the men with force on the tables and others with large knives and other utensils were doing something to them. Finally my turn came. Once on the table, I realized what was going on: the men were receiving examinations to find whether they had not hidden any gold in their insides.

From there, Gershon and his father Abram were led into the showers before being released to dress themselves with the clothes piled outside. Abram saw someone wearing his shoes and approached the man, complaining that his own shoes were too small and asking to trade, cleverly retrieving the few Russian gold rubles he'd stashed in the sole, rubles that could be traded for bread or cigarettes, the currency of the camps.

While Gershon and Abram were led to showers that pumped water, others were led to showers that pumped gas, their ashes blown up to the sky in gray columns that hovered over the camp, their smell an enduring memory for its survivors. For many years after the war, rumors circulated of terrors being inflicted on prisoners even after death. Corpses of Stutthof prisoners, it was said, were shipped to the nearby Anatomic Institute of the Danzig Medical School, where a professor named Rudolf Spanner was allegedly conducting grue-some experiments in the industrial production of human soap.

The rumors were false. But there is a "core of truth" to them, writes one scholar: limited amounts of soap were made from hu-man fat at the Anatomic Institute, where it was a by-product of the maceration process used to prepare skeletons and other anatomical parts for educational purposes. Most of the corpses used at the insti-tute came from a psychiatric institution and three prisons. In fact, Spanner himself later said that after obtaining the bodies of several Stutthof inmates—described as "Russian," not Jewish—he refused to accept any more on practical grounds. Specifically, in his words, "the material could not be used by the students due to the complete atrophy of fatty tissue and muscles." So badly were Stutthof prison-ers mistreated, even their remains had nothing more to give.

Gershon and Abram's fifth and final day in Stutthof was Friday, July 21, 1944. The night before, as every night, they had slept side by side on the ground—"Like herrings," Zayde would say—beaten if they broke formation and attempted to sleep in a more comfort-able position. That morning the prisoners assembled, as every day, for roll call. On this day, however, a selection was taking place not for work but for life. The ill and infirm were being steered into one group, the young and healthy, another. What happened next would become a central tenet of our family mythology.

When we were asked to tell stories about our grandparents in

Mrs. Salazar's fourth-grade classroom at Trinity School in New York City, one of my friends told a story about the time his grandfather got a haircut at the Waldorf. I told the story of how Zayde saved his father's life at Stutthof—not, in retrospect, the kind of lighthearted fare Mrs. Salazar had in mind when she handed out the assignment.

My grandfather would always say the person leading the selection that day was Dr. Mengele, "The Angel of Death," as he was called for his horrific experiments on Auschwitz prisoners. Stutthof archivists, however, have no record of any visits by Mengele. More likely the doctor my grandfather remembers was Otto Heidl, Stutthof's thirty-three-year-old chief physician, who had in fact preceded Mengele on the medical staff of Auschwitz before a promotion landed him at Stutthof.

I've heard the story so many times I can picture it in my head as I imagine it unfolded. Heidl, accompanied on either side by Nazi guards, calling up one prisoner after another, inspecting them up and down, squeezing their biceps, asking them to turn around, then rendering his judgment: "Left" or "Right."

Zayde's father Abram stepped forward, looking older than his forty-eight years, his appearance degraded by the dirty, tattered clothes he'd snatched from a pile outside the showers when he could not find his own.

"Left," Heidl said, directing him to the elderly group behind him.

Gershon came next. One month shy of twenty, he was scrawny but tough, his muscles taut. The years of shoveling, paving, and hauling showed.

"Right," said Heidl.

As he was marched to the edge of the camp, my grandfather never let Abram out of his sight. As he saw prisoners up ahead boarding the same wagonettes that had brought them to Stutthof days earlier and realized his own life was being spared, at least for now, he decided it was not worth living without his father. So when the guard told him the wagonette was full and he would need to wait for the next one, he came up with a plan.

He caught the attention of a young boy he had known in Schisch-maren. The guards, he would explain, paid little attention to young children, letting them run freely around the camp.

"Tell my father to meet me in the bathroom," he instructed, before requesting permission to use the bathroom himself.

Once there, the two men exchanged clothes—Gershon's idea being to make his father look a little less infirm, a little more like he belonged in the same group as his son. Then they ran back together toward the wagonettes and joined the men waiting to board the train.

It has always seemed unlikely that no one noticed the second prisoner returning from the bathroom. Holocaust survivors are, in my experience, exceptionally observant. My cousins and I would often joke that nothing can get past my grandfather. We can be talking about this or that family member as he sits nearby silently watching ESPN, when, with an offhand remark or a turn of the head, he'll let us know he's been listening to every word.

But if any other prisoners noticed Zayde returning with an older man, they said nothing, allowing the father and son their deception, one of the many times life and death in the highly mechanized, highly systematic Nazi killing apparatus ultimately came down to chance.

Along with Gershon and Abram, some two thousand prisoners—eighteen hundred men and two hundred women—departed Stutt-hof on the transport on July 21. According to Kommandantur Order No. 48, issued the previous day, once the wagonettes arrived in Tiegenhof, the prisoners were to board another, larger train that would transport them roughly seven hundred miles, bringing them from the periphery of the Nazi Reich to a village on the outskirts of Munich, the city revered by National Socialists as the "home of the movement." That village was Dachau.

8

Bubbie

Bubbie, photographed in a displaced persons
camp in Eschwege, Germany, around 1947.

O N A VISIT to Connecticut when I was sixteen years old, I decided to interview my grandparents about their experiences during the war. They didn't have any paper in the house—what little writing they did was on Perecman Jewelers stationery at The Store. So I took some notes on a couple of flattened shoeboxes I found in the basement.

What I wrote about my grandfather that day would be enriched over the years by many other conversations. But the few paragraphs I wrote about my grandmother Rivke—Bubbie, as I called her—reflect one of our only conversations about her experience.

A short time later, her cognitive abilities began a rapid decline, a symptom of the brain cancer that ultimately confined her to a La-Z-Boy in the living room, where she would sit, gazing blankly at the TV, cared for by a nursing aide and her stricken husband.

Some of what I recorded that day is merely a chronology of her story, from the time she was fourteen at the start of the war, until the time she was nineteen at the end. But I also captured her memories of how she had felt as a young girl being hunted by German troops.

There's this: "Bubbie hid between the walls while the Germans stuck bayonets through them. Bubbie remembers how scared she was watching through a hole in the wall as a German climbed into the attic to look for them." And this: "There were many times when she was so tired, hungry, frustrated and angry that she wanted to give up." And this: "She cried the first time she had to beg for food." And this: "Bubbie told me she just wanted to die."

Of the eight members of Bubbie's family—the Wexlers—only two others survived: her brothers Berel and Yale. I met Berel once, on a trip to San Diego, where he lived when I was young. We spent the day at the San Diego Zoo, with me racing ahead to see the animals while my mother and Berel trailed behind, catching up and telling old stories.

I got to know Yale better. He was a constant presence at Bubbie and Zayde's house—a quiet man with a toothy grin and smooth fingertips, their nails peeled off, the result of an accident on his Connecticut chicken farm after the war. Once I reproached my grandmother for raising her voice at him. She was being too hard on the old man, I said. She smiled, explaining it was the only way he could hear her.

I never talked to Yale about the war. But I would later learn that this seemingly vulnerable, fragile man had been a fearless, hot-tempered Polish army veteran and resistance fighter.

In the autumn of 1942, after the Germans established a ghetto in Bubbie's hometown—Postov, roughly seventy-five miles northeast of Vilna—Yale tried unsuccessfully to mobilize the Judenrat to back an uprising. Unable to fight, he decided that his family would hide. As he recounts in an oral history: "I decided to construct a bunker for my family and a few friends that would serve us during the troubled time. The bunker was underground and the entrance was in the shed in our backyard that looked out on the field. I built air-pipes into it, which let out on the field and which were so well disguised that from the outside you could not see them. When the Germans began the liquidation of the Ghetto, we went into the bunker—twelve souls—and we stayed there for 9 days."

The twelve souls included Bubbie's baby nephew—Berel's son— and a handful of cousins. As one of those cousins, Reuben, recalled, Yale was making a final sweep of the house before entering the bunker when he came face-to-face with a German by the front door. "He shoved the door in the German's face," writes Reuben, "and locked it. The German ran for reinforcements, and when they came back, Yale had already crawled into the hideout. The Germans searched everywhere. They shot into all the walls, floor and ceiling. They did not find the hiding place. Figuring that Yale had escaped through the back door, they left the house. While the Germans were yelling and shooting in the house, the baby boy started to cry. But someone put a hand on the baby's mouth, and he never cried again."

I remember hearing this story when I was a child, the pallid look on the face of the storyteller discernible to me even then. Some time later, I learned that it was Berel's wife, the infant's mother, who had smothered her own son. She and Berel would have two more sons after the war, one of whom was shocked to learn later in life that he had once had an older brother.

I imagine a day never passed when Berel didn't think of the child. Was he thinking of the boy that day in the San Diego Zoo? Was the child's sacrifice what made Bubbie's survival possible? Do I owe my own life to that terrible act of desperation?

In the bunker, the family had just a single weapon—a pistol— and at some point Berel's wife ran off with it, leaving the rest of the family defenseless. The act of betrayal was not forgotten. For decades after the war, Berel and his wife were not welcome at his brother Yale's farm. "Don't trust anyone except your parents and siblings," Yale and his wife would teach their children.

It's not entirely clear how the rest of Bubbie's family was killed. "They never liked to talk about how anyone died," one of Yale's daughters told me. "If it came up, they'd change the subject."

According to some accounts, Bubbie's parents Leah and Mendel were the first ones killed after everyone filed out of the bunker, betrayed by the child of the peasants who took them in. One of my grandmother's older sisters, Perke, I'm told, was raped and killed by the side of a road. The other, Sorke, was killed with her two little children. Somehow Sorke's husband survived, immigrating after the war to Israel, where he started a new life with a new family.

Once, after Bubbie had lost the power of speech, my mother showed her some photos of her onetime brother-in-law with his new Israeli family. Displaying a presence of mind we feared had left Bubbie, she tore the photos apart, one after another. Whatever memories they elicited, whatever feelings they stirred—sadness, resentment, anger—were so deeply engrained that they had endured, even after almost every other trace of her personality had departed.

There are multiple—and conflicting—stories about what happened to my grandmother's younger sister. I asked her about it once. I was sitting in the passenger seat of her car as she drove to my aunt's home in Cheshire, Connecticut.

"What was her name?" I asked. "What was she like?" I could see only Bubbie's profile, but I could tell the light had left her eyes. Tears started running down her cheek. "I can't remember what she sounded like," she said softly. "I can't remember what her voice sounded like."

As young children, we don't often see our grandparents cry. I don't think it had occurred to me that Bubbie *could* cry. I suppose I thought she was so old, had seen so much, she was beyond tears.

One of my memories from sleeping over at my grandparents'

home when I was a child is waking up early, as kids do, only to find my grandmother already in the kitchen, making me freshly squeezed orange juice. I always thought she rose early just for me, her *sheyner ingeleh*, as she called me, Yiddish for "handsome little boy."

Only later did I learn that even then, fifty years after the war, nightmares of all that she had endured still kept her awake. Bubbie, I realized, was up so early because she had been unable to sleep. My uncle would tell me that when he was a boy, he would sometimes be awakened in the middle of the night by cries from his parents' room. "She was screaming her sisters' names," he said.

After leaving the bunker, Bubbie, together with Berel and Yale, fled from one ghetto to another before joining the Jewish resistance in Narocz Forest, "a base for anti-German, pro-Communist Lithuanian partisans," according to historian Allan Levine. While the precise number of Soviet partisans in Eastern Europe at that time is impossible to determine—complete lists do not exist—some estimate there were roughly 350,000, including as many as 25,000 Jews, organized into hundreds of brigades.

One of those brigades—the one my grandmother and her brothers joined—was led by the Russian colonel Fiodor Markov, a former teacher, dressed, recalls one partisan, "like a general—epaulets, two [weapons]—one a German Luger and the other a Russian pepesha [submachine gun]. He had no faith in either and therefore wore them both."

I once paid a visit to the Bronx apartment of another member of Markov's brigade. Chaya Palevsky was in her eighties when we sat down for lunch. She offered me borscht and cold cuts, and we began talking about the war. "Have you seen *Defiance?*" she asked, citing the 2008 film starring Daniel Craig about the Nazi-fighting Bielski brothers, operating out of another forest not far from Markov's brigade. "That's what it was like."

My grandmother spent roughly two years in the woods. But I know virtually nothing about them. Unlike Zayde, whose every movement was dutifully tracked by his Nazi captors, leaving a paper trail I can follow to this day, Bubbie's journey was off the grid, stored only in her own memory. And she was unwilling or unable to talk about it. Even Zayde was left to piece it together from whatever stories her brothers told him.

All Chaya Palevsky remembers of Bubbie from this time is that she spent her days knitting, sewing, and cooking for the fighters. That another partisan had a crush on her and they became close. And that her brothers were constantly looking out for her, wary of the Russian fighters known to kill women who rejected their sexual demands.

Another story Chaya shared about her brigade took place in the fall of 1943. On orders from Soviet authorities in Moscow, Markov disbanded the Jewish units under his command and seized their weapons even as they prepared for a German assault. "Partisan intelligence reports," writes Allan Levine, "confirmed the rumors that had been circulating in the forest for weeks: that a Nazi force of more than 70,000 troops was preparing for a massive attack on the fighters' base."

As the Russian partisans prepared to flee north, the unarmed Jews were told they would be fired upon if they tried to follow. Forsaken, some two hundred of them—Bubbie and her brothers among them—marched deep into the woods, where, surrounded by marshes and swamps, they hoped the Germans would not find them. More than half of them were killed in the siege that followed. It was an experience I never heard Bubbie mention.

In the mid-1990s my mother and I went to Israel and came back with a present for my grandmother: a framed watercolor of the biblical Ruth, the name—an Americanized version of Rivke—customers sometimes called her at The Store.

The artist had rendered the image using strings of Hebrew calligraphy—excerpts that recounted the story of Ruth famously vowing to her mother-in-law Naomi: "Where you go I will go, and where you stay I will stay. Your people will be my people and your God my God. Where you die I will die, and there I will be buried."

It's a beautiful passage, perhaps the most eloquent depiction of loyalty in the Western tradition. And it is a fitting epigraph for the way everyone rallied around Bubbie when the end finally came. Three generations of Perecmans packed into her small room at Yale New Haven Hospital, clutching her blanket and holding her hand.

As her breathing slowed to unnaturally long gaps, family members would start wailing, assuming she had passed, until suddenly, unexpectedly, she'd take another breath and the cycle—silence, wailing, breathing, silence, wailing, breathing—would repeat.

At the time, the dramatic display of mourning made me uncomfortable, and I stepped into the hall. Looking back, I'm moved by the memory of Bubbie drifting off, immersed in the love of the family she had suffered so much, so early in life, for the chance to build. I hope she felt it. I hope, as she slipped away in those final hours, she dreamed dreams, and not nightmares.

9

Ringeltaube

Yad Vashem, Photo Archive, Jerusalem

Weingut II, one of the underground aircraft
factories that were part of Hitler's secret plan to beat
back an Allied invasion.

IN 1986, WHEN I was five years old, my mom won a several-
months-long research fellowship to study aphasia, a neurologi-
cal disorder, at an institute in Munich. My parents were already
separated by then, so the two of us packed our bags and headed to
Bavaria.

Most of my memories from our time in Germany are, naturally,
the memories of a child: The glockenspiel in the Neues Rathaus
with its large figurines twirling at appointed hours of the day. The
underground toy store in the U-Bahn station near the flat where we
were staying. The foreign sights, smells, and brands like Familia
Swiss Muesli that I love to this day.

But alongside these memories is another, more somber one, of the visit we made to Dachau. On the way back, my mother started feeling ill, an apparently psychosomatic illness induced by all the feelings—pain, disgust, terror—that the camp had triggered.

Before we left, my mother bought a guidebook at the visitors' center. It was in German, and I could not read it. But from time to time throughout my childhood, I'd pull it off the shelf and page through it, pausing on its black-and-white images of the words on the camp's entrance, forged in wrought iron, "Arbeit Macht Frei"—work sets you free. And in other shots, like those of prisoners pushing up against barbed wire fences, I'd search the faces in the crowds, looking for Zayde.

I visited the camp only once more, during a backpacking trip across Europe a few years out of college. I paced the rows where the barracks had stood, trying to imagine what my grandfather might have felt when he walked the same grounds more than sixty years earlier.

It is, of course, impossible. The passage of time makes the distance too great to cross. And in the end, we are left only with a sense of solemnity, of visiting what we feel to be hallowed ground.

That we cannot fully grasp the horror is a blessing—one that our ancestors who experienced it would surely have wished for us.

It is also, in a way, a curse, clearing the way for deniers to claim it never happened, and allowing the rest of us to grow complacent, to entertain the possibility, even for a passing moment, that everything we have—all of our rights, all of our freedoms—are somehow entitled to us, that they cannot vanish in an instant.

The site where I imagined my grandfather's imprisonment—Dachau Concentration Camp Memorial Site, the historic landmark twenty-five minutes outside Munich—is not, in fact, where he was imprisoned. The actual site of his incarceration, at least for most of its duration, was farther south, at one of Dachau's eleven Kaufering subcamps a few miles from Landsberg am Lech, where Hitler, jailed after his failed 1923 Beer Hall Putsch, wrote *Mein Kampf*.

The entry form my grandfather completed upon arriving at Dachau still exists, one of dozens of documents about him in the archives of Yad Vashem and the US Holocaust Memorial Museum. It is a single, yellowing sheet with printed text alongside handwritten notes—like the form a doctor fills out while asking a battery of questions.

At the top, alongside the printed word "Konzentrationslager," is a handwritten "Dachau." Next to the notation "Gef. Nr.," the number—my grandfather's Dachau identification number—85696. On the line next to "Beruf," German for profession, someone wrote "Uhrmacher," watchmaker. Next to the word "Nase," the notation "Kurs"—small.

At the bottom of the page is Zayde's signature, recognizable even now, its lettering a little more upright, with a little more bounce, than the signature on the birthday cards he sent me over the years.

My grandfather does not remember filling out the form. In fact, he has only one memory of his arrival at Kaufering: while the prisoners were standing in the forest, waiting to be admitted, an Allied plane flew directly overhead, firing a single shot that killed a single inmate—Ringel, the same Ringel who, as head of Schischmaren's Judenrat, had ordered Gershon's lashing after he left the camp without permission.

"We were so happy," Zayde told me. "You cannot imagine how happy the day was."

No, I'd think. I cannot know what it was like, standing outside a concentration camp and finding happiness in the death of one of my tormentors.

Whenever I asked Zayde about his time at Dachau, about how he spent his days, he would always answer the same way, explaining that he had helped build what he called an "underground airport." I had no idea what he meant. When I pressed him, he would simply wave me off. "What do you mean what do I mean?" he would say, as if the answer were obvious.

Then his face would settle into a smile, acknowledging the

impossibility of making his grandson comprehend it all. "You don't understand," he would say. He was right, of course. I didn't understand. In fact, I was sure something was getting lost in translation. I was sure he wasn't explaining it accurately. "Underground airport"—the term itself is an oxymoron.

And then, one day, I decided to take him at his word. I entered "underground airport" and "Nazi" into Google just to see what I would find, and was immediately led to the May 1958 issue of *Flying* magazine. Alongside stories like "Russia's New Look at Civil Aviation" and "The Problem of the Fly-Over" by rising political star Minnesota senator Hubert Humphrey, I noticed another, "Hitler's Last Dream: The Underground Airport," by Charles B. Harnett—a dream Harnett called "too late, probably, but cunning and well planned—the last spark of genius before the fire died."

The secret history of the project, one of the largely untold stories of World War II, began in the spring of 1944 after what's known as Big Week, a five-day Allied bombing campaign that targeted not only German airplanes but the entire German aviation industry. On the first day of Big Week alone—February 20, 1944—nine hundred and forty-one American bombers bombarded twelve German aviation factories.

By the time it was all over, the US Air Force had dropped about ten thousand tons of bombs on twenty-six German factories, slightly outperforming Great Britain's Royal Air Force, which had dropped roughly another nine thousand tons of ordnance around the city of Augsburg and other strategically important centers of German aviation. The result: four thousand German planes were destroyed, and German aircraft production was decimated by as much as two-thirds, according to one estimate.

The Reich's response was swift. Nazi air minister Hermann Göring established an interministerial executive committee—the Jägerstab—to carry out "the repair and relocation of the damaged factories with a direct authority and without any bureaucratic scruples." The Jägerstab would also, according to its founding orders, "contribute to the restoration and increase of fighters' production."

The Luftwaffe had a need for all kinds of fighters, from Focke-Wulf Fw 190s to Messerschmitt Me 109s. But the one fighter that captured the imagination of the Nazi High Command more than any other was the Me 262, the world's first operational jet-powered aircraft, "arguably the most important jet aircraft of World War II," according to historian Daniel Uziel.

A marvel of German engineering, the Me 262 was powered by twin Junkers Jumo 004 engines that yielded a combined speed of nearly 900 kilometers per hour. Further optimizing performance was an innovation later adopted by virtually every modern aircraft: the so-called swept wing, which protruded at an angle, rather than perpendicular, to the fuselage, thereby reducing drag.

It was the most advanced fighter of the dawning Jet Age, the crown jewel of the Luftwaffe fleet. No other great power—not the Americans, not the British, not the Soviets—had anything like it. Hitler himself had high hopes for the Me 262. It would be his answer, he told commanders, to an Allied invasion. With its startling speed and deadly payload—if, as Hitler demanded, the jets were equipped with bombs—the aircraft might be just what was needed to repel an Allied invasion long enough to move reserves into place.

The question, then, was not whether—but where—to build them. The likeliest candidates had been destroyed during Big Week. And those facilities that had withstood the bombings remained targets for future raids. After initially exploring an idea to foil a concentrated Allied attack by scattering production across civilian sites from glass-blowing workshops to chocolate factories, the Jägerstab began wondering if they had been going about their mission all wrong. Perhaps they shouldn't be looking for sites aboveground at all. Perhaps they should be looking beneath it.

Hitler loved the idea. According to minutes of a meeting at his headquarters in early March, he ordered the "generous and final transfer of German industry under the surface." Every corner of the Reich was scoured for subterranean spaces that might prove suitable for aircraft production. Caves, mines, church cellars, breweries—nothing was overlooked. Within two months, two hundred thousand square meters of underground space were ready to be repurposed. By August, one million square meters were ready, only a fraction of Hitler's ultimate goal: eight million square meters.

Perhaps the most ambitious single project was codenamed Ringeltaube, "wood pigeon." Carried out under the auspices of Organisation Todt, Ringeltaube called for the construction of three massive bunker factories: Walnuss II, Diana II, and Weingut II, the latter located near Kaufering in the Ingling Forest. Combined, the sites were expected to produce nine hundred Me 262s per month. "They said if we finished it," Zayde recalled, "Hitler would win the war"—a claim historians consider a gross exaggeration.

To build the bunker factories, O.T. relied on some thirty thousand Dachau slaves. "Their use within the Reich," writes one of the scholars of the sites, historian Edith Raim, "constituted a precedent that needed special authorization by the Führer because the Reich had been officially judenfrei since 1943. So important was the O.T. project to the regime that ideological reservations were overruled by economic considerations. Jews who would have been killed without scruples in 1942 or 1943 were now exempted from gassing and instead were deported to Germany."

There seems to exist, embedded in our cultural understanding of the Holocaust, the idea that prisoners who escaped murder simply languished in camps, passing their days with nothing to do. In fact, imprisonment was frequently a form of servitude. Often under O.T.'s direction, camps were mobilized to provide an ample supply of labor for the Reich's highest manufacturing and construction priorities—from armaments to aircraft to military facilities. Just as the slaves of ancient Egypt built the pharaohs' pyramids and the slaves of the American South built the cotton economy, Hitler's slaves built the Nazi war machine.

One of those slaves was my grandfather. I once asked him if he'd ever heard the names Walnuss II, Diana II, or Weingut II. He had not, insisting that the sites had been called Moll and Holtzmann. It took me some time to draw the connection: Philipp Holzmann and Leonhard Moll were O.T.'s German subcontractors for, respectively, Diana II and Weingut II.

Construction of the bunker factories, obscured from aerial surveillance by massive nets fastened to towering pine trees, involved shaping an estimated 740,000 cubic feet of gravel into a mound 787 feet long, 278 feet wide, and 93 feet tall. Tons of concrete were then poured over the mound until the coating was ten feet thick. Weingut II alone required an estimated eleven million cubic feet of concrete. Once the concrete dried, a tunnel was carved from one end of the mound to the other and tracks were laid for a small train to carry away the gravel, leaving a vaulting ceiling over a gaping cavern. Then the process was repeated again and again.

Upon completion, the three structures would have been large enough to house a roughly six-story building and enclosed by a roof camouflaged with greenery and trees. Due to shortages of steel and concrete, two of the sites quickly ground to a halt. Only Weingut II moved forward, but it remained unfinished at the end of the war. The best eyewitness description comes from a US Army major who came across one of the sites in late October 1945: "The factory is astonishing. It is an aircraft plant located in thick woods. The largest single unit in this plant is an enormous incomplete underground hangar. Railroad trains come in at ground level. At the bottom level of the hangar, you have to crane your neck to see the undersides of the railroad cars. Colossal is only a mild word to describe the structure. Only the Maginot forts that I saw in France can compare with this."

The toll on the prisoners is reflected in a single statistic, reported by an O.T. staff officer in December 1944: only 8,319 of the 17,600 inmates at the Kaufering camps were capable of even light work. So harsh were conditions at the Ringeltaube sites that prosecutors cited them as evidence of "the violation of the laws and usages of war" during a military court trial of Dachau personnel.

The conditions, according to the *Review of Proceedings of General Military Court in the Case of United States vs. Martin Gottfried Weiss et al.* (Weiss was Dachau's commandant), were especially difficult "for the night shift and the average night shift worker died from the severity of the work. Once a worker was shot because he fell asleep. Almost every day some dead were brought back to the camp. The prisoners were continuously beaten by the German foreman who even used iron hammers. Prisoners were pushed off the construction building which was about six stories high."

Whenever I asked my grandfather what it was like at the sites, he'd tell me about waking up each morning to find dead prisoners on either side of him. "*This* one was sleeping," he'd say. "*This* one was sleeping." And he'd tell me about the Hungarians, who arrived on a transport in September 1944. They had not, like Zayde, endured one camp after another before Kaufering. They had not had a chance to harden themselves, to adapt. Instead, they had come directly from their villages in Hungary.

In a way, my grandfather would say, he had been fortunate, adjusting to the increasing demands of his captors, like a climber acclimating to higher levels of altitude. Unprepared, many of the Hungarians simply gave up, their wills defeated, submerging themselves in large piles of empty cement bags, where their lifeless bodies would be collected and carted away.

There's another story my grandfather tells about the Hungarians. Their arrival brought news of the outside world for the first time in months, alerting inmates to the approaching Jewish High Holy Days. I've often struggled to understand how my grandfather could, after all he'd experienced, sustain his faith during—and after—the Holocaust.

When I asked him about it, he told me a story about visiting a friend in Connecticut after the war—a rabbi and fellow survivor.

"Where was God?" my grandfather asked. "Don't ask such questions," replied the rabbi. "There's no one to answer them."

That he would ask such a question reveals an uncertainty, a skepticism, he rarely shared with his family. And yet, whatever his doubts, he also seemed to possess what is perhaps the oldest, purest form of faith, defined by another community of believers as "the substance of things hoped for, the evidence of things not seen."

And so, on Kol Nidre, the eve of Yom Kippur 1944, in the darkness of Dachau—the very place and moment where God could not have seemed more absent—my grandfather set aside his daily allotment of bread and prayed, a living embodiment of hope over despair, dignity over degradation.

It is a story that reminds me of a passage by another Kaufering survivor, the Viennese psychiatrist Viktor Frankl. "After all," writes Frankl in *Man's Search for Meaning*, "man is that being who invented the gas chambers of Auschwitz; however, he is also that being who entered those gas chambers upright, with the Lord's Prayer or the Shema Yisrael on his lips."

10

The Watchmakers' Brigade

United States Holocaust Memorial Museum, courtesy of
National Archives and Records Administration, College Park, MD

One of the Kaufering camps after liberation. The sunken,
earthen-roofed huts were characteristic of the camps.

"WHY," I ONCE asked my grandfather, "did you survive? Why you—and not so many others?"

Zayde's answer: his mother's faith. In Stutthof, he learned after the war, Chaya had fasted every Monday and Thursday—days when the Torah is customarily removed from the ark. The power of a mother's prayers was the source of his survival, he'd say.

And yet his own stories suggest he was not willing to trust his fate to prayer alone, that what also contributed to his survival was the occupation scribbled on Gershon's Dachau entry form: Uhrmacher.

Ask Zayde how he started fixing watches for Nazis, and he'd tell you how he offered his services to the foreman of one of the

Ringeltaube worksites, who had a pocket watch in need of repair. Ask him where he intended to find the tools needed to fix it, and he'd tell you how he made them from what he found in a shed on the construction site. How he removed the handle of a slim saw, split the blade in two, and fastened the pieces together at one end to form a pair of tweezers. How he found a couple of three-inch nails, filing the ends down until they were thin and flat—screwdrivers.

And he'd tell you how, the following night, after the Germans discovered the tools during a pat-down while he was on line for dinner, the Lagerführer, the head of the camp, demanded to see him the next morning, outside camp in the woods. A sleepless night followed.

Abram watched through the barbed-wire fence as his son was escorted outside, certain he would be executed. Decades later, Zayde's eyes would widen in surprise and relief as he described the moment he saw two objects dangling from the Lagerführer's fingers—a pocket watch and a miniature clock. The moment he realized the Nazi would not be his executioner. He would be his customer.

"Fix these," said the German, "and you'll get a loaf of bread."

If he could repair them with his father, Gershon replied, they could finish the job in half the time. And that is how Zayde extricated himself and his father from what may well have been fatal shifts at Weingut II and Diana II. Once again, the loyal son had saved his father's life.

He'd always tell another story, too, about working for the Lagerführer. One day he was summoned to the Nazi's office. Again, he feared he'd done something wrong and was about to be killed. Instead, the Lagerführer had a gift for him. Zayde had repaired some clocks for the man's friends, and the Lagerführer wanted to reward him with a box of fine cigars; Zayde declined to accept them.

Remembering this story, I once made the mistake of asking Zayde if he'd ever had wine or alcohol in the camps.

"What a meshuggah question," he exclaimed. "How can you ask such a meshuggah question?"

Zayde and Abram were not the only watchmakers in the camp. Around the same time they were fixing watches for the Lagerführer, a prisoner named Dmitrijus Gelpernas remembers, another watchmaker "had a conversation with someone from O.T., and he told him there were several very good watchmakers here." Gelpernas continues, "We later learned the O.T. man gave him a watch to repair as a test and was pleased with his work. So came the idea to organize a workshop that would repair watches for O.T. staff, SS, and civilian workers."

The O.T. official sponsoring the watchmakers' brigade was a devout Catholic. And when a parsonage in nearby Unterigling agreed to house the workshop, the official arranged for the watchmakers to be transferred to another Kaufering camp—Camp III—which had a train that could take them to the town.

I once asked Zayde about the workshop. He was silent for a moment before answering—then described walking into the parsonage for the first time and heading down a long hallway toward the back, where the workshop was.

"At the end of the hallway," he said, "I see someone. Who's this? I wonder." He paused. "It was a mirror."

He walked up to it, raising and lowering his arms, not quite believing that the reflection—gaunt and pale—was his own. "I didn't recognize myself," he told me, his voice cracking, tears forming in his eyes.

The workshop was in operation only a couple months—months of lighter labor and larger meals that probably saved the lives of all its members. Then, suddenly, it was over. "One day," Gelpernas recalls, "a German delegation came from Dachau. When someone asked if I knew anything about the watchmaking proficiency test, I answered: 'Only in theory, I've never actually taken it.' I had made a rule for myself early on: never tell Nazis the truth. For the most part, I followed that rule. This time, I told the truth and no good came of it. A few days later, the watchmakers' brigade was liquidated."

On February 18, 1945, Gershon and Abram were transferred out of the Kaufering camps to another Dachau subcamp, this one in Augsburg. After the war, a commission was established to investigate the crimes that had been committed in the Kaufering camps. The commission—made up of Holocaust survivors, Landsberg city and district officials, and representatives of the International Committee of the Red Cross—estimated that the death toll across the camps was approximately 14,500, out of roughly 30,000 Kaufering inmates. A death rate of approximately one in two.

11

The Bicycle

Zayde, seated on right, with other survivors in
Schwabmünchen shortly after liberation.

B Y 1945 THE city of Augsburg, once renowned as a capital of
German watchmaking, had become a center of Luftwaffe aircraft production—and not coincidentally, a frequent target of Allied bombing. Dmitrijus Gelpernas, transferred to Augsburg on the
same transport as Gershon, recalled the ruined factory where they
were put to work making component parts for Messerschmitt Me
410s and Me 262s.

"Everything had been bombed and destroyed," he says. "Inside there were wooden tables on which prisoners were ham-
mering pieces of aluminum into different shapes. The work
was simple and difficult—the hammer was heavy and we had

to swing it all day—12 hours—on our feet and on an empty stomach."

The relentless bombing presaged the end of the war. In March, US troops had crossed the Rhine into Germany. In April, Zayde heard rumors of approaching American forces. "The Americans are far away," the capo in the Augsburg barracks had told him, a tip that Zayde interpreted—in the circuitous ways intelligence was surreptitiously communicated—to mean the Allies were, in fact, close.

On Sunday, April 22, 1945, Gershon and Abram were evacuated and led on what would stretch into a five-day death march through the woods of Bavaria—two of tens of thousands of prisoners led on similar marches toward the end of the war, a final attempt by Nazi leaders to deny their slaves the chance at liberation.

The one story my grandfather tells about the march is standing under a tree—famished from the long walk without food—eating leaves off branches until they were bare. "Like a skeleton," he would say.

"On the last day of our march," Gelpernas remembers,

we were lying on a hill in the woods, surrounded by guards who were all trying to tear off and destroy any indication of their status and rank.

Many of them tried to ingratiate themselves with the prisoners: "You know, don't you, I never beat anyone. You'll confirm that, right?" Everyone could feel the Americans were nearby. Soon a few Russian youths arrived shouting, "The Americans are down in the village."

At first, I noticed nothing. Then I saw the whole group of prisoners running down the hill, at first slowly, then faster and faster. By then, the SS guards had disappeared, and at the foot of the hill was an American tank and a soldier looking bewildered by the mass of people approaching him in tattered striped clothing, their hair cut short, dirty and half-savage.

They encircled him, everyone trying to shake his hand, everyone speaking to him in broken English, everyone trying to kiss him. I saw two big tears running down his cheeks.

My grandfather does not remember the US Army tanker's tears. He does not recall the bewilderment. But he does remember the exact words that soldier spoke in German for all to understand: "It's 3 o'clock on Friday, April 27th—you are free."

Over the years, I've come across friends, classmates, coworkers, and acquaintances with family members on the other side of the liberation experience—liberators, not liberated. One of them shared a story about an uncle who'd been a tanker like the one my grandfather had encountered in the woods. He told his family that some GIs were so appalled by what they had seen that they lined up surrendering Germans and executed them.

In a family like ours, where the scars of the war sometimes seemed like the subtext of every conversation, such extrajudicial killings would have been excused, if not condoned.

Everything relating to Germany was viewed with a certain amount of suspicion. On family outings, if we heard anyone speaking German, particularly men or women of a certain age, eyebrows would be raised and looks exchanged. "What were they doing in the 1940s?" we'd all wonder.

During one of my high school English classes, the question of the German people's culpability in the crimes of the Nazi regime came up during a discussion of war literature. My teacher listened aghast as I argued, strident in my certainty, that Germans who supported Nazism had ceded their humanity. "They were monsters," I proclaimed. Looking back on my teenage self, I'm reminded of one of JFK's favorite quotes, what Lord Melbourne reportedly said of Macaulay: "I wish I were as sure of anything as he is of everything."

I would often try to engage my grandfather on the topic of German culpability and the balance between good and evil in human nature. His answer was always impatient. "What are you talking about?" he would say. To him, such questions were overly abstract, hopelessly philosophical. The worthwhile question was not about German culpability, but the culpability of individual Germans. Not about human nature, but the nature of specific human beings, some of them evil, some of them righteous, and some of them defying easy categorization.

One remarkable quality of my grandfather was his capacity for generosity. He often told a story that occurred just a couple days after liberation. He and his father had made their way to a town called Schwabmünchen near the site of their liberation, walking along the side of the road as US troops tossed cigarettes and chocolates from the backs of military vehicles.

Upon entering the town, they knocked on the door of a house they came upon, and a woman answered, her ten-year-old son standing behind her. "Where was her husband?" I asked my grandfather. Captured or killed, he assumed. They asked if they could come in, wash up, maybe spend a few nights. "You won't kill me?" the woman replied. No, they said, they just needed a place to rest.

After a bath, Gershon prepared to head into town. Occupying US forces had directed Schwabmünchen's shopkeepers to give the freed prisoners whatever they wanted for the next twenty-four hours. He was going out to get some clothes and food.

The boy was waiting for him by the door. Would Gershon mind, he asked, getting him a bicycle while he was out? He, the son of a Nazi, asking my grandfather, a Jew, for a gift. Perhaps the boy was unaware of how Jews had been treated. Or perhaps he was all too aware, raised to believe he could demand of a Jew anything he pleased.

All Gershon knew for sure was that the boy's mother had done him and his father a kindness by welcoming them into her home. And so, a short while later, the two of them could be seen on the streets of Schwabmünchen, the Holocaust survivor, his arms loaded up with all the goods he could carry, and the little German boy, pride of his Nazi father, riding beside him on his brand-new bike.

12

Abraham and Lea Perecman

Bubbie and Zayde in a displaced persons camp
in Eschwege, Germany, in 1946. The deprivations of
war are visible; they are much thinner than they
would appear in later photographs.

SECRETS ARE SOMETHING of a family tradition. One of my aunts never told her son he was colorblind, and he didn't find out until his now-wife told him in his twenties. One of Mom's cousins once had surgery in Israel, not the United States, because her mother didn't want anyone to know she was sick. And no family gathering was complete when I was growing up without my mom or her siblings switching from English to Yiddish to discuss something they didn't want me or one of my cousins to understand.

For many years, the biggest secret in my family was that Bubbie and Zayde had two sets of names and identities. The first set of identities, their true identities, were known only to immediate family. Bubbie was Rivke Wexler, born on August 10, 1925, in Postov, Poland, and Zayde was Gershon Gubersky, born on August 14, 1924, in Michalishek.

To everyone else, Bubbie was Lea Perecman, born on June 4, 1927, in Wadowice, Poland, and Zayde was Abraham Perecman, born on June 2, 1921, in Ostrow, Poland. Perecman—not Gubersky—was the name on their drivers' licenses, passports, and any other form of official US government identification. It was the name they chose for the family business, Perecman Jewelers. And it was the name they passed on to their children and grandchildren, including me. My middle name is Perecman.

I don't remember anyone telling me explicitly not to reveal Bubbie and Zayde's true names and identities. I simply knew, from the way people talked about it—quietly, when no one was around—that their true names were a secret that our family was expected to keep.

It was not always easy. My mother once told me that when she was a teenager and went to the DMV for her driver's license, she had to call home to confirm what to put down when the clerk asked her mother's maiden name. To any suspicious friends or neighbors who asked why Zayde had a different last name from the father to whom he bore such a close resemblance, the answer was simple: he was adopted.

When I was a young boy, I remember answering the phone and hearing a voice on the other end, asking for my mother. "Who is it?" my mother mouthed across the kitchen. The man said he was another Perecman and figured we must be related. My mother frantically signaled to hang up.

Another time, during a visit to the Orthodox Jewish cemetery in Connecticut where much of my Perecman family is buried, one of my young cousins asked why our great-grandfather Abram's tombstone had a different name—Gubersky—from our own. My uncle quickly shooed him along with an unconvincing answer.

Keep the family secret, don't reveal the story—that was our unspoken mandate. What exactly the story was, remains unclear. To this day, the circumstances surrounding my family's transition from Guberskys to Perecmans remain murky, as Zayde preferred it.

I *do* know that the origins of the secret date back to the years just after the war, when Bubbie and Zayde were living in what's called a DP (displaced persons) camp in Eschwege, Germany. Gershon and his sisters had arrived in the camp on March 16, 1946, just in time to celebrate the Jewish holiday of Purim at a festive dance, where Bubbie and Zayde locked eyes for the first time.

One year later, they were married, holding their wedding reception in the Bavarian spa town of Bad Reichenhall, where they danced to the songs of a friend from Eschwege, fifteen-year-old Netania Davrath, who would go on to become a celebrated soprano, performing with the likes of Leonard Bernstein and the New York Philharmonic.

Gershon spent his time in Eschwege fixing watches with his father while running a small side business smuggling contraband into the camp. He would never reveal what exactly he was selling—my uncle thinks it was cigarettes—or how long he was selling them. When asked about it, he would just smile and change the subject. But that business was sufficiently good that he and his partners could buy a car to expand their market beyond the DP camp.

At some point, the car was pulled over by West German police, putting an abrupt end to their operations. My grandfather wasn't in the car at the time, but it was registered under his name, and the police were onto him. In fact, a police officer walked up to him in the DP camp and asked if he knew where to find a certain Gershon

Gubersky. Characteristically quick-footed, he replied he'd never heard of anyone by that name.

Fearing that any whiff of criminality would hamper their chances of immigrating to the United States, Gershon and Rivke felt they had little choice but to adopt new identities. According to Zayde, they were unable to find papers for a married couple, so they bought the papers of two unmarried adults, Abraham Perecman and Lea Ringel. The real Abraham and Lea had immigrated to Israel, where such documentation was not required.

My grandparents had briefly considered immigrating to Israel themselves, but living in Israel at that time—as so often since— meant more fighting, more war, and in Zayde's words, "We were tired of war." They wanted peace, so they chose America. "Did you ever consider staying in Europe?" I once asked Zayde. "No," he said. There was nothing left for them there. There was also another com-pelling reason for choosing America: Zayde's father Abram had de-cided to settle in New Haven, Connecticut, near a brother who had emigrated before the war, and Frumke and Blumke had joined him.

Gershon and Rivke applied for a marriage certificate under their new names, and on March 29, 1949, the couple formerly known as Gershon and Rivke Gubersky were married for a second time, of-ficially becoming Abraham and Lea Perecman, the names they gave to immigration officers upon arriving in the United States.

That was all I, or anyone else in my family, knew about the origins of our name until I started poking around in the archives of Yad Vashem a couple of years ago. There, researchers unearthed a correspondence that occurred over the course of a decade—from 1957 to 1967—on the multiple identities of one Abraham Per-etzman. The name, according to the International Committee of the Red Cross, was being used with modest spelling variations by no fewer than three different individuals, two of them living in Is-rael and one of them in the United States, with an address matching Bubbie and Zayde's in New Haven.

The practice of adopting another surname before immigrating was fairly common in those years, as it has been throughout history, a fact acknowledged in the correspondence. But it seems German reparations payments were at stake, and the Red Cross, as well as other parties, were trying to get to the bottom of the matter. Investigators seem to have settled on a certain Abraham Peretzman of Tel Amal, Israel, as the one true Abraham Peretzman, and facing the prospect of arrest, he signed an affidavit confirming it.

That, along with the fact that a German lawyer representing Abraham Perecman of New Haven—my Zayde—ignored repeated attempts at contact, seems to have persuaded the relevant authorities to drop the investigation. When I told Zayde about the investigation I'd uncovered and the references to his own lawyer in Germany, he replied that he knew nothing about it.

After discovering these documents in the summer of 2017, I decided to see if the one true Abraham Peretzman were still alive. With help from a friend in Israel, I managed to track down the telephone number of a couple living in Haifa listed as Dora and Abraham Peretzman.

The woman who answered spoke no English, but I could detect some Russian, so I called back a few days later with my stepmother Helen—herself a Russian Jewish refugee—on the line to translate. The woman, we learned, was Abraham's second wife. Her husband, she said, was hard of hearing, so we could not communicate with him directly. But I heard him in the background, answering the questions we passed on to his wife.

"Was he from Ostrow, Poland?" we asked. Yes.

"Was he born in 1921?" Yes.

"Had he been in Eschwege DP camp?" Yes, he confirmed.

This was the man, I thought—the Abraham Peretzman whose identity my grandfather had bought. (The third Abraham Peretzman, according to the documents in Yad Vashem, was Itzchak Finkelstein, born in 1908, and I assumed I was not communicating with a 109-year-old.)

Then we asked the more sensitive question. We knew he was aware of the multiple uses of his identity—he'd signed an affidavit about it, after all—but we phrased it in a way that would allow him deniability if he wasn't comfortable answering honestly. "Was he aware that his identity had been used by at least two other people?"

I could hear Dora ask the question, and I could hear the silence that followed. She came back on the line: "He says," my stepmother translated, "he was never aware of it. He's a quiet, reserved man," she continued, "and he doesn't talk much about those years."

Dora herself, his wife of nineteen years, had not known her husband had lived in a DP camp in Eschwege until this very phone call. These men, I thought—Abraham Peretzman and Abraham Perecman—still holding onto their secrets, still doing whatever was necessary to protect themselves all these generations later.

So, with their new identities, Bubbie and Zayde traveled to the port city of Bremerhaven on the North Sea and on December 30, 1949, boarded the USAT *General Stuart Heintzelman* for the transatlantic voyage to the United States.

The ship docked in New York Harbor on Friday, January 13, 1950. Their surviving family members had all preceded them, and a delegation of Guberskys met them on arrival. After a quick bite at a nearby diner, they made their way to Grand Central Station, where they boarded the train to New Haven, the city they had decided to call home.

Over the years, I'd ask my grandfather about his arrival in America—what it was like, what it meant to him. Each time, he'd reply the same way—with the same proud look in his eyes, and the same big smile—telling me how, one week to the day after he stepped off the USAT *General Stuart Heintzelman* onto American soil, he had a little watch repair shop, the forerunner of Perecman Jewelers, up and running on New Haven's Legion Avenue.

PART II

INHERITANCE

The past is never dead. It's not even past.

—WILLIAM FAULKNER, *Requiem for a Nun*

13

The Survivors of New Haven

Zayde with his sisters, Blumke, seated,
and Frumke, standing, in the 1970s.

I N 1979, HELEN Epstein published *Children of the Holocaust: Con-versations with Sons and Daughters of Survivors*, the first widely read book on the experiences of what are called second-generation Holocaust survivors. It has not been out of print since. "For years," Epstein begins,

> it lay in an iron box buried so deep inside me that I was never sure just what it was.
>
> I knew I carried slippery, combustible things more secret

than sex and more dangerous than any shadow or ghost. Ghosts had shape and name. What lay inside my iron box had none. Whatever lived inside me was so potent that words crumbled before they could describe.

Sometimes I thought I carried a terrible bomb. I had caught glimpses of destruction. In school, when I had finished a test before time was up or was daydreaming on my way home, the safe world fell away and I saw things I knew no little girl should see. Blood and shattered glass. Piles of skeletons and blackened barbed wire with bits of flesh stuck to it the way flies stick to walls after they are swatted dead. Hills of suit-cases, mountains of children's shoes. Whips, pistols, boots, knives and needles.

It might seem strange that a child should daydream about skel-etons and barbed wire. But I'm hardly surprised, because such day-dreams filled the thoughts of another little girl: my mother.

Images and stories of the Holocaust were a leitmotif of her child-hood. One of her earliest memories is sitting with Bubbie and Zayde in the living room of their home on Ellsworth Avenue in New Ha-ven, and watching a television documentary about the war. Mom still remembers the black-and-white reel of corpses being shoveled into mass graves. She was about five years old.

Back then, in the 1950s, Bubbie and Zayde were still absorbing as much as they could about the Holocaust. They'd known their own experiences, of course, and the experiences of family, friends, acquaintances, and strangers they'd come across in Europe and America. But it was only after seeing some of the early journalistic accounts, documenting the full toll of the suffering, that they could situate their own stories within the larger, terrifying picture.

Mom was one of four children in that house. Her oldest sibling is my Aunt Linda, Lila before her parents Americanized it. Among family, Linda is also called by her Yiddish name, Leah or Lehke. Next oldest is my mother, Ellen—in our family, Chaya, Chayke, or

Chayele. My uncle Mark and aunt Shirley—twins—are the youngest. Mark is always Mendel, and Shirley, either Sorke or, more commonly—and for reasons no one seems to remember—Shushie.

If these Yiddish names—Leah, Chaya, Mendel, Sorke—sound familiar, it is because they appeared earlier in these pages. Each belonged to a family member who died in the Holocaust. Leah was Bubbie's mother. Chaya, Zayde's mother. Mendel, Bubbie's father. Sorke, one of Bubbie's older sisters. (Bubbie's brother Yale gave the name of one of their other sisters, Perke, to one of his daughters, Americanizing it as Pearl.)

In the Jewish tradition, it is not unusual to be named after a deceased family member. But Mom and her siblings were not named after some distant relative who passed away after a long bout with illness, as often happens today. They were named after mothers, fathers, and siblings who had been slaughtered less than a decade earlier.

I always wondered how it felt to be living reminders of loved ones who had perished during the war. "I considered it a blessing, a mitzvah," Mendel once told me. "I never thought about it," my mom says. Maybe so. I suspect Bubbie and Zayde did think about it. How could they not?

Bubbie and Zayde had a somewhat conflicted approach to preserving the memory of the Holocaust in their home. They wanted their children to remember what had happened. The words "Never Forget" and "Never Again"—words that have lost some of their force with every subsequent genocide—felt like a commandment. And whenever Bubbie and Zayde came across something about the Holocaust on TV or in a magazine, they made their kids take a look. "This is what it was like," they'd say. "This is what we went through."

And yet they rarely talked about their own experiences. For much of Mom's childhood, her parents refused to say anything about the war at all, a not unusual feature of Holocaust survivor families. And their children learned not to push them. "Bubbie would start to cry if you asked about it," Mom remembers, as Bubbie had done one of the times I asked about it. And on those occasions when her father started to open up, Bubbie would interrupt. "Gershke," she'd say, "don't talk about all that."

The only times my mother remembers hearing them tell their stories were when friends or family members came over. *Then* the stories poured out, even as Bubbie did her best to shield her children. "Why don't you go in the other room," she'd urge when the conversation turned to the past.

Still, the past was inescapable. Most of Bubbie and Zayde's friends, especially in their early years in America, were Holocaust survivors, and many of their children's friends were children of survivors, too. All of their neighbors were also survivors. Up the street. Across the street. Bubbie and Zayde had left Europe, but they had chosen to raise their family in the Holocaust's diaspora.

Anyway, even if Bubbie and Zayde themselves were resistant to talking about the war, the same could not be said of Zayde's father, Abram, who lived with them and constantly talked about it. "Those were his bedtime stories," Mom remembers.

Abram was that rarity in a community of Holocaust survivors and their families: a grandfather. Most of Mom's second-generation friends had lost their grandparents in the war, and they treated Abram like some sort of celebrity. By all accounts, Abram enjoyed everything about it, captivating the neighborhood's kids with his tales and showing off a scar on his back that he claimed was from a Nazi's knife. (Zayde would later reveal that the scar was, in fact, from a surgery in Europe.)

It was only after Abram passed away from a heart attack in 1965, Mom says, that her father began opening up about his own experiences. It was as if what she calls a "transference" occurred. Zayde seemed to feel it was now his responsibility to preserve the memory of what had happened, of what they had endured.

By the time I came around, Zayde was happy to answer any questions, and starting around age ten or eleven, I'd ask about the war on almost every visit. Why would a young kid ask about such distant events? Well, the events never felt distant. They felt relevant, immediate, somehow. The Holocaust—its stories, lessons, scars—was always present on trips to Connecticut.

Sometimes Zayde would start telling a story about a friend of theirs who was also a survivor. Or everyone would start talking about politics or world affairs, and sooner or later, comparisons were being drawn to events of the 1930s or 1940s. Sometimes the subject came up when my mom or one of her siblings asked a question, seeking clarity about some foggy anecdote or wondering what a certain family member had done during the war. In Zayde's final years, my aunts and uncle would even bring friends to meet the man they'd heard so much about, like some sort of pilgrimage.

Occasionally, in retelling his story, Zayde would cut himself off, as if struck by the horror of his own experiences, incongruous amid the placid suburban lifestyle he enjoyed in Connecticut. "I feel like I have become a Holocaust denier myself," he'd say. "It's so hard to believe it really happened. But it did."

All of Bubbie and Zayde's grandchildren asked about the Holocaust, but I asked more than others. Mom encouraged me. "Why don't you call them and ask them directly?" she'd say when the subject came up in our New York City apartment. Or, "Why don't you ask them in person on your next visit?" she'd suggest, if it were about something particularly sensitive.

In high school, I told my guidance counselor I wanted to write my college application essay about Bubbie and Zayde. "Oh, don't do that," she cautioned. "Everyone who has Holocaust survivor grandparents writes about them."

It was bad advice, and I took it. But I couldn't shake the feeling that Mom's life, and my own, had been shaped by the Holocaust, even if I did not fully understand how.

The Holocaust left different marks on different members of my family. The husband of one of Zayde's sisters had a breakdown. He was the only one of eight brothers to survive; the others, along with his parents, never even made it to the camps.

I'd see him at Bubbie and Zayde's Passover seders—sprawling, noisy affairs with three generations of Guberskys and Perecmans spilling across the dining and living rooms, where folding tables and chairs, couches, and a piano bench had been arranged to accommodate the guests. Zayde sat at the head of the table, surrounded by his generation of survivors, followed by their children, and finally all of us grandchildren; the periodically empty seats at the table belonged to the women continually serving and clearing the places of the men.

I'd say hello to my great-uncle, and he'd simply nod and smile. I can't remember ever hearing him say a single word. Years later, I'd learn that the man would periodically wander out and fail to return, leaving his worried wife to send their son out to search the streets at night for his troubled father, who would invariably turn up, only to do the same thing all over again some time later.

Another extended family member was a survivor of Auschwitz. She, along with her sister, had been awaiting execution when the Russians freed them. At the moment of liberation, I was told, she and her sister had been kneeling over open graves that they'd been ordered to dig for themselves, their heads shaved bald in preparation for execution. After starting a family of her own in the United States, she forbade her children from playing with anyone who wasn't Jewish, so terrified was she that their friends would turn on them, as her own friends had turned on her. "Can you blame her?" everyone would say after telling the story.

"How were you different after the war?" I once asked Zayde. "How did the war change you?" "I was less religious," he replied. I tried to probe further.

What he meant, he explained, was that he didn't wear tefillin or fast every week, as he'd done in Michalishek. Nevertheless, "less religious" to this son of Michalishek still meant Orthodox in America. And when I was growing up, Mom and I, along with her siblings and my cousins, would often join him and Bubbie for Rosh Hashanah and Yom Kippur services at Young Israel of New Haven, then a large, vibrant congregation, dominated by Holocaust survivors and their families, where men and women sat separately while the kids played downstairs.

All of Zayde's children were observant Jews themselves, varying only in degree. I grew up in a kosher household with separate sets of silverware and dishes for milk and meat, as did many of my cousins. But Mom's faith, like everything else she did, also bore her own distinctive flair. My bar mitzvah did little to ignite my faith, but it led to a kind of spiritual awakening in my mother, who started attending synagogue weekly and observing the Sabbath, refusing to use the telephone or do work on Saturdays.

I once joined Mom and Zayde at Rosh Hashanah services at Shushie's synagogue in Cheshire, Connecticut. During the service, there is a prayer that congregants are called upon to recite silently while standing, sitting down as they complete it to allow the rabbi to continue with the service.

One after another, our fellow congregants sat down after a brief interlude of silent prayer, while my mom continued, moving her lips and davening at her own pace, which was evidently considerably slower than everyone else's. When everyone but my mother was seated, congregants in nearby rows started shooting her looks—and then shooting us looks for not doing anything about the woman preventing the service from proceeding. Even the rabbi himself began nervously glancing up from his text to see if she was close to finishing. She wasn't.

"Chayke, come on," Shushie began whispering. Still, she stood there. At last, even Zayde himself had had enough, embarrassed by the scene his daughter was causing. "Chayke," he said, loudly enough for nearby rows to hear, "sit down." Mom closed her prayer book and took her seat with an audible sigh, as if she'd been cut off prematurely.

The last time I went with Zayde to his synagogue, the shrunken congregation, holding fast to its Orthodox traditions even as the older generation passed away and the younger generation wanted something different, fit inside the back room of a storefront down the road from Perecman Jewelers on Whalley Avenue. By then, Zayde was the last Holocaust survivor left in the congregation, a survivor even among survivors, having outlived virtually the entire diaspora that had settled in New Haven after the war. An honored guest, he was invited to read from the Torah at every service he attended—a fitting tribute to the man who had fasted in Dachau.

I once asked Zayde how he had seemed to withstand the crucible of the concentration camps, why the experience had failed to break him even after it had failed to kill him. He told me about an old Yiddish aphorism that his fellow inmates in the camps would use to describe him: "Your mother prepared you well for adversity."

That resonated with me. I marveled at how well adjusted he seemed, at least most of the time. To the extent I saw his occasional flashes of anger, they were almost exclusively directed at his own family.

Still, such flashes were the exception. Most of the time Zayde was cordial, friendly, even playful, the picture of propriety, always taking great pride in his appearance and manner. The first—and for many years, only—suit I owned was a double-breasted wool suit, and the only knot I knew how to tie was a double Windsor, both of them courtesy of Zayde, who felt the more formal styles were the only appropriate ones.

Appearances mattered to Zayde, perhaps too much. When Bubbie's health began to decline, he refused to get a handicap placard for their car, lest other people know she was unwell. That meant she had to park around the corner from The Store, a couple of blocks away, even in winter, which she would always do without complaint.

Was such concern with appearances rooted in his wartime experience? A refusal to let others detect even a trace of weakness? An insistence on proclaiming his sense of self-respect, projecting a sense of dignity, after all the degradations he had endured?

One of Zayde's most conspicuous attributes, and perhaps his only unrefined one, was his manner of eating. As with countless other immigrant families from countless other cultural traditions, food played a central role in our family. My childhood memories of Bubbie and Zayde's home are memories of smells as much as sights— mun cake (with poppy seeds); bulkes (cinnamon rolls); cabbage stuffed with beef; and my favorite, lekach (honey cake)—Eastern European dishes and treats I've only ever seen at one other place: Gruenebaum's Bakery in an Orthodox section of the Bronx.

Watching Zayde eat was mesmerizing when I was a boy. It was a loud, messy, multisensory experience, not only for him but everyone around him. The chewing, the slurping, the way the fork or spoon would clank against his teeth, the way the food would get all over his mouth, crumbs and drops getting stuck in the folds of his cheeks, and the way he'd just leave it there, using a napkin only sparingly, when he was done, rather than cleaning up as he went along.

Eating with him made me think: This is a man who knows what it's like to go hungry, who doesn't so much enjoy food as attack it, hurling himself at it headlong, devouring every last crumb— except, of course, the debris all around him—as if this meal might be his last.

The food writer Joan Nathan once interviewed Zayde and his sister Frumke at a restaurant in New York City's theater district. "When I told them that I was interested in food during the Holocaust, they reacted with disgust," writes Nathan. "'Food? What food?'" Zayde asked.

"Then," Nathan writes, "he took the paper napkin off his lap and drew a piece of bread, dividing it into quadrants. 'This was our lunch—a quarter the size of a piece of bread for a German soldier.'" He'd always remember the prisoner who cut him on line for soup one night, depriving him of the last, chunk-filled ladle before the pot was refilled.

Frumke responded similarly, telling Nathan, "Dinner was soup, mostly water. Sometimes there was a little meat. For all we knew it was dog or horse meat." According to family lore, she had once slapped a capo in Stutthof for taking the rounded end of a loaf of bread that was rightfully hers, a story that filled me with admiration—and fear—of my larger-than-life great-aunt.

Until her final days, of course, Bubbie rarely talked about the war. But her nightmares may not have been the only way her trauma manifested itself. "She got angry and frustrated easily," Mom would say. "I remember sitting in her lap when I was little, maybe four or five. Whatever she was feeding me, I didn't want. She put her hand over my mouth and forced the food down. I felt like I was suffocating."

Mom also remembers another incident. Once, when she was about five or six, and the family was still living on Ellsworth Avenue, she let herself out and found her way to Zayde's shop on Legion Avenue—over a mile away, spanning several large intersections— before Bubbie noticed she was missing.

Was the reason for Bubbie's neglect innocent? Had she simply been tending to Mom's baby siblings and lost track of her older child? Or was the neglect a sign of something else? Was she lost in her thoughts? Distracted? Depressed?

Mom, at least, thought Bubbie struggled with depression all her life. I thought about what Bubbie herself had once told me, that she had been so tired, so hungry, during the war, she had wanted to give up, wanted to die.

Healthy responses to the unimaginable? Or early symptoms?

"I once asked her what she would do in the ghetto," said Mom. Bubbie told her she had been a housekeeper for a Nazi official. Every time she'd enter the man's home early in the morning, she'd find the other housekeeper, another Jewish girl her age, already there. "I was so impressed by her work ethic," Bubbie told Mom with a smile, copping to her own youthful naiveté.

"Housekeeping could've only taken a few hours," Mom replied. "What did you do when you were done?"

"I went home and went to sleep," she said, an answer my mom read as an early sign of depression. I'm not so sure.

One of the most influential studies on childhood trauma is the Adverse Childhood Experiences Study. Researchers have found that the number of traumas someone experiences early in life—their ACE score—is correlated with a range of health problems in adulthood, from heart disease to cancer. According to a 2014 study, writes author Paul Tough, "children with two or more ACEs were eight times as likely as children with none to demonstrate behavioral problems and more than twice as likely to repeat a grade in school."

I shared the ACE test with my mother. "How many childhood traumas did you experience?" I asked. "Three or four," she said, depending on whether Bubbie met the diagnostic criteria for mental illness, one of the test's questions. Whether or not Bubbie met those criteria, however, one other family member certainly did: Mom herself.

14

The Trauma Gene

With Zayde and Mom,
celebrating my birthday in the early 1980s.

S EVERAL YEARS AGO, I met a friend named John for lunch at
the Old Ebbitt Grill, a Washington, DC, institution across the
street from the Treasury Department. John had been a speechwriter
for George W. Bush, and we had met at a gathering of the Judson Welliver Society, a loose-knit association of former presidential
wordsmiths.

John and I loved to talk about American history. And at lunch
that day, we talked about some of the founding members of Judson
who had passed away in recent years, among them JFK's speechwriter and advisor Ted Sorensen and White House speechwriter
turned *New York Times* columnist Bill Safire. Standing with both
Sorensen and Safire years earlier, I'd heard Ted rib his old friend,

"Remind me, Bill, did you write for Nixon, or just Agnew?"—an instance of the good-natured teasing that was a hallmark of Judson dinners.

With their passing, and the earlier passing of fellow Judson founders Clark Clifford, Jack Valenti, and others, we had lost witnesses to—and participants in—some of the most consequential moments of the past half-century of American life.

Our conversation reminded John of a YouTube clip that he pulled up on his phone—a 1956 episode of the game show *I've Got a Secret*, where a panel is asked to guess the secret of an elderly man in a three-piece suit who walks uneasily onto the stage, leaning on a cane. Samuel Seymour, a panelist concludes after a few well-formulated questions, had witnessed, ninety-one years earlier, Abraham Lincoln's assassination—making him the last person alive who attended *Our American Cousin* in Ford's Theater that night.

Seymour, John told me, held an unusual, but not unique, distinction as the last living witness to a major historical event. In fact, John said, Wikipedia devoted an entire page to the subject, appropriately titled, "List of last survivors of historical events." That list began with Aristodemus of Sparta, last Spartan survivor of the Battle of Thermopylae, dead at age forty-nine in 479 BC. Among dozens of names after him are George Robert Twelves Hewes, last survivor of the Boston Massacre, Rebecca Tickaneesky Neugin, last survivor of the Trail of Tears, and James Marion Lurvey, last survivor of the Battle of Gettysburg, each of them marking the slipping away, beyond living memory, of history-bending events, the moment at which what had once been visceral, painful memories—of blood, cries, gunfire—lost the kinetic remnants of lived experience, and suddenly belonged "to the ages," as secretary of war Edwin Stanton reportedly said of Lincoln himself, hours after five-year-old Samuel Seymour saw the sixteenth president carried out of Ford's theater.

There is no entry on that Wikipedia page for the last living Holocaust survivor or last surviving veteran of World War II. Not yet.

Those names will appear soon enough. In fact, my generation—or perhaps our children's—may be the last to meet anyone who personally experienced humanity's bloodiest conflict.

And yet something of history's witnesses remains even after they depart. Something of what they endured outlives them. Their trauma does not, like them, turn to dust. It is bequeathed to us, their descendants, a part of our inheritance.

Native American communities speak of a "soul wound," the way the legacy of the genocide has contributed to a host of ills from one generation to the next. Harvard Medical School psychiatry professor Dr. Alvin Poussaint and journalist Amy Alexander have written of "posttraumatic slavery syndrome," and the physiological risks it has created for African Americans—high rates of heart disease, hypertension, and other stress-related illnesses—that, they write, are "virtually unknown to white Americans."

Much of the academic literature on what is now called "the intergenerational transmission of trauma" originated in the 1960s with Vivian Rakoff, then assistant director of research at the Jewish General Hospital in Montreal, who, along with colleague John Sigal, noticed that children of Holocaust survivors were visiting his clinic in particularly large numbers, and started wondering why.

"The parents are not broken conspicuously," Rakoff wrote, "yet their children, all of whom were born after the Holocaust, display severe psychiatric symptomatology. It would almost be easier to believe that they, rather than their parents, had suffered the corrupting, searing hell." He later added, "It was as if some curious contagion, some terrible experience, had been communicated to the children."

Over the succeeding more than half century, hundreds of papers have been written on the subject of intergenerational Holocaust trauma by researchers in Canada, the United States, Israel, and around the world. Many of these studies have been challenged on the grounds that their sample sizes are too small or their study designs otherwise flawed, compromising their results. And their findings are often inconsistent, even contradictory.

One, for example, shows that Holocaust survivor offspring display "a tendency to experience depressive symptoms, mistrustfulness, heightened anxiety, and difficulties in expressing emotions accompanied by difficulties in the regulation of aggression, stronger feelings of guilt and self-criticism, and higher prevalence of psychosomatic complaints."

Another found that Israeli veterans of the 1982 Lebanon War who were second-generation Holocaust survivors reported a larger average number of PTSD symptoms—particularly notable, researchers say, because all of the study's participants were said to be physically and psychologically healthy before combat.

Others reveal no statistical differences at all between second-generation survivors and control groups. In fact, a 2003 meta-analysis of thirty-two studies involving 4,418 participants conducted by researchers at Leiden University in the Netherlands and the University of Haifa in Israel found "no evidence for the influence of the parents' traumatic Holocaust experiences on their children." (The same researchers did find, however, greater differences among children "who were also stressed by psychological or physical adversities unrelated to the Holocaust experiences of their parents, such as combat stress reaction or breast cancer.")

Similar inconsistencies dog the literature on the so-called third generation—my generation. In one study, grandchildren of survivors were found to be overrepresented by 300 percent in a child psychiatry clinic population. In another, they are found to have higher self-esteem and fewer behaviors indicative of severe psychopathology. Research has also been done on other forms of third-generation World War II trauma. In the wake of the 2011 Fukushima nuclear disaster, Israeli researchers found, "Grandchildren of Japanese living in Hiroshima and Nagasaki showed higher fear of radiation exposure and higher level[s] of PTSD symptoms."

Dr. Yael Danieli pioneered research on intergenerational trauma. In 1975 she set up one of the first organizations devoted to helping second-generation Holocaust survivors and their children, and her

1998 *International Handbook of Multigenerational Legacies of Trauma* remains a foundational reference text.

"A lot of people have focused on the question of whether children of Holocaust survivors develop mental health problems," Danieli told me. "For me, it was never a question of *whether*. It is a question of *who*, *how*, and *how intensely*." The answer to those questions, she says, depends more on how such children were raised than on their parents' Holocaust experiences.

Early on, Danieli—who coined the term *conspiracy of silence* to describe Holocaust survivors' unwillingness to discuss their experiences—identified at least four ways survivors adapt to their traumatic histories. "Victim Families," she wrote, were characterized by "depression, worry, mistrust, and fear of the outside world." "Fighter Families" sought to "counteract the image of the victimized Jew." "Numb Families" were notable for "pervasive silence and depletion of all emotions." And "Those Who Made It," who deny the Holocaust's effects, were "motivated by a wartime fantasy and desire to 'make it big' if they were liberated, in order to defeat the Nazis."

I emailed the long versions of Danieli's descriptions to Mom and asked if any of them characterized her own upbringing. She emailed them back, highlighting phrases and sentences that resonated.

Under "Victim Families," she highlighted "worry, mistrust and fear of the outside world . . . Physical problems were far more acceptable . . . than psychological problems. . . . Families insisted that the inside doors of their homes remain open at all times. . . . Bottomless rage . . . only indirect, mostly intrafamilial, means to express and experience it. . . . Guilt . . . keeping many adult children from . . . expressing anger toward [their parents], or 'burdening' them with their own pain. . . . Surpassing their parents meant leaving them behind, and as [a] result often unconsciously destroyed their success and accomplishments."

Under "Fighter Families," she highlighted "Any behavior that might signify victimization, weakness, or self-pity was not permitted. . . . Pride was fiercely held as a virtue; relaxation and pleasure were superfluous." Under "Numb Families," "The children frequently adopted outside authorities and peers as family in an attempt to seek identification models and to learn how to live." Under "Those Who Made It," "Tended to deny the long-term effects of the Holocaust upon themselves and their children."

I asked my mother how she would classify Bubbie and Zayde's parenting, based on Danieli's terms. "We were a victim family," she told me.

"That," Danieli told me, "may be significant." Children in victim families, Danieli explained, are statistically more likely to develop what she calls high "reparative, adaptational impacts," a term Danieli developed that refers to how much children want to heal their own parents, how well they adapt to the world around them, and how much their family's traumatic history and its aftermath continue to affect them and their choices about the future.

"Why does it matter if she has high reparative, adaptational impacts?" I asked Danieli.

"Because," she told me, "high reparative, adaptational impacts contribute to generalized anxiety disorder, depression, and post-traumatic stress disorder."

SEVERAL YEARS AGO, a flurry of news stories caught my attention. "Study of Holocaust Survivors Finds Trauma Passed On to Children's Genes," read a headline in the *Guardian*. "Descendants of Holocaust Survivors Have Altered Stress Hormones," read another in *Scientific American*. "Can We Inherit Memories of the Holocaust and Other Horrors?" asked the *Daily Beast*. The possibility was haunting—and captivating.

Had the Holocaust left some sort of genetic stamp on my family? On me?

Much of the headline-garnering research was led by Dr. Rachel

Yehuda, director of the Traumatic Stress Studies Division at the Mount Sinai School of Medicine. So I called her up and started with the basics.

"How do you define trauma?" I asked. The definition, Yehuda explained, has evolved. PTSD itself, she says, is a condition intended to put a single label on disorders previously assigned a variety of names: combat fatigue, battered wives' syndrome, Holocaust survivor syndrome. Trauma is best understood, says Yehuda, as "a watershed event that defines your life and divides it into a 'before' and 'after.'"

Yehuda herself began studying it as a postdoctoral fellow at Yale in the late 1980s. After interviewing a Vietnam veteran suffering from what we now know as PTSD, she told her mentor, "I just can't understand whether trauma does this, or whether this is just who this person is." She wondered whether other trauma survivors displayed similarly long-lasting symptoms. "That," her mentor replied, "is a testable hypothesis."

So Yehuda tested it. She returned to the neighborhood where she had been raised outside Cleveland, Ohio—a neighborhood with a large community of Holocaust survivors—and discovered that these survivors, like Vietnam veterans she had observed, had low levels of a stress hormone called cortisol—levels that are associated with posttraumatic stress disorder and chronic pain and fatigue syndromes.

Survivors of extreme trauma—combat, rape—often say that the experience profoundly, irrevocably altered them, explains Yehuda; that they are not the same person afterward that they had been before. What she was beginning to understand was how that could be true at the molecular level.

In subsequent research, Yehuda found that "Holocaust offspring were three times more likely to develop post traumatic stress disorder, if they were exposed to a traumatic event than demographically similar Jewish persons whose parents did not survive the Holocaust." In another study, she showed that pregnant women who were inside or near the World Trade Center on September 11—specifically, expecting mothers with PTSD who were in their second or third trimesters—gave birth to babies who also had low cortisol levels.

Yehuda's research is part of an emerging field called epigenetics, Greek for "above genetics." In the 1940s English embryologist C. H. Waddington used the term to articulate what he called "the epigenetic landscape," a way of thinking about cellular development.

Today, the word *epigenetics* has come to mean different things to different people, from information passed from parent to daughter cells after cell division to information transmitted across generations. But perhaps its most widely understood definition refers to a layer of information that sits above the genome.

Dr. Michael Meaney of McGill University in Montreal, one of the fathers of what's called environmental epigenetics, helped me understand the role epigenetics plays in our lives.

"From an evolutionary development perspective," Meaney told me, "it is always in a parent's best interests to enhance the fitness of their offspring. If the environment shifts dramatically—if the food supply suddenly diminishes or levels of violence rapidly increase—we can't simply wait around for genetic changes to occur. There has to be some way of signaling our offspring that allows them to adapt to the new circumstances. How does that happen? That," continued Meaney, "is where we landed on the idea that epigenetic mechanisms could be the process through which parents signal their offspring."

How, I asked Meaney, could altered stress responses in second-generation trauma survivors help them adapt to their environments?

The answer, he said, started with birds. Studies of birds show that pregnant mothers in what are called high-predation habitats, where they are particularly likely to be prey, inject their eggs with high levels of a stress hormone called corticosterone, the avian equivalent of cortisol. When the eggs hatch, these baby birds tend to be more fearful, and in a high-predation habitat, birds that are more fearful, more cautious, are more likely to survive.

The findings aren't limited to birds. Researchers looking at developmental outcomes of children, Meaney told me, have found that in conditions of poverty and violence, those who are shy and inhibited are more likely to be successful. "Think about it," he said. "If you're in a violent neighborhood, being more fearful, less likely to take risks, might not be such a bad idea."

In its extreme form, of course, an intense response to fear and stress can produce all sorts of psychopathologies. But an elevated sense of fear, a heightened response to stress, is not, in and of itself, maladaptive. Under the right circumstances, Meaney was saying, it could be precisely the opposite. It could help a person survive.

The question of how, exactly, such epigenetic changes are passed down from one generation to another is the subject of vigorous scholarly debate. Decades after World War II, children of women who were pregnant during the Dutch Hunger Winter, the devastating Nazi blockade of parts of the Netherlands in 1944 through 1945, were found to have higher rates of obesity, diabetes, and schizophrenia. Even their grandchildren, studies showed, were at greater risk of metabolic disease. It was proof, some argued, of epigenetic inheritance.

Perhaps—or, perhaps not. Because girls are born with all the eggs they'll ever have to reproduce, grandchildren of Hunger Winter survivors may have been directly exposed to deprivation when they were gametes in the unborn fetuses of their pregnant grandmothers—the reason, Rachel Yehuda told me, researchers require four generations to prove epigenetic inheritance.

Dr. John Greally, director of the Center for Epigenomics at Albert Einstein College of Medicine, has studied the Hunger Winter case. "I believe it is possible that nongenetic mechanisms can propagate traits through the generations," Greally told me. "But we have no evidence to date that it occurs through so-called epigenetic mechanisms."

Michael Meaney points to what he considers a possible explanation of how epigenetic changes can be passed down. In a landmark study, he found that rat mothers who lick their pups less frequently produce pups who are more fearful and wary than do more attentive mothers—and those pups themselves grow up to lick their own offspring less. "Variations in maternal care," says Meaney, "literally modify the chemical environment in which the DNA operates."

Despite the provocative headlines generated by her research, Rachel Yehuda, too, acknowledges the absence of definitive evidence that epigenetic changes can be directly inherited. But she also believes all the focus on the question obscures larger truths surfaced by the emerging science.

"Ultimately," Yehuda says, "the challenge for each of us is using our own experiences—however painful, however traumatic—to make better versions of ourselves. Trauma forces us to employ a broader repertoire of responses so that we can meet the challenges in our environment."

Epigenetics, she says, is a part of that process, a part of that promise. "The whole idea behind epigenetics is that we're a work in progress. And that's a good thing—because it means we're responding on a molecular level to what's happening around us and making changes to the way our genes function. It means our experiences are working together with our DNA. And *that* means, if we don't like where we are in this particular moment, we can go to a new place."

15

The Bird in the Purgatorial Flame

Zayde with my mother, age 10, outside The Store in 1963.

LONG AGO, I accepted what I suspect every child of a depressed parent accepts sooner or later: that proximity to a suffering loved one does not bring understanding. That in some fundamental way, my mother was, and always would be, unknowable, a stranger down the hall, my closest, most distant relation.

"How did it all begin?" I once asked my mom. "When did you first see the signs of the illness?"

She told me a story from adolescence, after the family relocated from Ellsworth Avenue to a ranch-style home at the end of a cul-de-sac on Crocker Road in Orange—one of five moves they made before Mom was in high school, the common experience of an immigrant family moving up as their means expanded.

The frequency of the moves also made me think of the Red Cross investigation into the multiple uses of the Perecman name. I knew that the Red Cross had sent Zayde letters that he had never answered. Had Bubbie and Zayde been moving so often to evade authorities?

Behind the new house on Crocker Road was a patch of woods, and Mom would often go there to read alone, while her siblings played inside.

"I spent a lot of time alone back then," she would say. "I also had this photograph hanging in my room," she added. She found it many years later in the basement of Zayde's home. A solitary young girl is standing in a field at dusk, facing away, head down, arms clasped behind her. It's a portrait of loneliness.

I asked if there were anything else, any specific moments she remembered. "I don't know," she answered. We were having dinner at her apartment on the Upper West Side. She went into the kitchen to refill our plates. "Actually," she said by the stove, "there was *something*."

As the only girl in her Hebrew school class, my mom was always assigned the role of Queen Esther in Purim plays, seeding an early passion for acting. In high school, she had been cast in a production of Edward Albee's *Who's Afraid of Virginia Woolf?* at the Yale Dramatic Association, the Yale Dramat, the nation's oldest continuously producing college theater company. It was a coveted role, particularly for someone so young, in a cast that included future Tony Award winner Judith Light.

"Driving back to Orange from New Haven at night," Mom told me, "I would take these winding roads. And sometimes I would think to myself, What would happen if I kept going straight at one of the turns? What would happen if I just drove off the road?"

Family members also have their own stories. Mom's cousin Pearl tells of getting a frantic call from Bubbie when my mom was in high school. "Your mother was refusing to talk to anyone else," Pearl says. Pearl asked Bubbie if she could come the following weekend. "No," Bubbie replied. "You need to come right now."

For much of my mom's teens and twenties, siblings and cousins would get similar calls, expected to drive over or hop on a plane immediately, if Mom was having one of her episodes and there was a chance someone's presence might help.

In the absence of any other suicidal thoughts or behaviors, such incidents might be utterly routine. Suicidal ideation, say therapists, can occur in otherwise healthy teens. And what teen hasn't felt lonely or inconsolable at one time or another? Yet in light of what would come, it seems reasonable to conclude that such incidents were an early sign of mental illness, a green shoot of the twisted tree.

"What did Bubbie and Zayde think of her depression?" I asked my aunt Shushie. "How did they handle it?"

"It broke their heart," Shushie told me. "They didn't really know what to do. They didn't really talk about it. No one talked about it. With all of the stigma in those days, I think maybe they thought it wouldn't reflect well on the family."

I thought of trauma researcher Yael Danieli's criteria for different styles of Holocaust survivors. "Physical problems," read one, "were far more acceptable . . . than psychological problems." Anything that might signify "weakness or self-pity," read another, "was not permitted."

The episodes continued when Mom went away to college at Sarah Lawrence. Soon after she arrived, campus authorities referred her to a psychiatrist. It was the first time she was prescribed antidepressants. "What happened that sent you to campus authorities in the first place?" I asked.

"Why did something have to *happen?*" she replied. "Sometimes nothing happened. Sometimes I was just depressed."

Something *did* happen, however. Early in her freshman year at Sarah Lawrence, Mom told Zayde about an opportunity to perform off-Broadway. "I've always felt most alive in the theater," Mom once told me. Zayde, however, didn't consider acting a worthy use of her education or his money, and made her promise to give it up. "That was a hard time for your mom," Pearl told me.

Was that why Mom was prescribed antidepressants?

I asked one of Mom's college friends, Beth, what she remembered from this time. Beth and my mother met their freshman year and shared a mentor, Adda Bozeman, a widely respected scholar of international relations. "Adda immediately saw a fragility in Ellen," Beth told me, "that manifested itself in a rigidity about a lot of things, a sureness of right and wrong, a fear of questioning. She wasn't a particularly religious person, but we'd all be having a drink at Adda's house, and Ellen would say she couldn't come because she needed to go kosher her room. She set herself apart. It didn't stop us from liking her, but it was odd."

During her junior year, Mom studied abroad in Paris. I grew up on the stories she brought back, including the time she saw two elderly Frenchmen openly giving each other the Nazi salute on the street. Later, I learned something else about her experience abroad: in those days, tutoring took place in students' dorms, and one of her professors came a little too close during one of her lessons, an advance she says she rebuffed.

When Mom returned to Sarah Lawrence, she enrolled in a linguistics course at Columbia, commuting once a week from Sarah Lawrence's Bronxville campus to New York City. She had taken Greek, Latin, and German in Paris, and discovered a knack for languages. With acting off the table, she thought linguistics might be a worthwhile pursuit.

One of the course's instructors was a Columbia professor, Bob. He was fourteen years older, married, and well ensconced in a field my twenty-one-year-old mother was considering entering, and they soon began an affair. At Bob's encouragement, my mom applied to Columbia's PhD program in linguistics when she graduated. And with Bob's help, says Mom, she was admitted.

I asked Mom's friend Beth if she knew of the affair at the time. She couldn't recall, but it didn't surprise her. "Everyone at Sarah Lawrence was having affairs with professors back then—some of them even resulted in marriage. It was a time of sexual awareness for our generation," she told me. "Most of us were involved in our twenties with married men, often powerful men. Power would usually be contextual, not power as in a high-profile figure or someone having power over us. But power as in someone admired in our individual spheres. The married man thing may be related to the newfound independence not to marry early. *Cosmopolitan* magazine was our guide. We believed in the idea that women have a right to be attracted to more than one person in the course of a lifetime and maybe to more than one person at once."

Zayde certainly didn't see things that way. During one of Mom's visits to The Store, he rose from his bench at the sight of his daughter, his face purple with rage. "What you're doing is worse than what Hitler did to me," he shouted in Yiddish. Without saying a word, she turned around and walked out, never knowing who had told him of the affair.

Meanwhile, the depressive spells continued. Mom remembers sitting alone on a bench at Columbia around this time, her gaze distant, when she was approached by two Mormons. Recognizing a woman in need, they offered their faith as a remedy. She sent them on their way.

During one particularly bad spell, Mom called her sister Linda, then living in Boston, and asked her to take the next flight down. Instead, Linda called Bubbie and Zayde, urging them to go to their daughter at once.

"They claimed the air conditioning was broken in The Store, so they had decided to drive to New York to spend some time with me," Mom remembers. "We went out to dinner, and Pop encouraged me to have a glass of wine, which I thought was odd. After dinner, they offered to drive me home. Pop got in the back seat, which was also odd because he usually drove. Next thing I know, they're heading down the West Side Highway toward Connecticut. I started screaming. They were kidnapping me.

"They thought I was on drugs," says Mom. It was not an entirely misguided assumption; Mom *was* using drugs, though in her case, as in others, the drugs were not the source of the trouble but one of its symptoms. Bubbie and Zayde arranged for her to see a psychiatrist in New Haven for what they thought was a drug addiction; she returned to New York City shortly afterward.

The incident was particularly hurtful, I suspect, because Bubbie and Zayde's inability to help, despite their efforts, came at a time when Mom was desperate for support. After a two-year-long affair, Bob had stopped returning her calls—*after* he had persuaded her to transfer from Columbia to the City University of New York (CUNY), where, he assured her, she would receive a better linguistics education.

Mom was devastated. Her friend Beth and a few others, hoping to take her mind off things, invited her out to dinner. Mom did some cocaine. "After you do coke," she says, "there's a downer. I don't know if that's what it was. But the next day, I wasn't feeling well." "Not feeling well" is how Mom always describes one of her depressive spirals.

All she remembers is that at some point, she walked into her bathroom, opened her medicine cabinet, and swallowed a fistful of pills. Frightened by what she had just done, she called Bubbie. In those days, there was no call waiting, and she got a busy signal.

"I took that as a sign."

"A sign of what?" I asked.

"That I should keep going."

She emptied the bottle into her mouth.

"Apparently," Mom says, "I was typing up notes while I was taking the pills."

"A suicide note?" I asked.

"I don't remember. Maybe a note to Bob."

Somehow Mom heard the phone ring through the haze. It was one of her friends, Isabel. "For some reason," Isabel told me years later, "I just let the phone ring and ring that day, and after a long time, she picked up."

"I took the pills," my mom whispered. "I took the pills."

The door was open when Isabel arrived. She found my mother on the bed, faceup, spread-eagled, foaming at the mouth. Draping Mom's arm over her shoulder, Isabel carried her downstairs and hailed a taxi that took them to the closest hospital, Roosevelt, on the Upper West Side.

"I don't think I've ever fully recovered from it," Isabel told me recently, "that this beautiful, intelligent, amazing woman would try to take her own life. Something transpired that day, with me finding her like that, and it's a bond that can never be broken. I've worried about your mother for the rest of my life."

Among Mom's first words to Isabel were "Don't tell my parents." It was too late. Isabel had already called them. Bubbie and Zayde arrived at the hospital a couple of hours later.

"Well," Bubbie said upon walking into the room, "that was a stupid thing for a smart girl to do." Zayde took one look at his daughter and burst into tears. "They were so wounded," said Isabel, "so terribly shocked."

"The doctors told me," Mom says, "that if I hadn't made it to the hospital so quickly, I would've died."

Isabel picked Mom up three weeks later. She had been on a floor with other patients admitted for the same reason. "All these people were talking," Isabel told me. "And I'll never forget, your mother told me she now had a dozen other ways to kill herself."

When they returned to her apartment, the notes she had been typing during the binge had been thrown away. Her parents had tidied everything up like nothing ever happened.

"Did you ever talk to Bubbie and Zayde about it? Did they ever ask why you tried to kill yourself?" I asked.

"No," she says. "We never talked about it."

I called Beth and asked what she remembered about the suicide attempt. "I remember being utterly shocked," she told me. "We'd just had this completely lovely dinner. She'd seemed so happy, so calm, so at peace, less frenetic than she sometimes was. There was nothing unusual about it. I remember talking with someone afterwards who told me that's often the case when someone has decided to commit suicide."

That was, in fact, what had happened. It was not as spontaneous as my mother had made it seem, not the result of some cocaine hangover. "I remember talking with her a few weeks later," says Beth, "and she told me she'd made the decision quite some time before, and was having these sorts of dinners and lunches with friends as a way of saying goodbye."

I don't know when I first learned of Mom's suicide attempt. Mom herself doesn't recall telling me. Neither does Dad. As early as eleven or twelve, I knew there was something dark in my mother's past, something nobody wanted to talk about—like the story of the little baby smothered in the bunker behind Bubbie's home during the war. And even after I learned about it, I still didn't know any details. Not when it happened. Or why it happened. Or how it happened. None of that would come until I began asking questions in my thirties.

I cannot know with certainty whether—or how much—Bubbie and Zayde's experience during the war contributed to, or exacerbated, my mother's mental health problems.

And yet it defies everything in my life's experience—everything I know of my mother, her parents, and their relationship—to believe her troubles are wholly unrelated to the Holocaust.

Remembering what Michael Meaney had told me—that elevated responses to stress can be critical to survival—I wonder: What happens when a child inherits traits that are ill suited to her environment? What happens when the behaviors we get from our parents—behaviors that may have worked *well* for them—actually work *against* us?

OVER THE YEARS, Mom would wonder aloud why she, alone among her siblings, had been so severely burdened by depression. And whenever I tell people about my family, I am often asked the same question: Why her, and not any of her siblings? How did they escape it?

Family therapy has a name for the phenomenon: "the identified patient," or IP, typically considered an emissary from a family that is hurting, a personified cry for help. As T. S. Eliot writes in the play *The Family Reunion*: "It is possible you are the consciousness of your unhappy family, its bird sent flying through the purgatorial flame."

And yet I've always found it a strange question. Who can perfectly tease out the separate strands of genetics, birth order, environmental factors, and simple chance that can produce different outcomes in a family? Why are any siblings different from one another? Even in a family displaying signs of intergenerational trauma, why would we assume every sibling would be affected in the same ways?

I suppose part of the reason I've never found this difference from her siblings particularly surprising is also because it is part of a broader pattern. Mental illness isn't the only thing that distinguishes my mom from her siblings. She is different in virtually every other way, too.

Some of those differences—of taste, style, dress—manifested themselves early on. "Come here, Chayele, you're so beautiful and so smart," her grandfather Abram would always say, without any regard to the feelings of his other grandchildren. Displaying the same sense of style as a young girl that she has to this day, she would show up to family outings wearing a white linen dress when everyone else was in shorts or jeans.

Other differences ran deeper. The middle child, who never felt as loved. The actress, the artist, in a family with little interest in acting or the arts. The intellectual in a family focused, ever since Aaron Velvel Gubersky sent Abram to apprentice as a watchmaker in Vilna, on the vocational. The city dweller, the world traveler, fired by an inextinguishable wanderlust, in a family that, by and large, didn't stray from the suburbs.

My mom's older sister Linda would attend a junior college and work in customer service for a telephone company before settling down and raising two children with my uncle Marty, who ran a plumbing business outside Boston. Her younger sister, Shushie, would work at an accounting firm before settling down and raising three children with my uncle Jay, who ran a construction company in Connecticut.

Mom, on the other hand, was the first in her family to attend a four-year college and the only one of its women to be a full-time working mom (although she believed Bubbie, who earned her GED well into her fifties, might have done the same had the war not deprived her of the chance).

"I've always been the black sheep in my family," Mom says, the one who never felt like she quite belonged. "Chayke," says Mendel, putting it more gently, "marches to the beat of her own drummer." Mendel himself followed the beat of a more familiar drummer, training as a periodontist before marrying the hygienist in the office, my aunt Lisa, raising three kids, and starting his own practice in Bucks County, Pennsylvania.

Mendel, a Republican, is also my own personal bellwether of where an election is headed. As goes Mendel, so goes the nation. And he's not the only Republican in our family. In fact, virtually every member of my Perecman family is a Republican—except Mom (and me). Her political beliefs, in other words, are just another thing that sets her apart. I cannot think of a single seder or family reunion that has not been overtaken, sooner or later, by some political dispute involving my Mom, with my conservative cousins rolling their eyes and snickering.

By the time I came along, such reunions were a regular occurrence. When I was a boy, Bubbie and Zayde took us to Kutsher's Country Club in the Catskills, the Borscht Belt, where we'd invariably be joined by their best friends, Melech and Shifra. Melech—the physical incarnation of the cartoon Tasmanian Devil—always brought along a wooden case.

"What's that?" all of us kids would ask.

"A typewriter case," he'd tell us.

When we got a little older, we noticed it contained not a typewriter but a bottle of Chivas Regal and four drinking glasses.

"What did Melech do during the war?" I asked my mom as a kid.

"He killed a lot of Nazis," she replied.

I loved Kutsher's—the canoe rides, arcade games, cheesy dinner entertainment. Mom had no such escapes when she was a girl. Entertainment, she once told me, was heading over to New Haven Green, where her grandfather Abram would capture a pigeon and bring it home for her and her siblings to play with before releasing it.

Bubbie and Zayde had survived an ordeal in which the slightest deviation, the subtlest act of nonconformity, could result in untold horrors. And yet here was their daughter, the nonconformist, the free spirit who marched to the beat of her own drummer.

"Did I feel like I didn't belong, so I got depressed, or was I depressed, so I didn't feel like I belonged?" Mom once asked me, herself uncertain of the answer.

MY PARENTS MET the year Mom was hospitalized—1976, America's bicentennial, when tall ships from around the world sailed into New York Harbor for the commemoration.

Dad struck up a conversation with her in CUNY's cafeteria. He was working for the Westchester County Attorney's Office at the time, helping underserved communities find jobs. After getting a law degree from Columbia, he'd tried working at a firm, but hadn't lasted long.

This work, he told me, was more gratifying. And he was better at it, going on to build a career in human resources, first in the private sector and then, for most of his career, at the United Nations Development Programme, where he oversaw the hiring of UN resident coordinators, the top UN job, in countries around the world.

"What were you doing in the CUNY cafeteria?" I asked.

"I guess I was there to meet girls," he replied.

Things moved quickly, and Mom and Dad were married within a year, welcoming me, their only child, four years later.

"Did you know about her depression?" I asked my father, wondering how open my mother had been with him before they got married. We were walking down Broadway after lunch on the Upper West Side.

"Sure I did," he said, adding plaintively, "I thought I could help. With everything that had happened—the hospitalization, the drugs—your mother had grown apart from Bubbie and Zayde. I thought I could help bring them together."

I asked if there were any more suicide attempts he was aware of, knowing it was possible other incidents hadn't been shared with me. He remembered another suicide attempt while Mom was still in the hospital or immediately afterward—an incident Mom says didn't happen.

There was also another incident after they were married. "One time, her psychiatrist called me at work and told me to get back to the apartment as fast as I could," he recounted, his voice growing agitated. "Said it was a matter of life and death."

When Dad got upstairs, Mom was sitting on the floor, drunk, papers scattered about. She had been reading letters from an old flame. Not Bob. Another one.

He also told me something else, an early, and different sort of warning he'd received about my mom. At their wedding, Mom was dancing a little too closely with one of the guests—who exactly, neither Mom nor Dad remembers. Dad's grandmother walked over to him.

"Be careful," she cautioned her grandson, nodding toward my mom. "She's trouble."

16

All She Has

Courtesy of the author

With Mom on a trip to Rome in the mid-1990s.

MOM AND DAD separated around my fourth birthday. I don't remember how I learned that Dad would be moving out, but Dad himself never forgot it. "You were sitting on your mom's lap in the dining room," he told me. "You looked up at her and said, 'Can Dad still come to my birthday party?'"

Mom's therapist told her it would be good for my emotional health for me to take part in the move. Looking back, I'm not so sure. As I saw my dad hauling his furniture down the street, it dawned on me just what was happening. I started wailing.

Dad stayed close, moving just a couple blocks away on West End Avenue. According to the terms of their divorce, finalized a few years later, he and Mom shared joint custody—a win, Dad felt, at a time when mothers were typically awarded sole custody. What it meant in practice was that I'd see my father twice a week, on Wednesday nights and Saturdays, and we divided the holidays: the Frankels got Thanksgiving, spring break, and a summer trip to Bermuda; the Perecmans got the Jewish holidays.

In photos from those years, at school or day camp, I'm rarely smiling. I seem sad, angry, dejected. The split was, as these things go, civil. But like so many other children of divorce, I often felt caught in the middle.

Many times, sensing my excitement about seeing Dad and his family, Mom would say, with a level of resentment that always felt like something other than traditional Jewish guilt, "It would be nice if you could be so enthusiastic about spending time with me or Bubbie and Zayde!"

After one of our Wednesday-night pizza dinners when I was seven or eight, Dad said he wanted to come upstairs. I told him he wasn't allowed inside. I didn't have the maturity to question whether the rule was reasonable, or whether it was my place to enforce it. It was simply what Mom wanted—or at least what I thought she wanted—so that was the way it needed to be.

Dad, understandably upset, called me from a pay phone on the corner. I was furious at him for challenging me—or my mother. "You're the worst dad anyone ever had!" I yelled.

Mom would later tell me that, growing up, she and her siblings had always felt protective of their parents. Bubbie and Zayde had endured so much, she'd say, that it was her job, *their* job, to protect them from any further pain, a role Mom acknowledges she did not always fulfill. I felt the same way toward her—protective, defensive, her faithful, loyal guardian.

Throughout my childhood, I'd hear Mom's siblings refer to their sister as a "single mom." I always resented the phrase for what I took to be its implicit disparagement of my father. But it was true that I didn't live with him. I lived with my mom, and she, more than anyone else, raised me.

She was the one who rushed me to the hospital after one allergic reaction or another when I was young. The one who helped administer my inhaler when my asthma kicked up, who read bedtime stories and tucked me in at night. The one who sat with me in the mornings eating banana bread she'd made from scratch, and in the evenings over some *coq au vin* or *boeuf bourguignon* she'd learned how to make during her time in France.

She was the one who taught me right from wrong and disciplined me. "These people didn't pay to hear you cry," she once said sternly as I began screaming on the M104 bus down Broadway.

"You're all she has," Mom's siblings would always say. It wasn't true. Not really. She had her family, friends, a job, passions. But I understood what they meant. So when they'd nudge, at bar or bat mitzvahs, weddings, or over the Jewish holidays—"Go sit with your mother" or "Go dance with your mother, it will make her happy"— I'd always comply.

I could sense, in a way that children can often sense unspoken truths, that my mother's emotional health was somehow tied to how much of myself I was willing to give. And I could sense that her family understood that truth, too.

Many weekends, Mom would take me to see Bubbie and Zayde. She seemed happier up there, and I felt freer, too, relieved—at least for a short while—of looking after her, of being the fulcrum of her emotional equilibrium.

Every time, as we got ready to leave, Zayde would pull me aside and stuff a few twenty-dollar bills into my palm, as I'd seen him do with all my cousins. Mom herself would leave with a wad of hundreds, the only Perecman child Zayde supported so generously, so regularly, for so long. Mom cannot care for herself, the gesture told me; she needs help.

I knew early on that something wasn't quite right with my mom. Some days she'd return home from work happy to see me, eager to talk. Others, she'd go straight to her room and shut the door. When I was little, I'd put my ear up to the door or peer through the keyhole.

What is she doing in there? I'd wonder. Why isn't she coming out? Why is she leaving me all alone out here?

At a certain point, I stopped wondering. I came to accept that it was simply who my mother was. I remember thinking as a boy that I never knew which version of her would be returning home at night—the one who wanted to spend time together, or the one who wanted to avoid me altogether.

As I got older, the routine evolved. We'd eat dinner together in the dining room, and then she'd go into her room and shut the door. I always assumed she just wanted to watch TV alone. Later I learned she sometimes sat on her bed, crying softly. A common memory among my childhood friends is hanging out in my apartment for hours at a time, only to learn, much to their surprise, that my mom had been home the whole time, alone in her room.

Knowing what I know now about her own childhood, I can see that she was isolating herself from me, just as she had isolated herself from her siblings as a young girl. The result was a kind of loneliness in that apartment that both of us were unable to escape.

Throughout my childhood, into my teens, I would have this recurring nightmare: I was locked inside the apartment on the Upper West Side, unable to live my life, duty-bound to care for my mother. Duty-bound not to leave her side.

"It must have been hard, me shutting the door all the time," Mom would say apologetically, many years later. "I just didn't want you to see me like that. Would you have rather I didn't shut the door?"

I wasn't sure what to make of the question. Surely she didn't want me to see her like that, but I also suspect she didn't have as much agency over the decision as she was suggesting, that she felt incapable of parenting in such a condition.

Anyway, how was I supposed to answer?

What I wanted, I replied, was not to face that kind of question in the first place. What I wanted was her not to feel like she *needed* to shut the door.

Mom's self-isolation, her solitariness, was not the only unusual aspect of her personality. Once, after visiting a high-end psychic (I was not previously aware such a thing existed), she told me she had communed with her ancestors in Europe—family members who'd perished before and during the Holocaust.

I was unfazed. I'd grown up hearing her assert, many times, that she had been a French peasant in a previous life—a life, she would say, that ended tragically in drowning. That, she'd add with a confidence I always found perplexing, was the reason she'd feared the water for as long as she could remember.

I'd often tease Mom about another odd piece of behavior: she would frequently talk to herself, loudly narrating her thoughts on some subject as she paced around, the quiet in our apartment broken by a seemingly endless one-sided conversation. Over the years, I grew so accustomed to it that I'd simply ignore her, playing with my G.I. Joes or watching TV while she spoke loudly to no one in particular.

Other memories stand out too. From time to time, Mom would mention this or that family member or friend she was no longer speaking to. For a while, she even stopped attending services at her synagogue because, she explained, the rabbi had done something to offend her. I grew up believing that such spats, such fallings-out, were a common occurrence in life, until I experienced the stability of my own adult relationships.

All of the drama, the volatility, hardly seemed Mom's fault. She was, I knew, at the mercy of her emotions, subject to their fickle swings. When I close my eyes and transport myself back, I can still feel her frantic, anxious energy, still hear the harried tone of her voice, even if the specific details, the triggering events, have mostly faded from memory.

I asked my dad about the few years the three of us were together. The first memory that came to his mind: Thanksgiving Day 1982 or 1983, when Mom suddenly—and inexplicably—decided she did not want to spend the holiday with the Frankels, as they'd planned, and he was left calling his parents to explain that we wouldn't be joining them after all.

Still, I never saw these sorts of behaviors as anything other than idiosyncrasies, the sorts of unique personality traits all of us, in one way or another, possess. "Ellen being Ellen," as one Perecman cousin put it. Mom being Mom.

Sure, she could be dramatic, but wasn't that just the disposition of a natural-born actress, as she considered herself to be? Sure, she could be impulsive, but I certainly didn't mind when she suggested one night, as the Yankees game came on TV, getting a couple of seats in the bleachers. Sure, I worried about what often seemed a rather reckless attitude toward money, spending thousands of dollars on paintings she couldn't really afford, but I almost admired that can't-take-it-with-you, live-for-the-moment attitude. And I didn't complain when she spent that money on a summer trip to a fancy ranch in Montana.

Mom would sometimes tell me, when I was growing up, that when I was a baby, she'd look at me and think that she couldn't wait until I got older, old enough to have a real conversation with her, old enough to be a companion.

And as I grew up, that is what I became. I was her son, yes, and she tried as hard and as best she could to raise me right—and succeeded in many ways. But I sometimes think she was less capable of—less interested in—being my mom than my friend.

One of my high school classmates would later tell me he was always struck by what he called the "openness and honesty" of my relationship with Mom, the way I seemed so comfortable telling her the kind of details most teenagers work assiduously to keep from their parents: where my friends and I went at night, and what we did. She was open with me, too, introducing me to many of her boyfriends, who would often spend the night.

I valued the openness between us. Now I also wonder if it

reflected an unwillingness, or an inability, to set appropriate boundaries. "Sometimes you two felt more like roommates than mother
and son," recalled one of my friends.

"You did seem to often be frustrated by things she did," one
friend remembered. "You worried she'd embarrass you." No doubt,
a common teenage fear. One year, my high school girlfriend showed
up on my birthday, excited to surprise me first thing in the morning with a specially made gift—one of my favorite 1960s rock al-
bums, made out of chocolate—only to be turned away at the door.
"Adam is sleeping," my mother told her. "He won't like to be woken
up." Learning of it years later, I sighed and shook my head.

Looking back on all our years together under the same roof, I'm
struck less by the prevalence of any particularly memorable acute
episodes of mental illness than by their absence.

"I'm not surprised," one of Mom's cousins told me when I shared
that observation. "You were a calming force for her. Remember
how she didn't even change the answering machine when you left
for college?" It was true. The recording, informing callers they'd
reached "Ellen and Adam," remained the same until I was in my
early thirties, more than a decade after I'd left home. "Having you
in the house was good for her," she continued. "Things were bad
before you were born, and they got bad again after you left."

COULD BUBBIE AND Zayde's experience in the Holocaust help explain not only some of the darker elements of Mom's psyche but also
some of the lighter elements of her spirit?

During my conversation with Mount Sinai trauma expert Rachel Yehuda, she said something that stuck with me: "We need to
start focusing on what we gain from trauma, not just what we lose
from it."

It can seem almost a flippant statement. How can we speak of
the *gains* of growing up with traumatized parents? The *advantages*
of a trauma as incomprehensible as the Holocaust?

And yet, insists Yehuda, part of what it means to understand the way trauma unfolds is to recognize the good it can do for us, not just the bad.

For example, she says, children of Holocaust survivors are often moral torchbearers in their communities, working in helping professions and sounding the alarm in times of crisis. My own awareness of what Bubbie and Zayde endured has, I've always thought, made me more sensitive to the suffering of others. Mom says the same.

One of her first jobs after getting her PhD was as a researcher at North Shore Hospital in Long Island. I have faded memories of visiting her there in the mid-1980s, the tall plants in the lobby, the all-white offices. What I did not know as a little boy was that she was working with AIDS patients to study how the illness was damaging their brains and language skills—pioneering, even enlightened research at a time when much about the virus was still poorly understood, and those suffering from it were often targets of abuse and discrimination.

Of all the possible topics to explore with a PhD in linguistics, why choose that one? Had her experience as the child of survivors made her more compassionate to others in pain?

In our apartment when I was growing up hung a photo clipped from the pages of the *New York Times*: a picture of Mom getting arrested outside the United Nations, protesting the Bosnian arms embargo, which she felt unjustly hamstrung the Muslims against the better-armed Serbs. "That's my mom," I'd say, pointing out the photo to any friends who came over. "Standing up for what's right."

Mom always felt a certain affinity with the poor, the forgotten, the old and infirm, strugglers of every stripe. I've sometimes thought she's more comfortable in sadness and grief than joy. Sympathy, her natural state.

Does she see in them something of herself, something of her parents? Did our family's experience help open her heart to empathy, to service?

I want to believe Rachel Yehuda is right, that something good can come from something so unspeakably bad.

MUCH ABOUT MY mom's parenting, I now see, was a response to her own upbringing. Her childhood had been so controlled, so insular, with New Haven's community of Holocaust survivors and their families so suffocatingly small, that she was determined to give me the experiences and space she felt she had been denied. She let me ride the subway alone much earlier than my friends and towed me along to off-Broadway shows at theaters where she had subscriptions, and museum exhibits on weekends. In every way she knew how, she wanted to show me the bigness of the world.

In high school she took me to her beloved Paris, pointing out her favorite cafés, used bookstores, and neighborhoods before we went south to visit some of her friends in La Roque-sur-Cèze, a medieval village outside Avignon. I remember fields of sunflowers, a shimmering pool, and her friends' children playing outside by a large wooden table beneath a vine-covered canopy. Another trip was to Rome, where, after a few days craning our necks in churches and museums, we took a train to see the rubble, mosaics, and plaster ghosts of Pompeii.

One memory from that trip remains particularly vivid: Mom and I are rushing to catch a train, and she is pushing passengers out of the way to climb on board. Of course, she is hardly the only person on earth to get frazzled running late for a train. But I'll never forget the sight of the other passengers on the platform, staring at the woman jostling them with utter confusion, even disgust.

I sometimes wonder why I remember their faces so well. Perhaps it's because it was one of the first times I saw the way other people reacted to behavior that had seemed so familiar, so unremarkable.

For much of my childhood, Mom worked at an academic think tank in a midtown tower. Her AIDS research had taken a toll, she would always tell me, demoralizing her in those years before anti-retrovirals extended lives. And her college friend Beth—the same one who dined with her the night before her suicide attempt—had recruited her to run a fellowship program for postgraduate students. The job allowed her to travel around the world hosting conferences, and one time, she brought me along.

It was a trip to the Middle East, and she took me to the Church of the Holy Sepulchre in Jerusalem, waiting outside while I joined the throngs kneeling in the crawl space where Jesus was supposedly crucified. Then she took me to the West Bank, where our taxi slowed to a crawl as it approached the checkpoint to Ramallah, and we ate pita and hummus in an open-air restaurant to the sound of firecrackers or firearms (we couldn't tell which) in the distance.

In Istanbul, we visited the Hagia Sophia, and she pointed out the overflowing slums that housed so many of the city's densely packed residents. In Cairo, we smoked hookahs on the Nile before heading down to Luxor, where a guide took us into the desert grave of an ancient nobleman, the thousand-year-old paint on the cavern's walls as bright a blue and gold as if it had been applied earlier that day.

The world is vast, complicated, and messy, she was teaching me. But it contains extraordinary riches and beauty, as well, and I should recognize and appreciate it all.

Mom and I were not alone on that trip to the Middle East. We were joined by one of her boyfriends. I'd already grown accustomed to my mother's peripatetic romantic life. "My life," she once told me, in one of her periodic bursts of inappropriate candor, referencing a line from her Yale Dramat credit, *Who's Afraid Of Virginia Woolf?*, "has been a game of 'musical beds.'"

Sometimes the men stuck around long enough for me to get to know them. When I was in grade school, I thought she might marry an Italian man until she told me Zayde objected because the man was Catholic; I remember thinking how strange it was that my mom, a grown woman, would defer to her father on such a personal decision.

Other men came and went. Eating breakfast in the kitchen one morning as a teenager, I was joined by a man whose name I no longer remember. Mom had told me she had high hopes for the relationship. Even at that age, however, I could tell, after only a few minutes, that nothing would come of it.

When I was in fifth grade, Mom's then boyfriend, a music editor in Los Angeles, got me a small part in his latest project, Barry Levinson's 1992 film *Toys*. One of Mom's old friends had a wealthy mother with a spare one-bedroom apartment, a few floors below her own, on Sunset Boulevard, our base for the several-weeks-long adventure. Every day we'd head to the 20th Century Fox lot, where a soundstage had been extravagantly reimagined as a miniature city, festively decorated for Christmas, with artificial snow falling from the rafters.

I loved every minute of it. How could I not?

I even got to spend time with the film's star, Robin Williams, who seemed to enjoy talking with the kids on set more than the adults (and somehow spoke Yiddish well enough to converse with my mom). "He's just ingratiating himself with you to get to your brother," Williams teased costar Joan Cusack after she found me, lost, wandering around the lot.

I was only dimly aware at the time that the trip had set off something of a firestorm back home. I remember some trouble at school, where my principal and some teachers thought it highly inappropriate to withdraw me in the middle of an academic year. The loudest outcry, however, came from Dad's family, who filed a lawsuit, at one point threatening a restraining order prohibiting my mother from taking me out of New York State.

Dad was particularly outraged by *how* my mother had told him of her plans to take me to LA: at a birthday party, surrounded by my friends and their parents—a setting she had selected, he was sure, knowing he wouldn't make a public fuss.

All my eleven-year-old self knew of what was happening, I heard from Mom, who frequently vented about it, calling the whole thing frivolous. Ultimately a judge found in her favor, ordering Dad's family to pay Mom's legal fees, which they did.

Neither Dad, nor his parents, said a word to me about any of this at the time. But several years ago I came across some letters between my dad's father, Stan—who I called Pa—and my mom, dated a couple of years after the lawsuit.

"This is being written on Irene's birthday," Pa wrote on March 4, 1994, referring to my paternal grandmother,

> and it occurs to me, just between us, that Adam's Bar Mitz-vah would be a perfect time for the two of you to make up.
>
> There are lots of trite expressions I could use . . . "to err is human, to forgive divine" . . . "bury the hatchet" . . . "let by-gones be bygones," but without resorting to clichés, I believe this would be the appropriate time for you two to begin your relationship anew. I think it would be good for Adam . . . good for Irene . . . good for middleman me . . . and I know how sensitive you are to the feelings of others . . . so I think your forgiving Irene for any bad deed done to you would make you feel a lot better.

I have no idea why Mom blamed Grandma for what happened. Mom herself no longer remembers. Whatever the reason, she was not in a forgiving mood. "After reading your letter," Mom replied four days later,

> I feel compelled to remind you that you and your family brought a completely unfounded and intentionally hurtful le-gal action against me. Your mean-spirited accusations caused me great pain. Your threats engendered months of emotional distress. In the period since that event, I have seen no expres-sion of regret or remorse from any of you for your actions. Instead, I have seen only denial of responsibility.

She concluded: "At the very least, it seems to me that you owe me an apology. I also believe that you owe it to Adam to admit that it is you and not I that hold the blame for damaging what were until then perfectly amicable relationships."

Even now, my heart beats a little faster reading those words and remembering the intensity of her anger.

"Thank you for your thoughtful letter," Pa replied a short time later, trying to subdue the tempest his conciliatory gesture had unexpectedly set off. "I think we are slowly working our way out of this painful situation by clearing up what seem to be areas of misunderstanding on both of our parts."

Then he shared his motivations for bringing the lawsuit in the first place. "We were advised," Pa explained,

> on an authority you would not question that it was your intent to take Adam to California, and if the young man you were seeing there asked you to marry him, you would accept his proposal and move to California with Adam. Of course, what you do with your life is none of my business, nor any of our family's. But what is done with Adam's life is very much his Father's business and to a lesser but meaningful extent, his grandparents' business on your side and ours.

The authority Pa felt certain Mom would not question was, of course, me. Perhaps the intelligence I was disseminating was not as reliable as I believed it to be. Perhaps my mother was telling me things she had no intention of acting upon. I'll never know.

I do not blame Dad or his parents for bringing the lawsuit. I know Mom well enough to know her motives are not always clear, and her behavior can be unpredictable. I'm also moved by Grandma and Pa's determination to keep me close, their unwillingness to lose me. I would have been devastated to lose them.

"It always seemed to us," one of Dad's cousins, Nell, would tell me years later, *us* being her own siblings and parents, "that Pa was a kind of polestar for you, a steadying force, grounding you with everything going on with your mother and parents."

Nell was right. Pa *was* my polestar.

17

Polestar

Pa, teaching me how to write on a visit to Scarsdale.

THROUGHOUT MY CHILDHOOD, a pair of framed family trees hung on an upstairs wall in Grandma and Pa's Colonial-style home—white with black shutters—in the wealthy, largely Jewish suburb of Scarsdale, a short commute from New York City. I'd go up to them as a boy and stare at the rows of generations spanning the two sheets of beige paper, feeling a sense of pride. This is where I come from, I'd think. This is who I am.

I remember tracing the genealogical lines, following them from the outermost leaves at the bottom, where Dad's name—Stephen Baskin Frankel—appeared, up to the name at the very top, Meir Katzenellenbogen, a sixteenth-century rabbi in Padua—the Lucy of his tribe. The genealogical trees were printed before I was born, so my own name did not appear—an omission that was a source of disappointment when I was younger.

Grandma would often tick off the famous names on the trees' branches—Karl Marx, philosopher Martin Buber, composer Felix Mendelssohn, journalist David Halberstam. She was an Anglophile, the most faithful royal watcher on Brewster Road, and those family trees, I sensed, were her way of asserting a claim, however tenuous, to some notion of Jewish aristocracy.

Pa himself never showed any interest in the family trees, even though it was his bloodline they traced. All he ever shared about his own family was that he had been nine years old when he lost his father to Bright's disease, an early twentieth-century catchall for a wide variety of kidney ailments, and that his younger sister Phyllis had contracted meningitis as a little girl, debilitating her all her life.

Still, he never dwelled on the hardships he'd faced in his youth. The only side of himself he allowed me to see was the obnoxiously proud, obsessively doting grandfather whose sole purpose in life seemed to be adding kindling to the sparks of his grandson's dreams.

One of my favorite activities as a boy was curling up beside Pa and listening to his stories about the war. On Grandparents Day in fourth grade, I introduced him to my teacher as "Pa, the soldier," and urged her to let him share one of his stories with the class, which he did, as I stood proudly by his side. I even dragged him to an army-navy store once so I could pick out my very own child-sized camouflage uniform, and for a time I wore it whenever I visited Scarsdale.

Pa, I later learned, had been a reluctant warrior, championing the cause of peace as a student activist at Northwestern before the war. In the late 1930s, campuses across the United States were alive with, among other issues, pacifism and isolationism. Students reared on the terrors of World War I fighting and the influence of banks and munitions companies on Woodrow Wilson's decision to enter the war had little interest in sacrificing their lives in yet another European conflict.

Before my generation marched against Iraq and my parents' generation marched against Vietnam, the war babies, as Pa's generation was called before earning their more enduring name, were marching in the first mass student movement in American history.

Pa himself was helping lead the way, making the case for peace in "Frankel-y Speaking," his *Daily Northwestern* column, even appearing in the pages of *Time* magazine for his efforts to mobilize campuses nationwide into what he called "The All College Peace Front." At one of Northwestern's peace rallies, a crowd of one thousand gathered outside Deering Library, and members of the paper's editorial board planted a black-beribboned maple sapling, dubbed "the Peace Tree," to be cut down when the first among them was killed in some future war.

Pa's role at the rally, he told a reporter many years later, was writing the day's slogan—"We shall not fight in Europe"—an adaptation of the Oxford Oath, the pacifist pledge conceived by Oxford University's debate society (and condemned by Winston Churchill, who called it "very disgusting"). "That has its ironic twist," Pa told the reporter. "I believe I was the first of the bunch to be inducted."

Pa joined the ranks of Ohio's Thirty-Seventh National Guard Division, "the Buckeyes," serving as an infantryman in the South Pacific, where he rose to the rank of major and earned a box of medals that filled me with awe as a boy, and still does—most impressively, a Bronze Star Medal with "V" device for valor, the nation's fourth highest individual award for heroism in non-aerial combat.

That combat ranged from the Battle of Munda Point on the edge of New Georgia—the same engagement where JFK's PT boat was sliced in half—to the Battle of Manila, one of the bloodiest of the war, where an estimated one thousand Americans, sixteen thousand Japanese, and one hundred thousand civilians lost their lives, a death toll higher than in Hiroshima immediately after the atomic bomb.

Through it all, Pa documented his journey in precisely 1,232 telegrams, letters, V-mail airgraphs, and postcards to Grandma, the

Northwestern freshman he'd started dating when he was a senior. One thousand, two hundred and thirty-two letters—typed and handwritten, expressing exhilaration, despair, heartache, boredom, fear, and loneliness, written during R&R and short breaks in the action, mailed from beaches, jungles, transport vessels, palaces, volcanic islands, and coral atolls.

The simple act of writing a letter by hand, sometimes more than once a day, week after week, month after month, year after year, was a profound expression of love, no less remarkable for its ubiquity among the troops. That Grandma kept each of Pa's letters—storing them in three-ring binders where I found them in a closet decades later—was her way of reciprocating that love.

Pa never stopped talking—or writing—about the war. Some of the stories he wrote from the frontlines on a borrowed typewriter were published in the day's leading periodicals, from the *New York Post* to the *Saturday Evening Post*. And he kept up his writing after the war, lending an occasional hand as a speechwriter to Democratic politicians while working as a corporate vice president. Seeking a congratulatory note on the eve of my bar mitzvah, he reached out to an old acquaintance: JFK's legendary speechwriter, Ted Sorensen. Pa didn't know Ted well. They'd met only a few times at Democratic Party functions over the years. But that didn't stop Pa from making the request.

"My lone grandson is working on a project having to do with JFK and very much involving his speeches," Pa wrote. "Your name has, of course, surfaced quite a bit, and Adam has often asked questions about you." He proceeded to tell Sorensen about the birthday celebration and asked if Ted could sign a photograph for me, even suggesting a sign-off: "from one speechwriter to an aspiring one."

Sorensen, always happy to do a favor for a Kennedy loyalist, graciously wrote back, inflating Pa's role in a way he knew would widen a grandson's eyes.

"Your grandfather," Sorensen wrote, "my old friend and a valued member of the Kennedy team, has told me much about you.

Although I have no picture to send on the occasion of your Bar Mitzvah, I hope you will accept in its place this expression of congratulations and best wishes from a former speechwriter (and more!) to a future speechwriter (and more!)."

I framed the letter from Sorensen in my bedroom, as I'd seen Grandma and Pa do in their own home, where the walls were draped with signed photographs of progressive leaders they had known: Adlai Stevenson, Hubert Humphrey, George McGovern, Walter Mondale, Robert Kennedy. Their white clapboard Colonial, a veritable shrine to mid-twentieth-century liberal idealism.

The link between Pa and all of these national political figures was his brother-in-law, my great-uncle Newton Minow, known on our side of the family as Uncle Newt, who married Grandma's younger sister Josephine. Newt had served under JFK as chairman of the Federal Communications Commission, where he gained national attention for telling a gathering of TV broadcasters in 1961 that their profit center had become "a vast wasteland."

The middle of Uncle Newt and Aunt Jo's three daughters, Martha, would grow up to be a professor, and later dean, of Harvard Law School, where one day in 1988 she called her father, then a partner at the Chicago law firm Sidley and Austin, and encouraged him to hire one of her students as a summer associate—the only time, she says, she ever made such a call.

Sidley had already heard about the young man. And when that young man graduated from law school, the firm offered him a full-time job, which he called Uncle Newt to decline in favor of a career in public service. "Well," Uncle Newt replied, "I'll help however I can."

"I don't think you're going to want to help me," the man replied, informing Uncle Newt that he was taking one of the firm's top associates with him.

"See what you got me into?" Michelle Obama teased Uncle Newt and Aunt Jo when she saw them in the Green Room of the White House in December 2016, where Newt, along with Tom Hanks,

Bruce Springsteen, and Ellen DeGeneres, was being awarded a Presidential Medal of Freedom, America's highest civilian honor.

At family gatherings in the 1990s, Uncle Newt would tell us about this "bright young man" who, he was convinced, would be the first black president of the United States. Sure, Uncle Newt, I'd think, sure.

When Barack Obama ran for the US Senate in 2004, Uncle Newt made some calls to try and get me on the campaign. Nothing panned out, but when I finally met the then senator shortly after joining his presidential campaign a few years later, he referenced Newt's efforts on my behalf. "We've been trying to get you on the team for a while now," Obama said, his black White Sox cap pulled low over his forehead.

Newt's efforts on behalf of Stanley Frankel's grandson were as indefatigable as they had been on behalf of Stanley Frankel himself. The two of them were more than brothers-in-law—they were close friends, both raised in the Midwest, both veterans of the war, both deeply committed to public service. And Uncle Newt never hesitated to open doors for him.

Pa, however, never had the chance to work full-time in government. The presidential candidates to whom he was closest, the ones most likely to appoint him to some federal post—Stevenson, Humphrey, McGovern—lost, allowing me to joke, after working on John Kerry's unsuccessful 2004 campaign, that I was upholding the proud Frankel family tradition of working for losing Democrats.

Still, Pa found other ways of contributing, serving on LBJ's advisory commission to the Peace Corps, pioneering a YMCA youth project in Bedford-Stuyvesant, earning a Peabody Award for producing a short-lived news program, *Adlai Stevenson Reports*, with the sitting UN ambassador, and speaking out, whenever he could, on the causes he cared about.

Some years ago, perusing Grandma's scrapbooks, I came across a letter she had written on August 29, 1964, addressed, "Dear Mom and all." Over eleven single-spaced typed pages, she detailed the family's experiences at the 1964 Democratic National Convention in Atlantic City. Toward the end of the week, Grandma wrote, she and Pa sat in a box at the convention hall watching the then senator Hubert Humphrey's vice presidential nomination acceptance address.

"Oh yes," Grandma wrote, "by now I guess I told you that Humphrey's 'Not Barry Goldwater' was Newt's idea and 'the party of memory and the party of hope' was Stan's," referring to two passages in Humphrey's speech—the former, a riff on Goldwater's extremism; the latter, an adaptation of Ralph Waldo Emerson's phrase to contrast Republicans and Democrats.

When, four years later, the then vice president Humphrey was the Democratic nominee for president, Pa once again collaborated on a draft acceptance speech with Newt, who had been urging Humphrey to break with Johnson over Vietnam. "If I ever made the kind of speech you boys recommend," Humphrey told Uncle Newt and Pa, "Lyndon would cut my balls off."

Pa's proudest contribution to a politician was an essay he'd ghosted for Stevenson—"If I Were 21"—published in *Coronet* magazine in 1955. More than once Pa urged me to read it, to absorb its lessons, one of them on the importance of civic participation. "A genuinely free and an honestly informed people will ultimately triumph over intolerance, injustice and evil from without or within," he and Stevenson wrote. "But a lazy people, an apathetic people, an uninformed people, or a people too proud for politics, is not free. And it may quickly be a mob."

The Rolling Stones' Keith Richards has said that he knew what he wanted to do in life when he heard Elvis Presley's "Heartbreak Hotel"—and the sound of Elvis's lead guitarist Scotty Moore. "Everyone else wanted to be Elvis," Richards said. "I wanted to be Scotty."

That, more or less, is how I felt after Pa introduced me to the world of speechwriting: I could see the appeal of being the person giving the speech, but what I *really* wanted was to be the person writing it.

18

Three Generations of Frankels

Courtesy of the author

With Dad and Pa on our last trip to Bermuda in 1999.

I T WAS ALWAYS very important to me that you felt you had a
voice," my dad once told me. "That you felt you were heard."

When I'd see my dad on Wednesday nights, growing up, we'd
usually get pizza slices and Snapples at Perfecto Ristorante around
the corner from my apartment, and I'd talk to him about whatever
was on my mind.

On Saturdays, however, we had the whole day together, and
the way we spent it was entirely up to me. Sometimes that simply
meant picking what movie to go see. Other times, it involved chasing whatever new passion I'd developed—one year, baseball cards;
another year, comics.

On a visit to Dayton, Ohio, to see Pa's sister, we'd all made a
stop to see where Pa had lived as a boy, a large two-story home with

a big porch on East Harvard Boulevard, a leafy street not far from Yale Avenue, Princeton Drive, and Amherst Place—names befitting the big dreams once belonging to the neighborhood's parents. By the time of our visit, many of those dreams seemed elusive. Pa's childhood home was dilapidated and vacant. In the backyard were used syringes and something else, too: a bone.

Most parents, I suspect, would have told me to put it down immediately, go wash my hands, and scurry along. Not Dad. He could see I was transfixed, and he suggested we bring it back with us to New York City. An archaeologist he soon tracked down at the American Museum of Natural History explained to us that the bone belonged to a large bird, likely a turkey, that had last waddled around Dayton in the early twentieth century—the scraps of one of Pa's boyhood Thanksgivings?

Later, when I became interested in politics, Dad would take me on an annual trip to DC, where we'd get a room at the Tabard Inn off Dupont Circle, the city's oldest continuously running hotel, scan the papers every morning for what seemed like the most interesting hearings on Capitol Hill, and then go sit through them, spending the rest of our days in one of the inn's dimly lit sitting rooms, buried in our respective doorstoppers on US history, pausing every so often to share some particularly noteworthy nugget about whatever prominent figures or momentous events we were reading about.

"Why," I asked my dad, "was it so important for you to make sure I felt like I had a voice, like I was heard?"

He didn't need to think about it. "Because," he told me, "I didn't always feel that way growing up." Pa, he said, would sometimes make decisions for him rather than letting him figure it out on his own and find his own way. Dad told me that his father had arranged several internships for him when he was young, and reimbursed his son's employers for the costs.

"Why do you think he intervened like that?" I asked.

Part of the reason, Dad speculated, was Pa's own childhood. He'd grown up without a father, without a model for what a father could be, *should* be, so he'd invented one for himself, and the model he'd invented—perhaps the model he'd wished for himself—was hyperinvolved in the lives of his children. The father Dad described wasn't so much overbearing as overly eager to help, even if it might have been better to let his kids stumble sometimes so they could learn how to pick themselves back up on their own.

When I was in high school, I experienced for myself Pa's willingness to interfere in the normal course of life events if he thought he could help. I had applied to Northwestern's National High School Institute for its summer program in journalism. I'd heard about the program all my life—Dad had done it, as had other family members, and I'd always figured I'd do it, too, when the time came. So I applied, and I was rejected.

Pa was surprised, but for some reason less concerned than I was. He urged me to call Uncle Newt, a Northwestern trustee. It was immediately clear that Pa and Uncle Newt had already spoken.

"Apply again," Uncle Newt advised.

"Next year?" I asked.

"No—resubmit your application for this summer."

If I had been a little older, and a little less impressed by my own self-righteousness, I might've taken Uncle Newt up on his willingness to pull some strings on my behalf. I certainly didn't object when he made those calls to help get me onto the Obama campaign. But at the time I was a purist about such things, deciding I'd rather sink or swim on my own merits than reverse the admissions committee's decision.

The relationship between grandparents and grandchildren, of course, is usually far less complicated than the relationship between parents and their children, and my own relationship with Pa was rather simple: I adored him, and he adored me. With his war stories, public-spiritedness, and a Rolodex that, as far as I could tell, included everyone anyone would ever want to know, Pa was my role model.

The Perecmans, I sometimes thought, were who I *was*; the Frankels and Minows, who I *wanted* to be.

The Perecmans seemed confined to that cul-de-sac in Orange, The Store at 896½ Whalley Avenue, and the homes of assorted family members, virtually all of whom lived near one another in a relatively small patch of Connecticut. I could understand why Mom had found the smallness of it all so suffocating, and why she'd needed to escape.

The Frankels and Minows, by contrast, seemed to occupy an entirely different world. They'd gone to impressive schools, done impressive things, talked about important subjects, and contributed in meaningful ways to the life of the country. That was what I wanted to do. That is who I wanted to be.

Plus, spending time with the Frankels was just more fun. Trips to Connecticut usually involved spending hours at The Store without anything to do. While Zayde hunched over his bench, fixing watches or talking with customers, I marked time until I could head back to the house and watch TV.

Weekends with Grandma and Pa, on the other hand, were a boy's dream. "Bring your wallet," I'd tease Pa from the pay phone at the Scarsdale train station—my way of asking if we could stop at the toy store on the way back. He'd laugh and happily comply. There were milkshakes by the pool of their country club, baseball card shows at the Westchester County Center, and visits to the arcade and batting cages at Sportime USA.

Time with Grandma and Pa offered a balm for all of the bitterness that had passed between my parents, and the heaviness that hung over my apartment and Perecman family gatherings, where every conversation was always one anecdote away from the Holocaust.

It also offered a refuge from the volatility I was experiencing at home. In Scarsdale, I never had to worry about whether Dad or Grandma and Pa would want to be alone instead of spending time

with me—they always wanted to spend time with me. I never had
to walk on eggshells or worry I might inadvertently set someone
off; they were all so reasonable, calm, and level-headed, their behavior so reassuringly, blissfully predictable.

ONE OF THE best parts of being Grandma and Pa's grandson was
our annual summer trip to Bermuda. Every year, from when I was
three until I turned eighteen, Grandma and Pa would take Dad
and me on a pilgrimage of sorts to Cambridge Beaches, a sprawling archipelago of white-roofed pink cottages on the western tip of
the island, where we stayed in the same two adjoining cottages—
Hibiscus North and Hibiscus South—on every one of our fifteen
trips.

Each of us, I suspect, retains in our memory a place that's so special, so inextricably interwoven with feelings of love and happiness,
that it can sometimes seem less like a point on a map than a state
of mind. For me, that place is Bermuda.

Few photographs remain from our 1985 trip, the last one Mom
joined us on before separating from Dad. One photo shows the
three of us, me sitting between my parents beneath an ancient tree.
I can still remember posing for it. Mom and Dad had started fighting a few minutes earlier, and I'd begun to cry.

Mom displayed that photo in our apartment when I was growing up, and it always saddened me, all the more so because the unhappy memories it surfaced displaced so many happy ones.

Every afternoon Dad and I would head down to the marina, pick
out our fishing rods, pick up a carton of squid, and take a motor-
boat out to the reefs by an old shipwreck, sometimes getting lucky
with grouper or even snapper, and other times coming up empty,
cast after cast. We'd sit there for hours, rocking in the gentle cur-
rent, as Dad asked me about myself, the past year at school, my
hopes for the coming year, where I saw myself headed and how I'd
get there, drawing me out, getting me to talk about who I was and
what I wanted for myself.

Evenings in Bermuda had their own routines. When I was a boy, the island was hopping with frogs, and every evening, after dinner, Pa would change into his "World's Greatest Frog Catcher" T-shirt, and we'd grab small nets and scour the grounds of Cambridge Beaches, collecting frogs in a bucket and releasing them first thing in the morning.

As the years passed, the routine changed. Instead of frog hunting, we'd smoke Cuban cigars, usually H. Upmanns, Pa's favorite, and play penny stakes poker in our cottage. As our laughter and cigar smoke carried into the bedroom next door, Grandma would yell "Stan! Keep it down!" to no avail.

Then, after we'd played enough rounds for one evening, with our cigars still lit, the three of us—three generations of Frankels— would walk down a sloping green to a tranquil bay. And there, sitting beneath a starlit sky, small waves lapping our beach chairs, the two men I loved most in the world would invite me to dream about my future, telling me with an assurance I trusted implicitly that I could do anything I set my heart to.

Was the predictability, the regularity, the frequency, of the time I spent with Grandma and Pa born of something more than love? Was it born of concern? Years later Dad would confess, "I was worried that your mother's irrationality, her bad judgment, would have an impact on you." Did Grandma and Pa feel the same way? Was at least part of the reason I spent so much time with them a conscious effort on their part to be a mitigating, stabilizing influence?

The year after our last trip to Bermuda—my senior year in high school—I was admitted to Dad's alma mater, Princeton. Grandma and Pa told me how proud they were that I was following in his footsteps. I was, too. "Good genes," Grandma said, as she did after any accomplishment.

Some weeks later, Grandma and Pa wrote me their annual birthday letter—the eighteenth such message I'd received from them; the first was some doggerel they'd written on my birth. At the bottom of the page, they wrote, "As we look ahead to your college career with wonder but without reservation about your onward-and-upward progress . . . as we think and dream, we will thank Whoever Above gave you to us . . . and keeps watching over your charmed life . . . and you must know that when the time comes for us to join that Watcher in the Sky, we will still be with you in our undying love . . . forever and ever."

Every one of the eighteen letters that Grandma and Pa had written closed on a similar note, about their possible passing, evoking the lesson Pa had learned as a nine-year-old boy—and relearned in the Pacific—that life is fleeting, that the end can come at any time.

Pa's time came the following fall, several weeks into my freshman year. On October 13, 1999, he collapsed from a stroke in a classroom at Baruch College, where he was an adjunct professor. "Class had just ended," one of his students told the school's paper, the *Ticker*. "He bent down by the desk to pick up his bag, his head dropped on the desk, and he just stayed there."

Distraught students rushed to get help. An ambulance was called, and he was brought to New York University Medical Center. Little could be done. He had fallen into a coma from which he would never awake.

I was in my dorm room when Dad called that evening. I ran across campus, searching for one of my two close friends. Neither was around. So I went for a walk by myself, pacing the grounds and crying in the dark.

I visited Pa only once in the hospital. Dad and his siblings Nancy and Tom were there, and graciously gave me some time alone with their father. I went up to him and held his hand, watching his chest rise and fall at a mechanized pace. The doctors couldn't be sure he could hear me, but I crouched by his bed anyway, telling him, in between tears, how much I loved him. How much he meant to me. How much he had guided me. Then I said goodbye.

Uncle Newt came later that day, his face as sad as I've ever seen it. He stood over Pa's bed—lips pursed, shaking his head—a silent farewell to his old friend.

Grandma couldn't bring herself to visit the hospital. She couldn't bear the thought of seeing him like that, she told us—the upper-classman who'd wooed her sixty years earlier, the boyfriend she'd written day after day during the war, the husband she'd loved for more than half a century.

Pa would have understood. "Shock ooh on sawn goo," he would always say, bastardizing the pronunciation of the French adage. "To each his own."

Years later, spending the night at Grandma's Scarsdale home, I was awakened by what sounded like moans coming from her room downstairs. I crept to the top of the stairwell to make sure I was hearing her right. "Stan?" she was saying. "Stan? Are you there?"

On November 12, after a family decision to take him off life sup-port, Pa passed away. His ashes, it was decided, would be stored in a Westchester mortuary, where, despite the firm instructions he had always given with a wink, rules prohibited their placement in front of a television every Sunday so he could watch the Giants game. He died a couple of weeks before Bubbie herself succumbed to her own illness, just shy of his eighty-first birthday, December 8—the date his hero FDR called on Congress to declare war on the Empire of Japan.

19

The Monarch and the Footservant

With Ted Sorensen at the John F. Kennedy Presidential
Library and Museum in 2008.

PRESIDENTIAL SPEECHWRITING AS a craft dates back to the earliest days of the Republic, when Alexander Hamilton and James Madison drafted speeches for George Washington. But with the exception of a handful of presidents and a small number of aides, no single person has contributed as much to the shaping or perception of presidential eloquence as the man whose congratulatory letter Pa had secured on my bar mitzvah: Ted Sorensen.

The press called him JFK's "alter ego." JFK called him "my intellectual blood bank." Kennedy's 1960 opponent Richard Nixon, on whose enemies list Grandma and Pa proudly found their names, once told an interviewer, "You need a mind like Sorensen's around you that's clicking and clicking all the time," suggesting that JFK was a "puppet who echoes his speechmaker."

It's only a slight exaggeration to say that every speechwriter entering the profession aspires to be the next Ted Sorensen. "No," Sorensen would respond when he heard that sort of thing, "they just want to work for the next JFK." And that is true, as well.

I had only the vaguest notion of all this, however, when, in December 2001, Pa's ghost seemed to reach out from beyond the grave and place me opposite Sorensen at a lunch at Renaissance Weekend, the political, intellectual, and schmoozing extravaganza then held in Hilton Head, South Carolina, where I had been invited as a guest of my Minow cousins.

Sorensen's eyesight had been severely impaired, the result of a stroke several months earlier, and he was, he later told me, feeling discouraged. At the time of his stroke, he'd been in the early stages of writing his memoirs. But the historian he'd been counting on as his collaborator had abandoned the project, and the prospect of completing it on his own, particularly given his new limitations, seemed overwhelming.

In me, Sorensen saw—correctly—an eager pupil, grateful for the chance to absorb as much as I could from the master speechwriter. A couple of hours later, he offered me a job as his research assistant.

Ted initially thought the book would take two years to complete. It would take six. Upon publication in 2008, the *New Yorker*'s Jeffrey Toobin interviewed me for a short piece about it. I called Ted's dedication to the book "heroic," as inspiring as any words he ever wrote. It was. Despite one health crisis after another, from a ministroke, to prostate cancer, to a leaky heart valve, he never gave up on it, faithfully adhering to the elaborate process we designed as a workaround for his handicaps.

Whenever a thought struck him—in bed, at lunch, walking down the street—he would scribble a note on whatever he could find—a scrap of paper, a napkin—emptying his pockets whenever

I met him at his Upper West Side apartment or midtown office so I could store their contents in one of dozens of folders corresponding to different chapters or subchapters on our outline.

His poor vision was not, as Ted put it, a problem of the eyes. It was a problem of the brain. And he could see reasonably well under the right conditions. Sitting in his living room, beneath two bright lights, he would squint, angling the notes this way and that, until the text appeared clearly.

Then he would dictate into a tape recorder, and I would clean up the transcripts, reorganizing them into something resembling a chapter that each of us would then take turns revising until we felt sufficiently good about it to move on. "One foot in front of the other," Ted would say. "Just like a marathon."

"Have I ever told you the story of the Monarch and the Footservant?" he would sometimes ask. I'd heard it a dozen times, but I would always say no, just to hear him tell it again. The Monarch went everywhere with his Footservant, he'd say, and one day the Footservant told the Monarch he had heard him give the same speech and answer the same questions so many times, he could do it all himself. So they exchanged clothes, and the Footservant fooled everyone into thinking he was the Monarch, until one day he got a question he couldn't answer. "That question is so obvious," he finally responded, "even my Footservant can answer it!"

That, Ted would say, was like the two of us. After all our time together, I could answer any question about his life exactly as he would have answered it. "Well," he would say smiling, "*almost* any question." Sorensen, famously discreet, keeper of JFK's secrets, doubtless had many stories he never told, even to his Footservant.

Sometimes, sitting together, Ted would grow wistful, amazed by the progress we were making on a book both of us had occasionally doubted would ever be completed. "Can you believe," he would say, "all of this started with Stanley Frankel's note on your bar mitzvah?"

My relationship with Ted, however, was rooted in something

more than the adulation of a young acolyte for one of his heroes or the gratitude of an éminence grise for his loyal assistant. It was also rooted in a shared family experience: Ted's mother, too, had suffered from mental illness.

He opened up about it in his book. "Suddenly, mysteriously," he wrote, "it all changed. That beautiful mind, so precisely attuned to both maternal and civic responsibilities, so energetically full of both caring and intellectual instincts, careened off the tracks, like some fine timepiece racing inexplicably out of control." He continued, "All we children knew was that, at times, a totally different person, almost a stranger, lived in our house, neglecting herself and her family, with sudden, violent mood swings followed by uncharacteristic lethargy."

I never told Ted about my mom's troubles. At the time, doing so felt like a betrayal. But knowing that both of our mothers had endured mental illness—even if their diagnoses may have been different—made me feel closer to Ted, like we understood one another in a way few others could.

I remember thinking about the distance, in everything but geography, between my mom's apartment on West End Avenue and Ted's apartment on Central Park West, between the muddled, whimsical, stubborn way my mom sometimes made decisions, and the clarity and precision that Ted brought to every subject.

I later learned that Ted had once commented to one of his family members about the "loving loyalty" I showed my mom, perhaps an indication that he sensed something was amiss. I know of at least one instance where he experienced the kinds of impulsive bursts that so often characterized Mom's behavior.

A couple of months after Ted and I began working together, Mom called him. I barely knew Ted at that point. Mom herself had met him just once. But she was in a bad place. Her longtime employer, the think tank, had let her go, and she was considering a lawsuit.

Ted didn't practice employment law, but he was the most prominent attorney my mother could think of. So, without asking me or even a heads-up, she contacted him for some legal advice. I was in China at the time on a summer fellowship, and was alerted to the call by an email from Ted. I was mortified and dashed off an apology. He was gracious, and never spoke of it again.

Years later, after Ted passed away, I invited his former Kennedy-era secretary Gloria Sitrin and her husband Dave to lunch in the White House Mess, the elegant staff dining room in the West Wing. They brought along a folder, containing some items they suspected might interest me.

In the folder, buried among papers that had been stacked in their garage—exposed for decades to cold, heat, fumes, and pests—was, I recognized instantly, the oldest surviving draft of JFK's inaugural address. I could tell it was the oldest because the words, "Inaugural—Draft 2" were typed at the top, and Sorensen himself had told me he had torn up the first draft decades earlier, deciding, after consulting with Jacqueline Kennedy, that her late husband's legacy was not well served by having a draft of the iconic speech floating around with Ted's handwriting all over it.

When I told Obama what Ted had done, he smiled. "See," he said, "*that's* loyalty. Not like all of you guys. You're all like, 'Hey *New York Times*, I wrote *this* speech, I wrote *that* speech.' " We laughed. He wasn't wrong.

During my years in the White House I'd occasionally be invited, like other staff members, to speak to White House interns, who'd often ask the same question: "What made you decide to be a speechwriter?"

I'd start by telling them about my appreciation for the craft, my belief, as Sorensen wrote in his book, that "the right speech on the right topic delivered by the right speaker in the right way at the right moment" can "ignite a fire, change men's minds, open their eyes, alter their votes, bring hope to their lives, and, in all these ways, change the world."

Then I'd talk about how speechwriting offers a way of gaining access, regardless of age, at the highest levels in politics and government. To be a senior policy or political advisor typically requires decades of experience mastering a particular issue or battling it out in the political trenches. Speechwriters, by contrast, simply need to write well, and get along with the boss. Just look at Ted, I'd say—arguably the second most powerful person in the White House at age 32.

That's all true, of course. But there was also another, simpler answer to that question. Pa had been a speechwriter. And I wanted to be like Pa. After Obama's 2009 inauguration, my Minow cousin Nell and her husband David took me out for a celebratory lunch in DC. "It's such a shame Stan isn't here to see you in the White House," David said. "This was his big payoff."

20

Genealogical Bewilderment

With Mom and Dad at Cambridge Beaches in 1985.

I DON'T HAVE A lot of memories of Mom and Dad before they separated. Mostly, what I remember are fragments. That fight in Bermuda. The sound of Mom shouting. The crack of their bedroom door slamming. That, I think, is why I never really wondered *why* they split up. It wasn't like I'd seen their marriage fall apart; I'd never really known them as a couple.

That's not to say I *never* asked about it. Once, in high school, I raised the subject with my mom. We were sitting at our dining room table, having one of our nightly meals together.

She gave the beginnings of an answer before cutting herself off.

"No, I can't tell you that," she said. "You're too young."

"Too young?" I asked.

She wouldn't say any more—and I didn't push.

I also have another, older memory. I'm four or so, clutching my mother's hand as she lies in bed. She seems tired, sick.

"What's wrong?" I ask.

She says something about a baby.

Along with these memories are others, different ones. Growing up, I always thought it was strange how little I resembled my dad. I'd often go up to the mirror, scouring my features for similarities to his and feeling a rush of happiness, a sort of reassurance, when I'd find one. The way my cheek curved. The arch of my nose from a certain angle.

On those few occasions when someone *did* tell me how much I looked like my dad, I'd always be surprised. Maybe I *do* look like him after all, I'd tell myself.

All these memories lay dormant until, like some ghostly vessel exhumed from the ocean depths, they resurfaced sometime in early 2006. I'd moved back to New York City after working on the Kerry campaign in DC, and I was living at home while helping Sorensen finish the book.

Mom and I were spending a lot of time together, more than we'd spent since I'd left for college. I suspect anyone who has tried living at home after college has found it challenging. Even the closest relationships with parents can become strained with such proximity, as I was beginning to see for myself.

I discovered how sensitive, how easily offended, my mother could be—more so than when I'd been younger. How quickly a conversation could go sideways. Mom had been out of work for some time, and after one potential employer failed to get back to her, I told her it might be because they didn't have any jobs she'd done before. "You get hired to do lots of jobs you've never done before," she snapped. Of course I did, I thought. I was only a few years out of college. I'd never done *anything* before.

All those months together in that apartment meant a lot of

unstructured time to fill with conversations. And at some point, I broached the subject I'd raised at that dinner table all those years earlier—about why she and my dad split up.

I don't recall exactly why I raised it. I was dating my college girlfriend Laura at the time, and perhaps looking for clues about how to build a successful relationship. Or perhaps I sensed intuitively that certain things didn't add up, that certain things had been withheld from me.

I *do* remember that when my questions began, they were fairly innocuous, motivated simply by an interest in retrieving some missing parts of my family history. It was only after I saw how uncomfortable the whole subject made my mom that I began to grow suspicious.

"Why do you want to know that?" she said, head down, averting her eyes. We were sitting in my bedroom. It was dark outside, the end of a long day at Sorensen's apartment working on the book.

I kept pushing, telling her I wasn't sure why she was being so cagey. Finally, she started opening up.

"The truth is," she confessed, "I never really wanted to marry your father."

She felt helpless, she told me, like she *had* to go along with it. Bubbie and Zayde were worried, after their daughter's suicide attempt only a year earlier, that she would never again find such a promising match. As far as they were concerned, Dad's appearance in my mom's life was an unexpected blessing at just the right time.

"Isn't it amazing how awful things were a year ago, and how wonderful things are now?" Bubbie asked one of Mom's friends at the wedding.

Mom herself told me that on her wedding day, she sat crying in the bathroom of Young Israel of New Haven as guests took their seats in the sanctuary.

Still, something about Mom's answer left me unsatisfied.

The next time I saw Dad, I raised the same question: "Why did you get divorced?"

We were walking down Broadway, around the corner from Mom's

apartment, just outside the pizza place where we'd spent so many Wednesday nights when I was a boy. His answer was simpler, more direct.

"Well," he said, "your mother had an affair with Jason."

I was startled. Jason was Jason Black,* a man I'd known all my life. He'd been one of Mom's professors in graduate school, and a constant presence in my childhood, regularly attending birthday parties and piano recitals. A few times a year, Mom and I would join him and his wife at a dinner party at their Upper East Side home. I'd always known Jason as one of Mom's closest friends. But *just* a friend. Not a boyfriend.

"How do you know?" I asked.

He told me a story. "I was looking for a comb once," Dad said, "and I knew your mother kept one in her purse. She was in the shower, and while I was rummaging through her purse, I came across a letter. It said something about how she'd lost out to another woman for some man's affections. I took it to her in the shower, and I remember the ink running on the page as I held it there. She grabbed it out of my hands and tore it up."

He seemed to know the letter was about Jason.

"You know," Dad added, "your mother was once pregnant with Jason's child. I made her get an abortion. She didn't want to. I insisted."

Startled again.

Was that the baby, I wondered, my mother had told me about when I was a little boy, standing by her bed?

That pregnancy opened up a possibility that had never occurred to me before.

"How do you know I'm your son?" I immediately asked Dad.

"Because," he answered confidently, "I remember the night of conception."

Must've been *some* night, I thought.

What, I wondered, did my mother have to say about all this?

* Jason Black is a pseudonym.

When did her affair with Jason begin?

Had she *really* been pregnant with Jason's child?

Was she as certain as Dad that I was my father's son?

As soon as I returned home, I asked Mom about it. She was sitting in the living room, reading the *New York Times*. Irritated by my mother's lack of transparency, I told her I'd asked Dad the same questions I'd asked her, but that they'd led to different answers.

"Dad says you got an abortion when you were married," I said. "He says you were pregnant with Jason's child."

We were seated opposite one another, across a glass table, on Mom's bright red suede couches. The early-afternoon light poured in through the sixteenth-floor windows overlooking Broadway, brightening the pink walls and casting a glare off an impressionistic painting Mom loved of a man reaching up toward a bleeding heart.

She seemed perplexed. "I don't know where he's getting that. I *did* have a miscarriage once."

I hadn't anticipated that answer.

"Why would he make it up?" I asked.

"I don't know," she said. "That's bizarre. He must be misremembering."

"Seems a rather unlikely thing to misremember."

"Well," she said, "don't you think *I* should know? Bubbie took me to the doctor."

Of course she should know, I thought. But making up something like that was so out of character for Dad.

Depression, I now know, can damage the part of the brain responsible for memory. Is that what was happening? Was a lifetime of depression playing tricks on my mother's mind? Or was she just lying? Or was she right about Dad misremembering?

Even today, each of my parents insists on a different story—the whole episode a proxy for my inability to fully comprehend the messy saga that began revealing itself, slowly, in fits and starts, that afternoon.

"When did your relationship with Jason begin?" I continued.

She tried to wave me off. "Why are you asking that?"

"When did it start?" I insisted. "After I was born?"

Silence.

"*Before?*"

She nodded.

"You were having an affair with Jason before I was born," I said, repeating her words, registering them, processing the new information.

Enough. No more skirting the question I'd asked Dad.

"Whose son am I?"

So odd, to pose a single question—just four short words— knowing the answer can change everything. And yet, in that moment, the whole exercise seemed abstract. Surely, I thought, Mom would dismiss my question, just as Dad had. Surely I'd find reassurance in this conversation. Not something else.

Silence.

I asked again.

"I don't know," she said softly.

"Okay—whose son do you think I am?" I said, not quite believing this was where the conversation was headed.

"I don't know for sure," she tried.

I was beginning to lose patience.

"Surely you have an opinion, Mom," I said sharply. "A mother has a sense of these things. Who do you think my father is?"

She looked down.

My anger with her evasion was beginning to grow.

I asked again, "Who do you think it is?"

"Stephen is your father. He raised you. Why do you need anything more than that?"

That answer—insufficient, deflecting—made me realize, for the first time, that I would not be getting the reassurance I'd sought, that the answer to my question might be something I'd never imagined.

I asked again, my voice rising, "Mom, whose son am I?"

"Jason's," she said quietly.

"Jason . . . Jason," I repeated, letting out a long, lung-clearing sigh.

I didn't say anything for a minute or two. We sat there, silently. I sensed her looking at me, and averted my gaze. My jaw, my whole body, was clenched.

I wanted to climb out of my skin. I felt disembodied. I looked down at my legs, arms, hands. All of it suddenly felt so unfamiliar, like I was inhabiting a stranger's body.

In that moment, I felt undone. Twenty-five years of life—memories of Dad, Grandma, Pa, the Minows, Scarsdale, Bermuda, other family trips to Fort Lauderdale, Cooperstown—experiences that gave texture to my sense of self, that made me, I'd thought, who I am, who my friends, my family, knew me to be, that formed the bedrock of my identity—all of it unraveled in minutes, seconds.

How could she keep this from me? Didn't I have a right to know? Doesn't every child have a right to know who his father is?

"Who knows about this?" I finally managed. "Dad?"

"Of course not," she said. "It would break his heart."

"Isn't he entitled to know?" I asked.

"I didn't want to hurt him."

"Didn't want to hurt him?" I said. "You cheat on my father and have a son with another man, but you don't want to tell him because you're afraid of hurting him?"

She insisted she had been good to Dad. "I helped him move out of our apartment," she said. "I gave him our china."

"Gave him some china?" I said, incredulously. "Seriously?"

She was offended. I moved on.

"Did Pa ever know? Grandma? Bubbie and Zayde?"

"God, no," she said, visibly shaken by the thought.

"Jason?"

She nodded, biting her lip.

"Only Jason," I said—to myself as much as Mom—grasping, for the first time, that my mother and I were virtually alone with this enormous secret.

I thought of the Frankel and Minow side of my family—loving, raising, embracing me as their son, grandson, nephew, cousin. All the while, Mom knew I was not, and said nothing. I was appalled. She—and Jason—had played them, me, for fools. My whole life had been a lie.

"I forgive you," I said, surprising even myself.

How did I know I forgave her? I had not even begun to absorb the shock of what she had just told me. I had no idea how I felt.

Perhaps I said it aspirationally, somehow sensing that forgiveness, or at least an attempt at it, would be a part of the long, painful journey on which I'd just been so unexpectedly thrust. Or, perhaps I said it because I knew it's what Mom wanted to hear, and I wanted to give her that.

I immediately walked it back. "Maybe I'll call our rabbi and ask him about forgiveness. Maybe I'll ask his help forgiving you."

"Whatever you need to do," she said.

Words were coming out of my mouth, but they bore no connection to the rupture in my heart. Talk to our rabbi? I hadn't seen the man in years. What was I talking about?

I'm reminded of that scene in *The Princess Bride* where Wallace Shawn's character Vizzini drinks the Man in Black's wine and keeps chatting, oblivious that he has just consumed a deadly powder that will topple him over a few moments later.

"Were you ever going to tell me?" I asked.

"Maybe on my deathbed," she replied with a characteristically dramatic flourish.

Years later I would tell Rachel Yehuda, the Mount Sinai trauma expert, about this moment.

She could sense I was searching for some validation of the pain I'd experienced. In the aftermath of wars in Iraq and Afghanistan, psychological trauma seems so closely linked to combat that I'd felt reluctant labeling what I'd experienced as trauma.

Yehuda shared none of my reluctance.

"What you've experienced is a trauma," she told me. I felt better, lighter somehow, hearing her say that.

My conversation with Mom on the couch that day, I can now see, met Rachel Yehuda's definition of trauma, dividing my life into a before and after. *Before* I uncovered the lie. *Before* I learned the truth. And *after*. *After* I buried it. *After* I hid from it. *After* I began, haltingly, excruciatingly, grappling with it.

Still, even after I heard Mom answer with the name—"Jason"—I had difficulty believing her, accepting what she had told me.

Dad was not my father?

I thought of the days I'd spent in New York City after September 11. I'd come into the city from Princeton in the hopes of volunteering, only to discover there was no need. An MTA official had handed me an updated subway map detailing service changes in Lower Manhattan. I stared at it, struggling to comprehend the reality of a new subway map.

Subway maps can change?

I'd thought they were immutable, like the shape of a mountain. Or a person's parents.

I'd always thought of my mother as someone with a strong moral compass, the source of my own capacity for moral clarity. Now I no longer did. I no longer *could*.

I suddenly felt filthy—a filth that would linger for days, years. The kind of filth I couldn't wash away. Moral filth. I was, despite myself, complicit in this act of betrayal against my father, my grandparents, and a family—*my* family—I loved. I'd never escape the emotional instability, the impulsiveness, that were hallmarks of Mom's life, I now realized. I was a product of them.

I also felt complicit in her lies. *Her* secret was now *my* secret.

Telling Dad was unthinkable. I had a stepbrother, Greg, Helen's son from a previous marriage—a stepbrother I wasn't particularly close to, growing up as we had in different places, separated by too many years. But I was Dad's only biological child, his only *real* son, I'd sometimes thought in adolescence.

How could I tell Dad I was not his own blood?

"It would break his heart," Mom had said. I was sure she was right. Hadn't he told me himself that he'd insisted Mom get an abortion when he learned she was pregnant with Jason's child? Would he have wanted Mom to abort me if he'd known the truth?

Dad's heart, however, was not my only concern. I was also concerned about *mine*.

How could I be sure he would still love me as much? That he would still want to be my dad? That he would still want me in his life?

I knew Dad loved me. And it was difficult to imagine him abandoning me. But that is not what I feared, or at least not what I feared most.

What I feared most was something far subtler. The slightest change in the way he looked at me. A shift, imperceptible to everyone but the two of us, in the tone of our relationship. The glance, the gesture, that would let me know, silently but unmistakably, that the parental seal of unconditional love had been broken, that he did not, and could never again, see me the same way. As his son.

The thought terrified me. And I would live in fear of it, day after day, month after month, for years to come.

If Dad couldn't know, I certainly couldn't tell any other members of his family. It didn't seem right to share something so personal with his siblings, cousins, nieces, or nephew.

Anyway, I couldn't run the risk of them telling him.

And how could I tell Grandma?

This was a woman who would always say, every time I did anything that made her proud, "Good genes!"

The whole sordid story seemed incompatible with the genteel world my eighty-two-year-old Grandma inhabited in Scarsdale. On the bureau in Grandma's bedroom was a photo of me. The next time I visited, and every visit thereafter, I'd notice that my resemblance to Jason in that photograph was particularly striking, and feel guilty about it, as if the photo itself were some sort of perpetual offense committed against my grandmother even in my absence.

My mind went to other secrets in my family's past. I thought of

Bubbie and Zayde and the secret at the center of their lives, that their names—Lea and Abraham Perecman—were not their own.

Mom had been reared on that secret, instructed, from the time she was a girl, to guard it at all costs. She had been raised to be comfortable with deceit.

Secrets—vital for Bubbie and Zayde to survive the war, to create a new life in America—were now being employed by their daughter to raise another man's child, a perversion of a righteous vice.

I suddenly felt a strange new kinship with Bubbie and Zayde. I shared something with them, something no one else in our family shared—the experience of living under an assumed identity. The fear of being exposed, of worrying that the life I'd known would crumble if my true identity were disclosed.

How astonishing that my mother had managed to keep this secret, decade after decade. It could not have been easy. It must have required constant vigilance, constant subterfuge. It must have been emotionally, psychologically taxing.

How did she do it?

It was no coincidence, I thought, that Mom's lifelong passion was acting. Throughout my childhood, Mom would take acting classes, often rehearsing with acting partners in our living room, her attempt to create space in her life for the calling her father had made her abandon years earlier. Later, after leaving the think tank, she'd even launch her own theater company, translating Yiddish plays into English and producing them.

Theater, I knew, was her life. I had not, however, appreciated just how literally that had been true. Much of her life, I now realized, had been a performance, an extraordinary one that had kept all of us, even her own son, spellbound.

How would *I* sustain such a lie?

In *The Secret Life of Families*, psychiatrist Dr. Evan Imber-Black identifies four classes of secrets. First are sweet secrets—"Time-limited," she writes, "and made for the purpose of fun and surprise."

Second are essential secrets—the private language of a couple, for example, that fosters closeness and connection. Imber-Black cites an example: "In Edward Albee's play *Who's Afraid of Virginia Woolf?* we watch with horror as George and Martha shatter one essential secret after another." Reading that, I wondered whether the centrality of secrets in the play was one of the reasons it resonated so much with my mother.

Another class of secrets, writes Imber-Black, are dangerous secrets—when a child, for example, is afraid to speak up about being abused. And finally, toxic secrets. "These are the secrets," writes Imber-Black, "that take a powerful toll on relationships, disorient our identity, and disable our lives. They handicap our capacity to make clear choices, use resources effectively, and participate in authentic relationships."

Mine was undoubtedly a toxic secret, and its toxicity soon began producing physical symptoms. I started having a new recurring nightmare: I had a dark secret—I'd been complicit in a murder. And I lived in terror that my family, my career, would fall apart if anyone found out. For years I was puzzled by the nightmare, blind to its obvious symbolism.

Sleep, at least, usually offered an escape. Every morning, when any of us is lying in bed, there's a fraction of a second between unconsciousness and consciousness. In that fraction of a second, whatever anxieties we may feel, whatever stressors may be weighing on us, do not exist. For that fraction of a second, all is bliss.

I came to live for that fraction of a second. I'd wake up and feel serene, unperturbed. A moment later, the memory of the secret I was carrying, the realization that I was not my father's son, would come crashing back. With that weight, I grew accustomed to climbing out of bed.

Around this time, I had to travel to DC for a meeting at the World Bank, part of a project to supplement my income while finishing the book with Sorensen. I still remember sitting through it, in one of the building's antiseptic conference rooms, struggling to suppress the tears I could feel welling up in my chest, to hold back the torrent I was containing.

I left, proud of my own performance. That night, alone in my hotel room off Dupont Circle, I let it all out, sobbing in my bed, just a few blocks from where Dad and I had always stayed on our trips.

In the days and weeks after my conversation with Mom, I retraced my childhood and found new patterns, new meanings, everywhere.

For my eleventh or twelfth birthday, Jason had bought me a black Spalding outfielder's glove. Kids that age, especially future major league baseball players, as I considered myself to be, often have an encyclopedic knowledge of the prices of sports equipment. And I immediately recognized this particular glove as one of the most expensive I'd seen on a recent trip to a sporting goods store.

Even at that age, I found it strange that Jason would buy me such an expensive birthday gift. Something about the whole thing made me uncomfortable, and I never used the glove, opting instead for a mitt my Dad gave me.

I thought about the trip Mom and I had taken to LA when I was a kid. The apartment we'd stayed in, the one owned by the mother of Mom's friend?

Jason's mother—my paternal grandmother, I now realized. Mom and I had gone to see her once during our stay. I still remember her luxurious apartment with its sunlit living room and pastel furniture, the warmth of her smile and the way she greeted me. Like she knew me.

Did she know I was her grandson?

Suddenly, for the first time in years, I thought about my parents' lawsuit, and Mom's anger toward Dad and his family. She had the nerve to be upset with *them*, when our host in LA was my secret family?

That summer I'd spent with my mother in the South of France, at the home of one of her friends?

It belonged to Jason and his third wife Marie, who lived there with their young son Daniel, my half brother, I suddenly realized.

One night during that trip, we'd been invited to dinner at a nearby vineyard owned by one of Jason and Marie's friends, a son of New York banker Felix Rohatyn. On the bookshelf, I'd noticed *A Thousand Days*, Arthur Schlesinger Jr.'s study of the Kennedy presidency. I found Uncle Newt's name in the index, and proudly pointed it out. Felix Rohatyn's son was unimpressed.

Now, I wondered, did my mother flash a knowing smile during my little boast?

Later, I also learned that a form of subterfuge had taken place in advance of our arrival: a photo of Jason at my age had been removed lest I discern a resemblance.

Another time, during a sleepover in high school, a friend was awakened in the middle of the night by a strange sound. I lay gurgling, unconscious, on the floor. I was rushed to the emergency room, where it was determined I'd had a grand mal seizure.

The doctors never identified the cause, perhaps because I was too embarrassed to tell them that the night before, pregaming for a party, I'd consumed a few too many packets of ginseng energy pills from the local Korean market.

MRIs, EKGs, even a spinal tap, followed. Through it all, Jason— then a professor affiliated with the hospital—was a constant presence, talking with doctors and updating my mother and me.

For the first time in years, I thought of the gift Jason had given me when I graduated from high school, a first edition of British philosopher R. G. Collingwood's *The Idea of History*. "I very much admire the work of Collingwood," read his accompanying note. "He writes a good deal about the role of memory, the revisitation and reconstruction of the past." A newly relevant topic, I thought. The note was signed, "With great affection, Jason."

Later, I learned that Jason had helped cover the cost of my lavish bar mitzvah celebration at Dezerland, a now-shuttered New York City venue with arcade games and bumper cars.

I thought of the summer I'd spent in high school as a reception-ist at Jason's office, and the books, edited by my mother, that sat on her living room bookshelf.

As a boy, I'd page through them, impressed. Mom, the editor. Now I suddenly recalled one of her mentors at the time: Jason. What had once made me so proud now seemed sullied.

Everywhere I looked, there he was, hiding in plain sight.

In college I'd managed, with help from a friend I'd made on a White House internship, to secure a junior role at the 2000 Demo-cratic National Convention in Los Angeles.

My roommate for the week?

Jason's daughter Roxanne, a few years older than I, who had a small studio apartment. One day, Fabio called while she was out. (Yes, that Fabio.) When I told her, she rolled her eyes. "Ugh, again?" I would tell that story repeatedly in college, never suspecting that she was my half sister from one of Jason's previous marriages.

Did she know I was her half brother?

All my life, I'd been an only child. I was now astonished to dis-cover I had at least three half siblings, one half sister and two half brothers—the young one, Daniel, I'd met in France, and another, Roxanne's brother, Jacob, also several years older; Jason had been married to Roxanne and Jacob's mother at the time of the affair.

Once, in high school, Mom had asked me to spend a day with Jacob, and we'd walked around the Upper East Side. Did he know about me? Or had my mother been trying to foster some sort of fraternal connection between two people who had no idea they were brothers?

Other incidents surfaced. During a *Doors* phase in high school, I'd joke with friends that I was Jim Morrison's long-lost child, al-beit, considering my prudish aversion to drugs, the improbably so-ber one. Mom played along and laughed.

Another memory: I was in the car with Grandma and Pa, talk-ing about some recent event, a birthday party maybe. Grandma asked who was there. I gave some names, one of them Jason's. "Oh, he *was*, was he?" she said, glancing at Pa.

What did *that* mean? I now asked myself. Did she know about the affair? Know I was his son?

These memories, newly understood, constituted a sort of alternate history of my life, a kind of shadow biography. My past suddenly appeared differently, like I had been given the key to a secret code.

On that trip to Rome with Mom in high school, I'd made her trek across the Eternal City to one centuries-old church after another, in search of Caravaggios. Something about the Italian master's work resonated. Later I read a biography, Peter Robb's *M: The Man Who Became Caravaggio*, detailing, from what little we know of the man, his hard life, revolutionary artistry, and the messages he sent with his brushstrokes.

I read about *The Conversion of St. Paul*—Paul, prostrate, reaching skyward beneath the horse from which he had fallen—painted to hang, as it still does, alongside Annibale Carracci's *Assumption of the Virgin Mary* in Rome's Cerasi Chapel.

The work, writes Robb, "sucked your eyes away from the tasteful Carracci altarpiece into an hallucinatory *mise en scène* that had the pony's bony workaday rump projecting massively and indecorously toward Annibale's glossy, demure and untouchable heaven heading virgin. From the altar what you mostly saw was horse's arse."

My whole life, it now seemed, was like that painting, where the trained eye sees a composition, along with veiled meanings, invisible to the novice. My eyes were now trained. Now open.

I knew I could no longer stay at my childhood apartment. It was no longer *my* apartment. No longer *ours*. It was now *her* apartment. My girlfriend Laura had a place on Central Park West that her family used occasionally, and she told me I could stay there as long as I needed.

I moved in a short time later. Physical distance, I quickly realized, was insufficient. I needed emotional, psychological distance. I had no interest in anything my mother might have to say, any excuse or apology she might attempt to offer. I wanted nothing to do with her. I wanted her out of my life. I felt a fury I had never known before, a rage with a life of its own. I was helpless before it.

Years later, Laura would tell me she had suspected the truth about Jason even before I learned it. She mentioned a Hanukkah party Mom had held at her apartment. I was running late, and she arrived ahead of me. Jason was there, and my mother had introduced them. Laura was immediately struck by the shared resemblance and mannerisms. "I felt so sad for you, for your dad," she would say.

She also told me something else. She said I changed after that conversation with my mom. That it almost frightened her, how angry I was, how I cut my mother off over the months that followed. "You were shut down and had a wall up," she remembered. "You were so angry that you felt she in some ways deserved to feel pain from the break in your relationship and didn't deserve your forgiveness."

I still have emails my mom sent during that period. "I know I have caused you tremendous pain," read one. "I will honor your wish that I not bring this up again. And though it won't make your pain go away, I just had to tell you that you are more important to me than my life and that all I have ever wanted for you is a life of love, fulfillment and complete and utter lack of suffering. Please believe that if you can."

Here is another: "I just wanted to remind you that I love you more than words can convey. I will never forgive myself for causing you such pain."

"Dear Adam," she wrote in still another,

> I am lately feeling a growing distance between us, and it makes
> me very unhappy. In spite of the fact that I know I've let you
> down as a mother, I thought we had found a way to leave that

issue in the past and move forward. I now worry that we have
not and that I am losing you. I can't rewrite history—much as I so
wish to God that I could. All I can do is try to be a good mother
going forward. I hope you believe that I am doing the best I am
capable of. That may not be good enough. But know that I love
you with all my being and I love you the only way I know how.

"Mom," I replied later that night, "When I said I forgave you, I thought I was expressing how I really felt. In fact, it made me feel a lot better to say it. But the truth is, I don't. I may someday. But not now. I wish I could offer you more than that, but I can't—it's simply how I feel."

Sometime later, walking to the subway station at Seventy-Second Street and Broadway, I got a call. Seeing it was Mom, I stared at the number, letting it ring, debating whether to answer. As soon as I picked up, I knew instantly that something was wrong. She had been crying.

My first thought: Has Zayde died?

"Can you come over?" she asked.

"Why?" I replied, coldly. She didn't say. A sense of guilt kicked in. "Okay," I managed. "I'll be right there."

The door was unlocked when I arrived, the apartment silent. Mom keeps her apartment meticulously well organized, everything in its place, and I could tell something was off the moment I entered: one of the wooden chairs from the dining room had been pushed into the living room. Mom was perched on it, knees under her arms, rocking back and forth. She was biting her bottom lip so hard I thought it might bleed.

The light from the midday sun struck her face, her whole demeanor expressing the fragility I'd heard on the phone.

I asked questions. She said nothing.

When she did speak, her voice was barely audible, just above a whisper. She seemed so vulnerable, like some baby animal that had been separated from its mother and lost its way.

Who *was* this person?

All the time we'd spent together over the years, all the moods I'd seen her in, I'd never seen anything like this. This was a version of my mom I did not recognize.

An eerie, unsettling calm hung over the apartment. This woman was coiled tight. An explosion is coming, I thought.

Her whole being cried out for sympathy. But I could not offer it. I did not want to help her. I felt not compassion but anger. Resentment. For making me come there in the first place. Then I felt guilty for the thought.

"Are you okay?" I mustered. "How long have you been feeling this way?"

She just rocked back and forth, her eyes skittish, flitting from me, to the floor, back to me, to some unknown point on the wall, out the window.

Is *this* what mental illness looks like?

I knew about Mom's suicide attempt. I knew about her depression. None of it prepared me for this. There's a certain distance between knowing and understanding. And I'd never understood that the woman who had raised me, the woman I loved as my mom, was the same woman who could be capable of taking her own life.

It just didn't make sense. She never struck me as that sort of person—as if I had any idea who that sort of person was.

Now, at last, I understood. This stranger, this version of Mom, *this* is the person who takes her own life. I was terrified.

And I felt responsible. Oh God, I thought, did I do this? Is she afraid of losing me?

I knew she had recently split up with a boyfriend. Was that part of the reason, too? Did she feel like she was being abandoned by everyone around her?

I knew I could not leave. She was in no condition to care for herself. And leaving would only confirm her fears, might push her closer to the edge.

Should I call a doctor? An ambulance?

I called her brother. Mendel lived outside Philadelphia. Of all Mom's siblings, he was the one who understood her best—or was at least the most clear-eyed about the gravity of her mental health problems.

I didn't need to say much. He understood immediately. "I'll be there as soon as I can," he said. "Stay with her. Don't leave her side."

"Don't leave her side," he repeated.

Slowly, Mom started coming back, returning to her steady state. My presence seemed to calm her. Even though I was icy, and she could plainly see I wished I were someplace, *anyplace* else, this was the most time we'd spent together in a while. And it made her happy.

Mendel arrived a few hours later. He must have hit the road as soon as we hung up, I thought. That's Mendel, the loyal brother.

After making a few calls, he suggested taking my mother to Mount Sinai Beth Israel's psychiatric emergency room on the Lower East Side. I sat in the hallway while he talked with the doctor.

Sitting there in that ER, I should have felt overcome with sadness over my mom's state, wanting nothing more than to take care of her. Instead, I was furious. At her. At the situation.

What the fuck? I thought. Am I not even allowed to be angry with her without worrying she's going to kill herself?

A couple of days later, I called Mendel to update him on his sister's progress. He didn't want to talk about *her*. He wanted to talk about *me*.

"Let me tell you something," he said. "I saw how you were treating Chayke. It wasn't right. She's your mother. You were a bad son."

Fuck you, I thought. You have no idea.

It was the first instance of the rift between my mother and me forcing a rift with the rest of her family, none of whom knew anything about what had transpired between us. Telling Mendel, or any of them, felt like an act of betrayal against my mom, and for all my anger, I couldn't bring myself to do it.

Over the coming weeks and months, I tried to be more responsive. I'd check in on Mom more regularly. God forbid she tries to kill herself, I kept thinking. I need to reassure her that she hasn't lost me, that I still love her.

The psychiatrist my mother had seen in the ER that day told her to come back. She liked him, so she did. In time, Mom asked me to join one of their sessions.

"Maybe it will help our relationship," she pleaded. I felt I had no choice but to go along. Her health, her safety, depended on it.

All I remember of these sessions is sitting in the therapist's office on the Lower East Side, barely able to contain my anger, almost incapable of even articulating the source of it all, of uttering the words—Mom has lied to everyone about who I am—as if vocalizing it would make it true.

One day in February 2007, as Mom and I were walking out of her therapist's office, my cell phone rang. It was a fellow speechwriter from the Kerry campaign, Jon Favreau—"Favs," as everyone called him.

Favs and I had stayed in touch after Kerry's loss. He had gone on to write speeches for Barack Obama, the newly elected junior senator from the state of Illinois. And as speculation ramped up, following the publication of *The Audacity of Hope*, that his boss would run for president, I let him know I'd do anything to help.

I'd read *Audacity*. It inspired me. This, I thought, is what politics is *supposed* to be. This is the kind of leader Sorensen had told me about.

Sorensen himself was an early supporter. What first drew him to Obama, he told me, were Obama's critics, who claimed he was too young and inexperienced. That he had somehow been disqualified for the presidency based on some attribute of his birth.

It all sounded very familiar to Ted. "What they're saying about Obama is the same thing they said about JFK," he would tell me, remembering the anti-Catholic bigotry that had dogged Kennedy's candidacy.

In early January, as staffing for a prospective Obama campaign was being sketched out, Favs and I had exchanged emails. "I think

I might be getting a deputy on the campaign," he wrote. "You interested?"

It took me all of seven minutes to reply. "Favs, am I interested in being your deputy? Are you fucking kidding?"

Obama himself, however, had not yet declared he was running, and no official job offer had been made.

This call from Favs, as we were leaving the therapist's office, was what I'd been waiting for.

"Hey man," he began. "I talked to Gibbs," referring to Robert Gibbs, Obama's communications director at the time. "Why don't you come out to Chicago and we'll figure something out."

That was about as formal as things got with Favs. It worked for me.

Never in my life had I wanted to be a part of something more—or live in New York City less—than at that precise moment.

I arrived in Chicago several weeks later, in March 2007, less than a month after Obama announced his candidacy on the steps of the Old State Capitol in Springfield, Illinois, and just a few days short of my twenty-sixth birthday.

PART III

HEALING

γνῶθι σεαυτόν ("Know thyself")

—ANCIENT GREEK INSCRIPTION,
Temple of Apollo at Delphi

21

Hope

President Barack Obama with Zayde and my family at
the White House in late 2011.

T HE ARC OF the moral universe is long," read the words on
Obama's Oval Office rug, "but it bends toward justice."

But how long exactly?

At what angle does it bend?

How can we measure the distance between where we stand and
the arc's end? Between us and justice?

I had expected, in the aftermath of the 2016 election, that my
sense of history would be constructive, assuring me that the arc
would soon bend back, that in due course we'd see the disaster
curtailed.

Sometimes, however, I would find myself unable to find any
cause for reassurance, any source of encouragement, my attention

drawn to darker aspects of our national identity, patterns of behavior that illuminate my own family's journey.

How was it, I often wondered as a boy, that so many seemingly good, hardworking men and women were so unable, unwilling, to stand up to the moral rot at the core of one of the world's most advanced societies?

How was it Bubbie and Zayde's friends could turn on them and acquiesce in the ghettoization and murder of their classmates?

Complete answers to those questions remain elusive, as I suspect they always will, perhaps even to survivors themselves.

And yet to be alive and awake in the second decade of the twenty-first century, as democracies around the world face the threat of backsliding, is to understand, just a little more easily, just a little more clearly, how quickly things can go awry. How many unfathomable scenarios lie on the other side of history's innumerable sliding doors. How many forces, good and evil, swirl around in our own natures, our own societies, battling one another for primacy.

I think sometimes about the more worrying developments in this country and approach the brink of despair. Then I remember something else: 2008. I remember that we are a country that elected Barack Hussein Obama with a majority of the popular vote. Twice. I remember the passage Favs and I inserted into that Iowa caucus night speech all those years ago—a passage, an idea, our boss had articulated so many times before. "Hope," read the speech, "is not blind optimism.

> It's not ignoring the enormity of the task ahead or the roadblocks that stand in our path. It's not sitting on the sidelines or shrinking from a fight. Hope is that thing inside us that insists, despite all evidence to the contrary, that something better awaits us if we have the courage to reach for it, and work for it, and fight for it. . . . Hope is the bedrock of this nation; the belief that our destiny will not be written for us, but by us; by all those men and women who are not content

to settle for the world as it is; who have the courage to remake the world as it should be.

Hope—the message Barack Obama offered our country and the planet, the word Zayde spelled on that hospital alphabet chart, the middle name my wife and I gave our daughter. Along with whatever trauma has been transmitted across the generations, hope, too, is a part of my inheritance.

TODAY THE MEMORY, the image, most closely associated with '08 is Grant Park. Crowds of thousands. Cheering, chanting in the streets. Wide, teary eyes absorbing the stunning fact of the United States of America, riven by race, electing its first black president, whose beautiful family would now live in a home built by slaves.

And yet, as inspirational as that night was, as much of a claim as those two words—Grant Park—will always hold on my heart, one other word will always mean more: Iowa.

It may be difficult now, in the aftermath of two Obama terms, to recall just how unlikely his victory was, just how deep the feelings of doubt ran from the moment he declared his candidacy.

Once, sitting with Sorensen at his country house outside New York City—its name, "Serendipity," announced on a wooden sign in the driveway—he had said of 1960, seemingly out of nowhere, "I can't believe we won. He was so young, so inexperienced. Everyone was against us. All the party leaders. Eleanor Roosevelt. I can't believe we won," he repeated, a wistful look in his eyes.

In the early days, all of us on the Obama campaign felt a similar sense of improbability. During the summer and early fall of 2007, when Hillary Clinton was ahead as much as nearly thirty points in national polls, fretful supporters would spam our in-boxes. "Where's the Obama of '04?" they'd write. "He needs to show more energy on the stump."

"Here's Barack's email," Favs, exasperated, would yell into his laptop. "Why don't you tell him yourself!"

Symbolizing the nadir was an op-ed I'd drafted for Obama in October, rejected by one outlet after another, each of them unwilling to publish a candidate with such a small chance of winning. Finally, we submitted it to what all of us assumed would be a sure thing: the *Hilton Head Island Packet,* a small South Carolina paper, distributed, I was told, under the doors of rooms in local hotels. No dice. Evidently, even the *Hilton Head Island Packet* felt Obama was not sufficiently newsworthy to grace its opinion page.

Iowa is where everything changed. In November, Obama delivered his Jefferson-Jackson Dinner speech in Des Moines, one of the most important of the campaign, a draft of which I'd pulled an all-nighter writing with Favs and Ben Rhodes, who'd joined the campaign a few months after me.

I was not there to see Obama give the speech. I'd flown home for my Dad's sixtieth-birthday celebration. I spent the evening constantly checking my Blackberry for live updates from Veterans Memorial Auditorium, where Obama was speaking, and feeling an overpowering sense of complicity, of duplicity. Here I am, I kept thinking, celebrating Dad even as I withhold the truth of my identity, even as he doesn't know I'm not his blood.

Keeping the secret was difficult enough while I was in Chicago, separated by hundreds of miles. I'd exhale after every phone call with Dad, relieved I'd made it through another one without inadvertently saying something that led to a question that led to an answer that somehow tipped him off to what I'd been hiding. Each conversation was like one of those medieval maps where sea monsters lay lurking for explorers venturing too far off course.

Face-to-face was that much harder. My presence itself seemed like an affront.

Shortly after I returned to Chicago, I was dispatched to Des Moines while Ben traveled to New Hampshire, supporting the Iowa and New Hampshire press offices, respectively, while Favs traveled with Obama as he barnstormed those states.

Five days before the Iowa caucuses, Favs arrived in Des Moines, and we started talking about Obama's caucus-night speech. The primary guidance we'd received was from our campaign manager, David Plouffe. "Make it about the organizers," he'd told Favs.

Quickly discovering we couldn't concentrate with all the noise in our Des Moines headquarters, we moved to a quieter location, a small conference room inexplicably located in the back of a nearby coffee shop, the Village Bean. There, we holed up writing for the next couple of days, periodically wondering whether the *Newsweek* reporter seated just on the other side of the door was eavesdropping.

We'd settled on the opening early, including the line, "They said this day would never come." Favs wasn't sure Iowa was the right place to use it. "Maybe we should hold on to it for the Inaugural," he suggested.

"Who knows if we'll make it that far?" I replied, less confidently.

Our writing process on that speech was not altogether different from any of the many other speeches Favs, Ben, and I wrote together on that campaign. We talked it through, paragraph by paragraph, line by line, inspiring, challenging, editing one another as we went.

"What's the story we're trying to tell?" we'd ask each other. "What are we *really* trying to say here?" "Where do we go after this?" "What's the right transition?" "Is the arc right?" "Is the cadence right?" "Should we bring it down a little before building it up at the end?"

A cottage industry has emerged to advise politicians, CEOs, and other public figures on writing and delivering powerful speeches. Mostly, the advice boils down to speaking slowly, enunciating clearly, and emphasizing a few words or phrases. Rightly so. That, more or less, is about as much as many public speakers can handle.

Obama was operating on an entirely different level. We were thinking through not only words, but beats. Not only tone and structure, but rhythm. "Ever watch Obama speak from behind the podium?" a campaign friend once asked. "Look at his feet. He's dancing."

Our job, as I saw it, was to write speeches commensurate with Obama's extraordinary abilities, speeches that could inspire others to believe in him as much as we believed in him. As much as I believed in him.

We didn't always hit the mark. One morning on the campaign, Favs greeted me with a sympathetic look. "See David Brooks' column?" he asked. It was about a speech I had written—"A Speech," read the headline, "about Nothing."

Sometimes, however, we got it right. "Cooking with grease," we'd say, borrowing an expression from Donna Brazile. In the Village Bean, we were cooking with grease.

On the afternoon of our second day of writing, January 2, we suddenly remembered that Obama was scheduled to speak that night at a rally, his last before the caucuses the following day. Taking a break from the caucus speech, we started brainstorming some rally remarks. Obama's stump could serve as the foundation, but we wanted to enliven it somehow, make it new.

"What about Yes We Can?" Favs asked, referencing the motto of Obama's 2004 Senate campaign. I loved the idea.

"Iowa," read the speech that Obama would deliver that night to a packed high school gym,

in less than twenty-four hours, you have the chance to change America.

You have the chance to do what all the cynics are saying can't be done.

They're saying that all of you who've never caucused before won't caucus now—that you'll stay home because your disappointment with what our politics has become means you don't have hope for what our politics can be.

But tomorrow is your chance to stand for a politics of possibility—a politics of hope. Tomorrow is your chance to say, "Yes we can."

That was the first time Obama used the phrase in a prepared 2008 campaign speech. And that is why it was on our minds when, a few days later, Favs, Ben, and I decided, on a call to discuss the following week's New Hampshire primary night speech, to close with a big Yes We Can riff about generations of Americans who'd believed in, and achieved, the impossible.

After the 2008 election, the *New Yorker*'s Ryan Lizza reported that Obama had told his incoming political director, Patrick Gaspard, "I think that I'm a better speechwriter than my speechwriters. I know more about policies on any particular issue than my policy directors. And I'll tell you right now that I'm gonna think I'm a better political director than my political director."

For all the eye-rolling that quotation induced on the speechwriting team—and it induced quite a lot, both at the time and later—I never felt Obama was being unfair or inaccurate. He *was* a better speechwriter than any of us.

I got a closer look at Obama's writing in the White House, where he was a short walk away, than I'd had on the campaign, where edits usually came in a quick call or email.

"Something about this draft just doesn't feel right." That, or something like it, is probably the most frequent feedback a speechwriter ever receives, and it is typically accompanied by precisely zero suggestions on what to do about it.

I never heard Obama utter those words. In fact, I was always struck by the precision of his edits. If a certain sentence or structure had problems, he'd tell us exactly how to fix them. During one Oval Office meeting, he leaned over my shoulder as I scribbled his edits as quickly as I could. "Actually," he said, pointing to a colon I'd inserted, "that should be a semicolon."

Occasionally, his edits were offered conditionally. "That's just my suggestion. Do what you think is best." No need to worry, Barack Obama, my twenty-something-year-old self would think—I'll take your edit.

On most speeches, we'd get line edits without any overarching feedback on the quality of the draft. (He was too busy to offer it, and we didn't expect it.) But if a speech were mediocre, he'd let us know. "Pedestrian, but serviceable," he once told us. And he'd also let us know if he thought we'd done a particularly good job.

Sitting with the candidate in a hotel suite in Denver on the eve of the 2008 Democratic National Convention, Favs, Ben, and I, along with a recent addition to our team, Sarah Hurwitz, who'd written for Hillary Clinton in the primaries, talked over some final changes to his nomination acceptance speech.

As we were wrapping up, Obama looked at us. "Hasn't Favs done a great job leading this process?" he asked. We agreed.

Obama got up to leave, and turned to Ben. "Didn't you help on Biden's speech?"

"Yes," Ben replied.

"That was a great speech."

"Thank you, sir," said Ben.

Obama took a few steps toward the door. "Sarah," he said, looking back. "Didn't you help Michelle on her speech?"

"I did."

"That was great, too," said Obama, taking a few more steps toward the door.

Turning back one last time, he looked at me. "Frankel," he said, and paused—unable, in that moment, to think of another speech I was writing, "I know you're working on something great, brother," and started chuckling. Characteristically inclusive, he hadn't wanted any of us to feel left out.

In the White House, where the size of our speechwriting team multiplied, collaborations among speechwriters became mostly impractical, and each of us gravitated toward separate portfolios. Outside the necessary allocation of policy and political speeches, I also cultivated something of an unusual niche, including eulogies.

"Soothing Pain with His Pen," read the headline of a profile in the *Los Angeles Times*. "The first thing we do when prominent people pass away, after we mourn their losses," David Axelrod wryly told reporter Peter Nicholas, "is we call in Adam to begin work on the appropriate remarks."

I also cultivated another portfolio—history, civil rights, faith—speeches that permitted, perhaps demanded, a more elevated tone, a different vocabulary, rooted in values, ideals, principles.

"The presidency is not merely an administrative office," Governor Franklin Roosevelt told a reporter before entering the White House. "That's the least of it. It is more than an engineering job, efficient or inefficient. It is preeminently a place of moral leadership."

Working with Obama on these speeches allowed me to make, I felt, a small contribution to his moral leadership of the country, of the world.

I also had another motivation. These remarks rarely drew the same scrutiny from senior advisors as policy or political speeches. On the list of White House communications priorities, where an event's importance typically reflected its likely impact on the day's news cycle, these speeches were simply not at the top.

One person who seemed to reject that prioritization, however, was Barack Obama. And taking the lead on these topics, I knew, would allow me to collaborate with him in a way that was, almost uniquely in the White House, free from the involvement of others.

Speeches that might have been entirely conceived and exclusively written by a speechwriter under any other president received from Obama large quantities of that scarcest of presidential resources—time.

One obscure speech that received such abundant presidential attention came in early 2010, when Obama agreed to speak on Martin Luther King Weekend at Vermont Avenue Baptist Church, near the White House. The speech would take place days before Scott Brown's victory in the Massachusetts special election to fill Ted Kennedy's seat threw health-care reform in doubt.

It was not lost on America's first black president, of course, that his frequent collaborator on civil rights speeches was white. "Go as far as you can on this," he had instructed on another set of remarks after tasking me with writing about some of the challenges in the

African American community. "There may be some things you may not feel comfortable saying that I need to write myself."

Occasionally, when I asked if he had any guidance on a particular speech, he'd say, "I think you've got this one," and move on to the next item on the agenda. Never, I should add, did I feel as confident hearing those words as he seemed to be delivering them.

He did not, however, express such confidence on this speech. He asked me to identify a moment of triumph followed by uncertainty in the civil rights movement, which, with help from King biographer Taylor Branch, I did. And he told me he wanted to reflect on the high hopes that had accompanied his own election, and the lessons King could teach us about heeding our vision in the face of the uncertainties of our own time.

The draft included a line about the "hard winters" endured by "the slaves and the freedmen who rode an underground railroad, seeking the light of justice under the cover of night." I thought about my own family's hard winters, the ones Bubbie and Zayde had endured so many years earlier.

Talking over a draft with Obama, I was struck by a passage he asked me to add—and later, reworked several times. A passage that had nothing to do with Martin Luther King Jr., the civil rights movement, or the challenges facing the United States in 2010. A passage that was personal. "Folks ask me sometimes," he wrote, "why I look so calm. Fact is, there are times when the words hurt. There are times when the barbs sting. There are times when it feels like all the hard work is for naught, and change is so painfully slow in coming and I wrestle with my doubts. But let me tell you—it's faith that gives me peace."

I saw Obama regularly in the White House, often several times a week. Occasionally, a few times a day. Rarely did I see him open up. I was moved, then, reading this passage, to get even this small glimpse into his emotional life.

When I left the White House in late 2011, I gave the president a gift: a 1935 first edition of *An Interpretation of Christian Ethics* by

Reinhold Niebuhr, a theologian he admired. I'd first learned about Niebuhr years earlier from Pa, who would often recite his Serenity Prayer. Inside the cover, I included a note. What had been so meaningful about the past several years, I wrote, was the chance to serve not only a president I so deeply believed in, but a man I so deeply admired.

As proud as I was of serving the most progressive president since the era Sorensen helped usher in, of all the meaningful changes the Obama administration delivered and pursued in the United States and around the world, I was equally proud of serving a man who displayed so much integrity, who hewed so closely to such a high ethical standard in his own life.

Reflecting on that note today, I'm struck by the way I distinguished between Obama the president and Obama the man—a distinction I drew partly, I think, because of what was happening in my own personal life.

At a time when I was reeling from decisions I considered grossly unethical, I had a boss who conducted himself in a way that was unfailingly proper, a paragon of how to act honestly, respectfully. A model family man, lovingly devoted to his wife and daughters.

Obama was not only a moral leader, a role model, for the country and the world, I now see. He was also a role model for me.

WHEN I MOVED to Chicago in March 2007, I was one of two speechwriters on a scrappy campaign few people gave much of a chance. When I left the White House in the fall of 2011, I was one of nine speechwriters for an incumbent president gearing up for reelection.

During the intervening years, our speechwriting team had shared fairly cramped quarters—adjacent cubicles, followed by a small office, then a larger office, and then a small office again—sitting only a few feet away from one another, hour after hour, day after day, month after month.

Many of the hours we were not working were also spent together, playing Guitar Hero at Favs' Chicago group house, singing karaoke, or out at some bar in DC, mindful of the advice Obama had given some of his young staff days after his victory. "I'm not saying, Don't have a good time," he advised, urging us to represent his new administration well. "I'm saying, Have that fifth beer at home."

And yet, at no time during all those hours in all those days in all those years did I confide in any of my Obama friends about the truth I'd learned before joining the campaign. The only people I'd told, in fact, were a few of my oldest friends from New York City, who had known Mom, Dad, and me since I was a boy. In Chicago and, later, DC, I was essentially alone with my secret, wary not only of sharing it but even of thinking about it too frequently.

I was certain that if I gave voice to my thoughts—"Before I left for Chicago, I feared my mom might kill herself," "Mom and I are barely speaking," "Dad doesn't know I'm not his son"—I'd need to face those realities. Deal with them. And I wasn't ready for that emotionally or psychologically.

If I so much as acknowledged what had happened, I thought, if I gave any space to the pain, sadness, or anger I felt, I would be unable to contain them. Unleashed, I feared, they'd swallow me up, and I'd lose control over my life and any ability to focus on my overriding, all-consuming objective: being as good a speechwriter for Barack Obama as I was capable of being.

Convinced I was unable to confront my truth and serve Obama at the same time, I chose the latter and postponed the former, burying it deep down where I hoped it wouldn't cause any trouble.

In the early days of the campaign, there had been occasional opportunities for Obama to meet staff members' parents. I never told Mom and Dad about them. If I'd invited Dad, I'd need to invite Mom, and I wasn't willing to do that. I simply hoped no one would notice that my parents didn't visit as often as others'. Since everybody was so busy, nobody did—or at least, nobody mentioned it.

Mom did visit once. Eager to bridge the distance between us, she kept asking when she could come. At a certain point, I relented.

During a standoff in my apartment, I told her I wished she hadn't made the trip. Around the same time, I started feeling lumps in my armpits. Frightened, I saw a doctor. "It's from stress," he told me.

Even calls with Mom were stressful. I'd spend time prepping for them, like a trial attorney prepping a big case, running through a list of questions she might ask and possible follow-ups, trying to think through how I'd respond in a way that would avoid unintentionally triggering her or provoking her to lash out or, equally worrisome, go silent on the other end.

Years later, I surveyed some of my Obama friends about whether they sensed what I was going through. "I never did," Favs told me. "We were all such brooding writers, always stewing, always staring at blank screens, trying to figure out what to say." The only time he, or Ben, noticed anything was wrong, they told me, was when Laura and I broke up toward the end of the campaign. "I guess you also just hid it really well," Favs added.

For a while in the White House, I shared a narrow office with another speechwriter, Jon Lovett. "Jesus Christ," he would occasionally yell. "Would you stop sighing?" At the time, I thought nothing of it. Now, I wonder if my sighing was a release of the heaviness I was carrying around.

Speechwriting, in a sense, offered an almost poetically inspired escape from grappling with everything. At a moment when my sense of self had been shaken, my job required inhabiting someone else's identity and perspective. At a time when I'd lost my voice, my professional success depended on adopting another's.

Years later, after Obama had left the White House, I stopped by his personal office and shared with him everything I'd been going through when I was on his staff. I was moved by his interest and empathy. Most of our interactions during the years we worked together had been businesslike. He was the president, I was a staffer, and there was work to be done.

This visit was different. It was the longest conversation we'd ever had about something other than a speech. "How'd you figure it out?" he kept asking after I told him about the revelation. "Is your dad black?" I laughed. By then, I could laugh about it.

As the 2012 election approached, I was handed a DNC laptop and Blackberry—on top of my government-issued laptop and Blackberry and personal devices—a requirement for me, a federal employee, to write Obama's remarks at political events.

Staff for presidents facing reelections have a choice: leave before the campaign ramps up or stay until it's over. Ducking out midway is not acceptable, and at that moment, I wasn't sure I had another campaign in me.

I'd been in the job longer than most White House speechwriters, and didn't feel I was serving the president well anymore. Once you've written a president's speech to an organization's annual gala three years in a row, how do you make the fourth stand out?

During a farewell reception for a colleague in the Diplomatic Reception Room in the White House, I made a crack to Obama about the chore of writing the weekly address. (I was not the only speechwriter who considered it a chore, although I was, admittedly, the only one dumb enough to complain about it to Obama.) The president rightly reminded me that even what were considered the dregs of speechwriting assignments garnered a large audience and needed to be taken seriously.

I'd always believed that the moment a White House staffer stops appreciating the privilege of being there, it's time to go. That seemed like it was beginning to happen.

Typically, when staff members leave an administration, they get what's called a departure photo with the president, often bringing family members along for the occasion. I invited everyone: Mom, Dad, Helen, Zayde, and Grandma.

It was the first time Mom, Dad, and I would be together since I'd learned the truth of our relationships. And, anxious about Dad picking up on the tension between Mom and me, I was counting on everyone's preoccupation with seeing Obama to get us through the day without anything coming up. I was right—it did.

Mom and Zayde arrived early, and I took them to lunch in the White House Mess. "Not bad for a Michalishker," Mom said to Zayde, who smiled as we sat down.

Upstairs, we waited in the West Wing Lobby as other departing staff members cycled in and out of the Oval Office. One of my friends managed Obama's schedule, and gave us the last departure photo of the day so we'd have a few extra minutes with the president.

"I'm Jo Minow's sister," Grandma said as Obama invited us in, and he gave her a big hug.

"This is my grandfather, Mr. President," I said, introducing Zayde. "He's a Holocaust survivor."

"It's an honor to meet you," Obama said as Zayde clasped the president's hand with both of his.

I appreciated the graciousness of the president's greeting, and tried to take the moment in, reflecting on the sweep of Zayde's life, from Michalishek to Kaufering to America, the idea of this man, this former Nazi slave, standing with the president of the United States in the Oval Office.

Lined up before the Resolute Desk, Obama's photographer snapping away, I felt an almost manic restlessness I was doing my best to disguise. I wasn't entirely successful. At one point, Mom asked if everything was okay. "Yes," I lied. In truth, I was in the throes of an identity crisis.

22

Who Am I?

Courtesy of the author

With Zayde and Pa in 1982.

ONE OF THE books I read to our two-year-old daughter before
bedtime is the children's classic *We're Going on a Bear Hunt*, by
Michael Rosen and illustrator Helen Oxenbury. "We're going on a
bear hunt," writes Rosen in one of its refrains. "We're going to catch
a big one. What a beautiful day! We're not scared. Oh-oh! A forest.
A big, dark forest. We can't go over it. We can't go under it. Oh, no!
We've got to go through it."

Each of the refrains introduces a new obstacle—"A swirling,
whirling snowstorm," "A narrow, gloomy cave," "A deep, cold river"—
that a family can't go over, can't go under, and must go through.

Like all the best children's tales, it contains a resonant truth,
equally applicable in adulthood: that we must confront the challenges, however daunting, in our lives. And toward the end of 2009

I began applying that truth in my own life, finally recognizing that I could no longer evade the dark forest that had arisen before me, the dense woods, thick foliage, and strange, frightening creatures that now lay in my path.

The catalyst for my decision was prosaic: a breakup. Her name was Stephanie, and we met in the spring of 2009 at a birthday party for one of my Obama friends. Steph herself was part of the extended Obama family. Her sister Jen was then deputy White House press secretary and an old friend of mine from the Kerry campaign. And Jen, along with another speechwriter, Cody, who knew Steph from grad school, had been conspiring to set us up.

Jen later said she knew we were right for each other when she heard me remark one day on the campaign that I didn't read fiction because, as I put it, there were too many "real things" to read about—a cringe-worthy statement she had only ever heard from one other person: her apparently equally benighted sister.

I had some awareness, then, of the matchmaking scheme being hatched when Cody offered to make the formal introduction. Steph was standing by a bar lined with red and blue plastic cups and bottles of cheap alcohol, the only kind we could afford on our government salaries. She had recently finished her master's in public health, and was working at an NGO while preparing to embark on her PhD at Johns Hopkins that fall.

I was immediately taken with her. Her eyes cut right through me, and her self-assurance put me at ease. She was brilliant, beautiful, public-spirited, and utterly unimpressed that I was an Obama speechwriter, which made her all the more attractive.

Things moved quickly in those early months—at least, as quickly as things could move, considering I'd often disappear for days at a time, working on a speech or traveling with Obama. But just as the relationship started getting serious, I panicked. I didn't have the wherewithal to work through my feelings of doubt or uncertainty, and I took the only action I felt capable of taking: I broke up with her.

"It's me," I told her. "You're incredible."

"Don't worry," she replied with her customary self-confidence. "My self-esteem is intact."

Mine, however, was not. "We're on suicide watch," the speech-writers cracked—a joke they might not have made had they known my mother's history.

I was bewildered by my own reaction to my decision. *I'd* broken up with her, I thought. Why was I so full of regret?

That breakup was my canary in the coal mine. I could not know then that Steph would be the woman I would marry, the mother of my children, or the best friend who would carry me through the gathering storm. But I somehow sensed that I would never be the kind of father or husband I wanted to be unless I quieted the upheaval inside.

I'd never told Steph about any of what had happened with my mom. So, on a call a few days later, I opened up and shared every-thing with her, hoping she might give me another chance if she knew what I'd been going through. Steph wisely encouraged me to see a therapist, and I did, ultimately finding someone I could talk to and trust.

On the campaign and during my first months in the White House, I'd kept a lid on everything, fearful that if I gave my emotions any space, they would swallow me up. My fears, I now discovered, had been well founded. The more closely I examined myself, the more time I spent thinking and talking about what had happened, the more unsettled and disoriented I became.

One of the features of being a White House speechwriter is the hurry-up-and-wait nature of the job. When we were working on a speech, we were completely consumed, isolating ourselves to pro-duce a draft, allowing interruptions only for information gathering or the periodic mind-clearing break.

But in the hours or occasional day or two when we didn't have a speech to write, we essentially had nothing to do. Given the way the White House worked, with everyone always focused on the im-mediate priority and events changing quickly, we couldn't really get started on the next speech. So we'd sometimes find ourselves with hours of free time. And precisely in those moments—moments the other speechwriters were stealing to unwind—I felt most uneasy. Without the preoccupation of writing a speech, I was a mess.

During my sophomore summer in college, I'd circumnavigated the globe on a fellowship, savoring all of my time alone spent in reading, journaling, reflecting. Now I was unable to sit with myself in peace. My mind was newly frenetic, and I had a constant tightness in my chest, a galloping heartbeat, and recurring shortness of breath, like some kind of chronic panic attack.

Long runs around the Lincoln and Jefferson Monuments or Rock Creek Park helped, at least for brief periods. I even signed up for the Marine Corps Marathon when I realized the psychic benefits the training regimen would yield. But inevitably, the next day, if not sooner, the dizzying disorientation would return.

"When the crisis of the French Revolution came," writes Oxford historian J. M. Thompson, "the kings' statues in Paris were pulled down and broken to bits: and it is said that the crowd, who expected to melt them down into an infinite supply of copper money, stood around angry and astonished; for they were all hollow inside, no thicker than a single coin."

I felt like one of those statues. Hollow—my apparent mass, volume, an illusion.

I'd always prided myself on being a person of strong opinions, someone who knew where he stood and wasn't afraid to say so, someone who could hear clearly his own inner voice. Now all I heard was static and noise. I seemed incapable of answering even the most basic questions about my opinions, interests, or desires, anything that required my personal take on something. I had lost all access to what those preferences were, to what I thought about anything. It was as if all of my beliefs, all of my views, had suddenly been erased. And I didn't know why—or when or if I would ever retrieve them.

Into this void rushed an overpowering, frightening sense of

self-doubt. I felt my life unfolding without me, like I no longer had any agency over it. I second-guessed every decision, no matter how mundane, sometimes to the point of paralysis. One particularly vivid memory is crouching in the aisle of an airport bookstore, stricken with panic over the choice of what book to buy.

And I felt so alone. The person I most wanted to tell was Dad. But I couldn't do that without also telling him what had precipitated the crisis I was experiencing, and I wasn't willing even to consider such a thing.

I was too angry to talk to my mother. And too embarrassed, even ashamed, to confide fully in friends, and especially Steph, certain I would drive her away after she had agreed to give me a second chance.

Occasionally I'd go down a rabbit hole, spending hours online, searching Google or Facebook, for whatever photos I could find of Jason and his children—my half family.

I would gaze at their faces, looking for any similarities to mine, just as I'd searched my own face as a teenager for similarities to Dad's. Only now, I found such similarities everywhere. My half sister and I have the same nose, I thought. My half brother and I, the same chin.

Sometimes I'd walk up to a mirror and lose myself in it. Five. Ten. Fifteen minutes would pass as I stared at my reflection. Who is this person? I'd wonder, even as I was struck by the oddness of the thought.

In my face, I saw a stranger. I look like this *other* family, I'd think. Not *my* family.

I couldn't help remembering Zayde walking into that parsonage in Unterigling for the first time and mistaking his reflection for someone else at the end of the hallway. Under vastly different circumstances, two generations of Perecmans failing to recognize ourselves in a mirror. What strange symmetries history reveals.

Years later I told a friend who had been raised by his adoptive family about all the time I spent in front of a mirror. "I went through something similar," he told me. "But I went through it in fifth or sixth grade." *Before*, not *after*, his identity was formed. I was doing the process in reverse. I was relearning who I was, all over again.

I started thinking about my name: Adam Perecman Frankel. A perfectly fine, if fairly generic Jewish name.

Now nothing about it seemed generic, nothing simple. I was not, at least biologically, a Frankel, nor had I ever been adopted.

Was I a Black?

Then there was my middle name, Perecman, the name Bubbie and Zayde had bought in the DP camp for safe passage to America. Gubersky was Zayde's true surname, the name Bubbie had adopted after their first marriage, before acquiring their new identities.

Was my name, in fact, Adam Gubersky Black?

Strange thought.

Who is Adam Gubersky Black? Would he have been a speechwriter? Would I have been different with a different name?

All of these questions now cast my relationship with Pa in an entirely different light, too. The conflict between my parents when I was growing up had led me to seek out the comfort of Pa's company. But now, I wonder, had I also sensed that Dad wasn't my biological father? Is that part of the reason I was so close to Pa? Because I'd gone searching for another father figure?

At the same time, as I reflected on Pa's life, I began thinking about what Dad had once told me, that the loss of Pa's father at such a young age had led him to be hyperinvolved in the lives of his children and grandchildren.

Were Pa's trauma and my own reaching out and interacting across the generations, across time and space?

Occasionally I also wondered something else. Was the reason the revelation shook me so profoundly simply shock from the magnitude of the lies? Or was it more than that? Was it because I'd always identified so closely with my Frankel family? Because I'd always wanted to see myself more as a Frankel than a Perecman?

If I hadn't drawn so much of my identity from my dad's side of the family, from the Frankels and Minows, would the revelation have hurt so much? Would I have been so shaken by the vanishing of any genetic link to them? If I'd wanted to be different from them, would I have found comfort in the revelation?

LOOKING FOR STORIES of other people undergoing the kind of identity crisis I was experiencing, I tracked down Naomi Cahn, a family law expert at the George Washington University Law School.

Cahn introduced me to the term *genealogical bewilderment*, an idea articulated in 1952 by British psychiatrist E. Wellisch that refers to the possible identity problems arising from ignorance or uncertainty about a person's birth parents. Our conversation also led me to another term I'd never heard—LDA, for late discovery adoptee, a person who learns, usually after age eighteen, that he is not the biological child of the parents who raised him.

"I found out what I'm called," I gleefully announced to Steph. "I'm a late discovery adoptee."

She gave me a puzzled stare.

"But you're not adopted," she replied.

I was crestfallen.

"Well . . . I mean . . . you're not," she said.

I thought about it for a moment.

"Fair point," I said. We both laughed.

Rather little research has been done on the experience of late discovery adoptees or donor-conceived children, and what little exists comes from Australia. I found a report—"Why Wasn't I Told? Making Sense of the Late Discovery of Adoption"—published by the country's oldest charity, the Benevolent Society, which found that some LDAs "experienced feelings of loss that their family was not their biological family, and questions of 'who am I?' overwhelmed them. The late discovery of adoption," it continued, "forced one to confront deep-seated identity issues and to grieve for the person whom one thought one was."

There are, of course, differences between my experience and the experiences of LDAs or any adoptees, as there are between adoptees and donor-conceived children. And yet, in testimonials of late discoverers' experiences, I recognized my own story. "My whole life," wrote one, "was a lie." "The sense of loss, anguish and bafflement about my own identity were overwhelming," wrote another. "I had become terrified every time I looked in the mirror and saw someone staring back at me who I didn't recognize."

Reading these testimonials, I felt less alone. Like my feelings were normal and my response to the revelation not altogether different from how others had reacted after experiencing something similar. And I suspect many others *will* experience something similar, as at-home DNA kits like 23andMe make it easier than ever to determine where we come from—and where we don't.

PERHAPS INEVITABLY, THE turmoil in my head and heart began to migrate out into the world, producing a series of real-life consequences. I've often heard some version of the maxim "Don't make any big decisions when you're emotional."

It is sage advice that I proceeded to reject extravagantly. The first big decision was leaving the White House and considering what to do next. The choice came down to either leading a new national education nonprofit that the Obama administration was helping establish, or joining the office of New York City's public advocate, Bill de Blasio, who was then considered a likely mayoral candidate in the upcoming election.

I'd lurch from one opportunity to the other, changing my mind every day, sometimes every hour. I'd call up Uncle Newt and my dad for advice and hang up, thinking I'd made a decision, only to reverse it a short time later.

Shortly after de Blasio offered me a role, I called him back to accept. "I want to help make you mayor," I said. Twenty-four hours later, I sent him a note saying I needed to talk.

I hadn't fully thought through how to make things work with

Steph in what would now be a long-distance relationship between New York and DC. She was away on an overseas trip with some friends, and when she'd left, I'd told her I would be accepting the nonprofit job. Informing her by phone that I'd suddenly changed my mind confused and upset her.

Not knowing how to extricate myself from the mess I'd just created in my relationship and waffling about the job itself, I created another mess, telling de Blasio I would be rescinding my acceptance.

I don't recall exactly what I said. Whatever I mustered was doubtless inadequate. How could I explain why I'd changed my mind? Even *I* didn't fully understand.

"Wow, you look like shit," Lovett told me when I showed up to work the next day. We went out to lunch. I shared some of what I was going through, as much as I felt I could. He didn't say much, but I appreciated him listening.

I spent the following weekend with my Minow cousin Nell and her husband David at a Virginia estate where they were housesitting. I remember sitting by the pool, wishing I could tell them everything—about Mom, about Dad. I was so close to the Minows, especially Nell, and I knew it would help to open up to her. But how could I tell Dad's cousin the truth when Dad himself didn't know?

Many White House staffers spend considerable time thinking through what to do after such an exhilarating experience, a high-class problem for each and every one of us. My problem was different. It wasn't simply that I didn't know what I wanted to do. I didn't know who I was. I'd lost the thread of my own narrative.

I thought of one of Uncle Newt's sayings: "Make sure the person you are, the person you want to be, and the person other people see are the same. When they're not, you've got problems."

I was sure the person people saw was not the person I was, but I had no idea *who* that person was, much less what I wanted to be.

23

The Gamblers

Steph and I on our wedding day in Bermuda.

A MID ALL THE tumult that was roiling my life, Steph patiently stuck with me. And yet her patience was not infinite. She knew I had lost my way, but she loved me, knew I loved her, and wanted to know where things were headed.

I could not tell her because I did not know. The same indecision that had gripped me over the de Blasio opportunity returned. During a long flight back from a conference in Arizona, I had a panic attack. My heart rate accelerating, my mind frantic, I started to sweat and looked around, wondering if anyone noticed the passenger sitting unnaturally still, trying to act normally as my psyche went into freefall.

Folding down my tray table, I took out a pen and paper and started writing. Maybe if I wrote down how I was feeling, I thought, I'd be able to bring some clarity to everything.

I drew up a list of pros and cons of getting married—in hindsight, a rather telltale sign that perhaps I shouldn't have been making such a consequential decision. One minute, the pros seemed to be winning. The next, the cons. I must have swung back and forth three or four times before the plane landed.

When I got home, I called Dad for advice. I held back, worried that if I revealed the extent of my inner turmoil, it would lead to a conversation exposing the secret I'd been carrying around.

Still, he offered what seemed like good advice, and it spoke to me. "Marriage is always a gamble," he said. "But it's worth it." What I couldn't tell him was that if I proposed, I would not be gambling on *Steph*. Both of us would be gambling on *me*, on the likelihood of me finding a way out of my morass.

I hadn't returned to Bermuda since my last trip with Grandma and Pa when I was eighteen, saving the experience for something special, someone special. Now, I had both. On a beautiful day at Cambridge Beaches—by a secluded bay where I'd snorkeled with Pa as a boy—I proposed.

I knew all was not right in my head and heart, but I didn't want a future with Steph to be a casualty of it. Steph was the first person I'd dated who I felt I could be happy with for the rest of my life.

When we started to talk timing, Steph said she didn't want to rush things, that she wanted a long engagement because she wanted to finish her PhD before getting married. That, I now know, wasn't the only reason. She was also giving me time to work through everything.

But the consequence of my deepening relationship with Steph was a widening rift with my mother. Mom began to displace her tension with me onto Steph, blaming her for what was transpiring between us.

Some of the difficulties were to be expected from a Jewish soon-to-be mother-in-law whose family did little to hide its disappointment about my marrying a shiksa, a "gentle," as Zayde always pronounced the word *gentile*.

"Is she a yid?" was his first question when I told him about Steph. A few years later, he took out the beautiful engagement ring he had made for her—"Made special," as he would say. "The first diamond they sent was not good enough, so I sent it back," Zayde told me, rightfully proud of his impeccable standards.

I gazed at it, telling Zayde how grateful we were, how meaning-ful it was to have a ring he had made himself.

"Now, do something for *me*," he said. "Promise me you'll have her convert."

I was silent for a moment.

As I stood processing the unexpected request, I almost admired Zayde for making it, for trying to extract something for the favor he had granted me and Steph with the ring. Deals like that, large and small, were a part of who he was, how he had survived the war, how he had made a life for himself afterward.

Still, I couldn't help reflecting on the gap between us, of genera-tions, worldviews.

Had he *met* Steph? I couldn't *have* her do anything.

Zayde's old-world views on gender roles were not well suited to the twenty-first century, or at least, the twenty-first century in our apartment.

"I'm sorry, Zayde," I said. "But that's not something I can promise."

I could hardly begrudge Zayde his disappointment that I was marrying outside the faith. As far as I was concerned, the man got a pass on that subject.

But I had a harder time shrugging off comments from the rest of my family, especially after the way Steph's family had welcomed me and after watching Steph, a lapsed Catholic, try so hard to show respect for our family's traditions. As we sat around my mother's dining room table over lunch one day, I told Mom how Steph had bought Grandma eight little presents, one for each of the days of Hanukkah.

"Well, I've always thought that sort of thing was stupid," my mother replied, as Steph's heart sank.

Later, after our daughter was born, Mom gave the baby a plastic *shofar*, which we inadvertently left behind. "Steph doesn't want their daughter to learn about Judaism," she told her siblings.

"Chayke," her brother Mendel responded, "don't be silly. They left it behind by accident."

Zayde himself knew where to place the blame for the absence of Jewish traditions in our home. "I think it's your fault, not Stephanie's, that you haven't joined a shul," he told me.

He was right. I felt little attachment to religious rites and traditions, despite my guilt at knowing Zayde had nearly given his life for what I was treating so casually.

On top of these difficulties were others. Perhaps not every mother has complicated feelings on the eve of a son's marriage, but my mom certainly did. As her only son, I was the sole object of whatever maternal energy she had to give, and she had always depended on me for emotional support. I was all she had, as my family always reminded me. She wanted to be happy for me, but I also knew she felt our relationship would soon change forever.

The earliest indication came around the time of our engagement, when family members began asking me why I'd suddenly shut my mother out of my life. While I was on the Obama campaign and in the White House, nobody had asked why my mother and I saw so little of one another. They simply assumed it was because I was busy. Now I had no such excuse, and it made no sense to them. All they saw was a son who seemed to have lost interest in spending time with his mother just as Steph was entering his life.

One evening, as we sat in the car outside the Milford station waiting for the train back to Grand Central, Uncle Mendel turned to me and said, "You know what they say, 'A daughter you have all your life, a son until he gets a wife.'"

What was I supposed to say? *Well, Mendel, the reason my mom and I don't see much of each other has nothing to do with Steph. It's because I'm still pissed at your sister for cheating on my Dad and lying to me about my identity for most of my life!*

I wasn't yet ready to have that conversation. So the questions continued, encouraged by my mother, who frequently vented to her family about how little I saw her, knowing they didn't have all the facts, while claiming I'd chosen Steph's family over my own.

"You know, you could come to Connecticut just to see Zayde," my mother and her siblings said on more than one occasion, resentful that we combined our visits with a stop to see Steph's family in Stamford or Grandma in nearby Scarsdale. As if the act of trying to see other family members on the same trip somehow diminished the respect we were showing Zayde—or my mom.

It was, perhaps, standard Jewish guilt—only, given all the variables, with a particularly sharp edge.

It also felt reminiscent of the way Mom had made me feel as a boy about spending time with Grandma and Pa. "You know," she had always said, "you could be as happy to see Bubbie and Zayde as you are Grandma and Pa."

Unsurprisingly, the period leading up to the wedding offered perfectly engineered flashpoints in the ongoing drama. My mother hosted one engagement party at her apartment, and we organized another on a day when some of Steph's out-of-town friends could be on the East Coast. Mom had a conflict that evening—an "unbreakable" one, she told us—and soon alleged that the decision to hold the party on that date had been made deliberately to exclude her.

At one point, Mom threatened to boycott our wedding if we didn't hold the ceremony after sundown on a Saturday or on a Sunday, as prescribed by the Jewish faith. We held fast, and she backed down.

Another time, a call about wedding invitation lists, a tricky subject even in a well-functioning family, quickly erupted. Steph and I were in Colorado, on our way to see a movie with some old friends. I nodded to Steph to go ahead while I finished the call in the car.

Mom was fuming over our decision to cap, due to costs, the number of Perecmans we were inviting to the wedding, and was taking the whole thing personally. Anytime she disagreed with something, she took it personally.

"You don't know the meaning of family," she snapped.

"*I* don't know the meaning of family?" I shot back. "You cheat on my dad and have me with another man, and you have the nerve to say that to me?"

Not, in hindsight, particularly constructive comments for either of us to make.

When Steph and I finally got married, nearly two years after I proposed, I felt lucky to see her at the end of the aisle and take her hand for our first dance—fittingly, to fun.'s "The Gambler." And yet, along with the love I expressed in my vows was also a note of gratitude, an acknowledgment of all I was still grappling with, all she was helping me grapple with, her confidence in our relationship, in me, a raft I clung to during that difficult time.

"Steph's feet are so firmly planted," I said before assembled family and friends on a Bermuda bluff overlooking the Atlantic, "she keeps both of us grounded"—revealing, perhaps more than I intended, that I was not yet fully whole.

Even now, looking back on our wedding, I sometimes think of the turmoil my mother experienced over her own marriage. My marriage is different. I was not rebounding from a suicide attempt when I got engaged. And every day, I feel thankful that Steph married me.

But I hate the fact that I can discern even the trace of a comparison, the messiness of my mother's past clouding what I'd always hoped would be a moment of unblemished happiness.

24

The Perecman Way

From left to right: Aunt Linda, Mom, Aunt Shushie,
and Uncle Mendel as children in the late 1950s.

P ERHAPS I COULD have navigated everything better—the land
mines of an interfaith union, the feelings of an unmarried
mother watching her only son get married—had there not already
been so much upheaval on account of everything else. But as things
stood, all of these issues, and the ones that sprang from the revelation, fed on each other, forming a toxic cyclone of family discord.

It probably didn't help matters that I continued to ask about Jason, refusing to settle for the limited details my mother had already
shared. One of the truisms of crisis communications is to rip off the
Band-Aid and get every piece of bad news out all at once. Releasing it little by little only prolongs the pain. Mom, however, did not
subscribe to this approach, dripping out facts, one at a time—none

voluntarily, all reluctantly—over months, even years, one agonizing conversation after another.

After Steph and I moved back to New York City in the summer of 2013, I'd occasionally stop by my mother's apartment so we could have some of these conversations in person. They were always fraught, always risky, full of invisible tripwires. Once, trying to make small talk, I told her about a dinner some friends were hosting to welcome Steph and me back to New York. The news was met with a scowl and an abrupt end to the conversation; she was bitter she had not been invited.

Still, I needed to know more about what had happened. So I braced myself and waded in. During one conversation, she explained that her relationship with Jason had not been, as I'd always assumed, a fling. In fact, she told me, it had been a years-long affair, evolving into something of a romance. "Aren't you glad you were conceived in love?" she asked.

I sat there in stunned silence—eyes narrowed, jaw limp.

Of course not, I thought. I wished I were conceived by my father.

I wanted desperately to be my father's biological son. He was my dad. That's how I felt. That's all I knew. And I wanted that to be the genetic truth of our relationship. In an almost primal sense, I wanted him to be a part of me, and me a part of him, our father-son bond written into our DNA.

That conversation with Mom was one of many where I was reminded of how wide a gulf existed between her way of seeing things and mine.

Was she *really* saying I should be happy about what had happened?

Really trying to justify it?

I couldn't tell.

Every expression of remorse, every apology, was accompanied by an explanation that seemed like an excuse, an unwillingness to fully own up to what she had done. "It's not you that has been living the lie," she wrote in one email.

It's me. I don't say that as a way of casting myself as a victim
but just because it's true. And while I do think that to a large
extent I was a victim back then due to my own profound
insecurities and extremely low self-esteem, I absolutely
recognize and take full responsibility for my hurtful actions and
for making you feel betrayed. But please try to understand that
I was in no way intending to betray you. As stupid as it may
sound, at the time my psyche was such that I had no way of
fighting against the choice I made. It was as if the choice were
made for me.

Today, I try to read those words with sympathy and compassion
for the woman my mother is describing. But I often grew impatient
with the "sorry, but . . ." formulations, with what I perceived to be
her insistence on playing the victim.

During one conversation, her feelings of victimhood about everything that had happened years earlier bled into her feelings of victimhood about how I had supposedly chosen Steph over her and my
Perecman family.

"What are you talking about?" I responded, exasperated. Many
times, Steph had told me how much she admired my mom, even
related to her—both of them PhDs, both of them service-minded,
both of them unafraid to cut their own path.

The conversation grew more heated, Mom's sense of victimhood
and my own, Mom's sense of betrayal and my own, forming a sort
of emotional Chinese finger trap from which neither of us could
escape.

"Oh, poor you," I finally said, my words dripping with cruel
sarcasm. "My heart breaks."

"Get out!" she screamed, rising from the couch and marching
me to the door. "Get the fuck out!"

The whole ordeal brought out the worst in me.

Later, after reading about intergenerational Holocaust trauma, I
recognized that Mom's feelings of betrayal may have been partly a

reflection of her own relationships with Bubbie and Zayde, relationships that can best be described as "enmeshed," a term frequently applied to survivor families, where boundaries between parents and children are loosely defined or nonexistent. In such families, writes one expert, overinvested parents can "make it difficult for their children to grow emotionally, and separate from them, as this would be perceived as disloyal in a family sensitive to loss."

During one lunch, Mom told Steph I no longer resembled the son she had raised, sharing an incident I remember only vaguely. When I was in high school, Mom returned from an overseas trip with some sort of sickness that kept her bedridden for days. During that time, she told Steph, I stayed home with her rather than attending an all-school assembly where I was scheduled to be recognized with some award.

That, Mom explained, was the sort of son she had raised, one who would sacrifice his own needs for hers—like Mom herself, along with her siblings, was doing for Zayde, as one illness after another slowed but failed to fell him.

All of the Perecman children played their parts. Shushie helped out at The Store every day. Years earlier, Zayde had taught her watchmaking, though only after her brother, Mendel, proved a disinterested pupil. "I should have started with Shushie," Zayde would say, acknowledging the error of his old-world ways. Aunt Linda rented a place nearby so she'd have somewhere to stay on visits from Florida. And Mendel regularly drove up from Pennsylvania to spend time with his father.

But only my mom was there, sleeping in a room across from Zayde's, every weekend and usually much of the week. Her Yiddish theater afforded her that flexibility; after leaving the think tank in the early 2000s, she'd never again have such a steady income, living off some retirement savings to avoid drawing down the modest resources of the theater. Zayde, meanwhile, continued to give her stipends. She was caring for him. But he was caring for her, too.

All that time alone with Zayde wasn't easy. He could be a tough person to look after, barking demands or barging in on his daughter. Because the doors in the house had no locks, he could enter any room at any hour without knocking, and sometimes did.

On those rare occasions when Mom told him she might need to skip a weekend due to some prior commitment in the city, he berated her and told her—ordered her, really—to cancel her plans. I thought of one of Yael Danieli's criteria for victim families: "bottomless rage . . . only indirect, mostly intrafamilial, means to express and experience it."

I never fully understood their relationship, but everyone could see that their codependence was unhealthy. Mom cared about her father deeply and wanted to be there for him. But there was an ambivalence there, too, that suggested that her caretaking was an attempt to make up for something. Perhaps she felt she'd put Zayde through a lot with her suicide attempt, her divorce, and who knows what else. Perhaps she felt she had never lived up to his expectations of a daughter, and this was her last chance to get it right. This time, she'd be the kind of daughter he'd wanted her to be.

"You don't need to go up there every weekend," I'd say, concerned about all the time alone with Zayde—and away from the theater that gave her days order and purpose, much as The Store did for Zayde. "You're allowed to have your own life."

"I know," she'd say, and dutifully trek up again.

Their relationship resembled that of a little girl and her father, not two adults. In a way, it seemed that my mom had never grown up. Maybe Zayde had never let her. Maybe, in trying to help her, to protect her from the world and from herself, he had never allowed her to become her own person, despite her independent streak.

Was that part of the reason my mom and I were closest when I was a teenager? Back then, I was not only one room away, there whenever she needed me, but I was myself impressed by her impulsive, live-for-the-moment, do-what-feels-right approach to life. Because, in a way, we were the same age?

I admired Mom for her devotion to her father even as I knew

she expected the same from me. But I could not give it, continually failing what seemed like repeated loyalty tests. More than once she called me at work or on a weekend, asking me to drop what I was doing and pick up some medication at a pharmacy around the corner from her apartment, even though she was perfectly capable of getting it herself.

Another time she fell on the sidewalk and scraped herself badly. She called me at work, frantic. Before I could ask where she was, or how badly she was injured, she hung up on me, outraged I had not, upon simply hearing the agitation in her voice, rushed to her side. Over the next few hours, I called and texted repeatedly to see how she was doing. I got no reply. Later, I learned she had gone to a walk-in clinic, where she had been stitched up and released a short time later.

The next day, I picked up an angry voice mail from Aunt Linda.

"I can't believe you wouldn't go to the hospital when your mother needed you," she yelled into the recording. "You only have *one* mom."

Somehow, on the journey from Mom's lips to Linda's ears, a walk-in clinic had morphed into a hospital.

I called Linda back immediately, my voice rising as I made my way through a crowded sidewalk in the Flatiron District.

"I really don't need this shit from you," I yelled as passersby looked on. "You don't know anything about our relationship. Did my mom tell you she hung up on me before I could ask where she was? Did she tell you I tried calling and texting and she didn't respond?"

"No," Linda replied. "I didn't know that."

"Of course you didn't," I said, particularly exasperated because Linda knew I was right. Of all the siblings, she had the least patience for my mom and her tendency to create drama.

In truth, there was another reason I didn't rush to Mom's side that day. I had some reason to be skeptical about what appeared to be her frequent medical emergencies.

Years earlier, when we were barely speaking, Mom had called

me up one day to say she had been stricken by an inexplicable and unbearable pain in her legs. I rushed over and practically carried her downstairs and into a taxi, which took us to Beth Israel Hospital downtown, where one of her friends was a physician. Mom insisted she could not even step out of the cab, so I ran into the hospital lobby, borrowed a wheelchair, and pushed her upstairs. In the waiting area, she stopped talking about the pain and began asking what was new and how things were going at work.

When her friend finally called us back, Mom's pain had vanished, and she seemed entirely uninterested in the exam. She just wanted to talk to me. Her friend and I exchanged a knowing look.

Of course, Mom's family did not have any of this context. They didn't know what lay at the heart of much of the conflict, what sometimes felt like the original sin. Part of me wished I could tell them. To throw it back in their faces after years of being on the receiving end of their judgment and scorn. But it was also about more than proving them wrong. I loved my Perecman family. And I hoped sharing the truth would bring us closer and restore our relationships.

Years later, I finally overcame my fear that disclosing the truth to her siblings was a betrayal of my mom. Zayde was still alive, but I knew they wouldn't say a word to him about it, that they'd keep the secret, as Zayde himself had raised them so well to do.

I decided to talk to Mendel first and gave Mom a heads-up.

"After everything he said to me all those years ago," I told her, "I want him to know why I was so mad at you, why I am still angry."

"Okay," Mom replied.

The call with Mendel had been years in the making. From time to time, I'd think about it, almost looking forward to it, wondering if, when the time finally came, it would be as gratifying as I'd hoped, if I'd get his acknowledgment that I hadn't been a bad son, that I'd been doing my best in a tough situation. I longed for that vindication.

"Remember when we took my mom to the emergency room that time?" I asked, my cell phone pressed hard against my ear as I paced back and forth in my living room.

"Of course," he replied.

"And remember how you gave me shit for not being a good son?"

"Yeah," he said, "I remember that, too."

"Well," I told him, "there was a reason I was acting that way."

When I finished the story, there was a long pause.

"I'm sorry to hear about all that," he said. "Thank you for telling me. It makes me feel better about how everything went down back then."

As far as my aunts were concerned, I told my mother I didn't care who told them, as long as one of us did. She decided to, which, in retrospect, was probably a mistake. Who knows what she said to them? How much responsibility, if any, she took? What, if anything, she conveyed of the pain she had caused?

Looking back on it, I wonder if I'd wanted her simply to tell her sisters the facts, that I'd been the product of an affair. Or had I wanted something more? Had I wanted her to tell them how sorry she had been for lying to me all those years, for throwing my life into chaos?

To this day, Shushie has never raised the subject with me. The only time we've ever discussed it was when I called her a couple of years ago to ask why she had never said anything to me about it.

In fact, after one of Shushie's daughters asked about it, Shushie's initial response was—astonishingly—to deny it.

"Where did you hear that?" Shushie had replied. "That's not true."

I was startled when my cousin told me the story, but I also understood my family's protective instincts. Mom was their sister, and they had her back in the only way they knew how.

I first learned that lesson as a boy. Years earlier, my mother had said something I felt was disrespectful toward some of her cousins. I'd gone up to them afterward and apologized on her behalf.

Mendel had witnessed the whole thing, and pulled me into a room.

"Don't ever apologize to anyone on your mother's behalf," he scolded me. "You're her son. Your job is to defend her."

I almost respected it, the strength of that loyalty.

I tried to model it, too. At an Upper East Side bar in high school—one of the many that accepted our fake IDs—I once came across a prep school thug who had, just a night earlier, thrown a buddy of mine down onto the pavement, repeatedly kicking him in the gut.

"Where are your friends?" I asked, knowing he hadn't acted alone.

"I can get them here in a few minutes," he said.

"Do it," I told him, immediately regretting my words.

Who did I think I was?

Thirty minutes later, two dozen white faces and North Face jackets could be seen outside the bar on Second Avenue.

One of them stepped forward, and a circle formed around him. "Who wants to go 1D?" he asked. The guy was a champion wrestler—a fact I did not know at the time, just as I did not know that "1D," for "1 deep," meant one-on-one. But I understood his meaning well enough.

I looked around at my friends, all of whom were bigger and tougher than I, all of whom had been making all kinds of threats the night before about what they'd do if they ever stumbled across the guys who'd beaten up our buddy.

Well, here they were. And my friends had suddenly fallen awfully quiet.

Oh, for God's sake, I thought. Someone needs to stand up for our friend. I called this fight, so I guess it will be me. I walked into the circle.

The next thing I remember is waking up in the bar with a pack of ice on my eye. A visit to the ophthalmologist confirmed no bones were broken, but I had a black eye for weeks.

Mom and her family were proud. "You were a loyal friend," Uncle Mendel told me. "But next time, throw the first punch."

Mendel never forgot the incident. At my wedding more than a decade and a half later, he went up to some of my high school friends and gave them a hard time for not getting my back in the same way I'd at least tried to get theirs.

I'd always prided myself on being loyal—to my friends, to my family. That was, after all, the Perecman way, going back to all those times Zayde had saved his father's life during the war. And yet this whole experience was making me wonder, what does loyalty even mean?

Was it loyal of Mom to lie about my identity because she felt like she was protecting me? Or disloyal because I had a right to know?

I also wondered, was it loyal of Mom's family to keep her mental health problems a secret? Not to talk about them outside—or even inside—the family? To pretend they didn't exist?

Was it loyal of Bubbie and Zayde to clean up Mom's apartment after her suicide attempt and never speak of it again, like nothing ever happened? Or disloyal because the stigma, the lack of openness, may have simply made matters worse? Would loyalty, in fact, have demanded acknowledging her illness openly, getting her the help and support she needed?

Is it disloyal to write a book like this, as some Perecman family members have told me? Or loyal to my wife and children to expose all these secrets in the hopes of helping our family heal and move beyond them?

And if I *am* being disloyal, so what? What's the price a person should pay to adhere to a family's code of loyalty? If an act of disloyalty is the best path, the only path, to healing, is it *necessary* to be disloyal?

I grew up unquestioningly adhering to my family's code, never talking about the origins of my Perecman name, never sharing anything about my mother's suicide attempt.

But would my mother and I have been on better terms, would all of us have been better off, if we'd abandoned that code altogether?

If we'd just acted in accordance with basic values of honesty and transparency?

And I'd occasionally wonder something else, too: Was I paying the price for my family's refusal to manage my mother's issues appropriately? Had their almost uniform insistence that nothing was wrong allowed her problems to fester, spilling over into the messes that had caused such havoc in her life, and mine?

I'll never know. I do know, however, that my perceived acts of disloyalty continued after Steph became pregnant.

We took a class for expecting parents, and learned that first-time mothers can be in labor a long time—hours, if not days—so there was no need for family members to rush to the hospital.

"It's not like the movies," the instructor told us, "where someone goes into labor, and the next minute, out pops a kid."

Over dinner with Mom, I raised the subject, treading lightly, fearful of how the conversation might go.

"It probably doesn't make a lot of sense for you to be at the hospital right away," I said, wary that her extended presence would add needless stressors during a sensitive time. "We'll call you and let you know when's a good time."

Her entire demeanor changed instantly. "Will Steph's mom be there?"

"Yes, probably," I replied. "It's her mom."

"Well, I'm *your* mom."

"Right," I said. "But you're not going to be holding Steph's legs during labor. We want you at the hospital, Mom. I'm just saying, it probably doesn't make sense for you to come right when we get there."

For months, even years afterward, my Perecman family would return to this exchange.

"Why," one family member after another would demand, "wasn't your mom allowed to visit you all in the hospital?"

"What?" I'd reply. "Not allowed to visit the hospital?"

Is that what she was telling them?

Slowly, after it was too late, I began to recognize that what had begun as a rift between my mother and me was now driving me and my Perecman family farther and farther apart.

More hurtful than anything I heard from Mom's siblings was what I heard from Zayde, the sole member of Mom's immediate family still in the dark about the origin of so many of the problems.

"It's not right, the way you're treating your mother," he said during one visit, his disappointment palpable.

I changed the subject.

He raised it again on another visit, at his favorite lunch spot, Athenian Diner III. Uncannily observant, he had sensed—in a way none of his children ever had—that my mother had hurt me. He just didn't know how.

"Forgive your mother," he said. "Whatever she did, forgive her."

What could I say to this man, then in his early nineties, who had nearly lost his entire family in the Holocaust, parting with his own mother at Stutthof and never seeing her again, tearing up more than half a century later at the mere mention of her name?

How could I tell him the truth?

It would have destroyed my mother. Destroyed their relationship.

Zayde, I'd always suspected, was, more than anyone or any*thing* else, the reason my mother had kept up the lie, the person she most feared with the truth. His old-world judgment would have been damning—and final. And that was too high a price to ask my mother to pay.

I felt obligated to protect their relationship, even as Mom continued to stoke his displeasure and disappointment, knowing he didn't have the full context of everything that had happened.

One day, I finally confronted her about it. I pleaded with her to stop feeding him damning stories about my mistreating her and not spending time with her when he didn't know the full story.

Why, I asked her, would she want to inject all these strains into what might well be the last years of my relationship with him?

"What do you want me to do?" Mom replied. "*Lie* to him?"

The breach with my Perecman family became so great that in an attempt to salvage it, I composed a thousand-word email to my mother's siblings. "Last week," I began,

> I went up to Orange. I wanted to spend time with Zayde and we went out to the diner. Over the course of the meal, he got worked up and said to me, apropos of nothing:
>
> "I never thought I would say this to you, but you're not good to your mother. When she was in the hospital, you didn't visit her. And now she's not even allowed to come to the hospital for the birth of your daughter while Steph's mother is being invited. It's your daughter, too."
>
> Needless to say, this was a pretty stunning and deeply painful thing to hear for a variety of reasons, not the least of which is there is not a shred of truth to it. [I should have been more precise: there was a *shred* of truth to it—a shred that had been wildly distorted.]
>
> Quite frankly, I do not feel that I owe anyone an explanation of anything regarding my relationship with my mother, but my and Steph's relationship with you (and our soon-to-be daughter's relationship with you) is important to us, so I think it's time to offer everyone a bit of context, since the facts are clearly being distorted beyond all recognition.
>
> For a couple of years, I barely spoke to my mother. This was after I extracted from her the truth of my identity. After much pain and reflection, I have finally accepted this. It is also true, as all of

you who have known my mother for so long know, she is a troubled woman. There is no shame in that, and it doesn't affect how much I love her, but it is a reality.

Why am I sharing all of this with you?

Because as best I can tell, you have believed what she has been telling you to varying degrees.

This needs to stop. I've known this sort of gossip was going on for the past couple of years but, quite frankly, dismissed it because I didn't think you'd believe it or that it would affect your view of us or my relationships with you. Clearly I was wrong. The distortions that are coming back to me second- or thirdhand via Mendel, Linda, and Zayde are incredibly hurtful to me and Steph.

Why on earth would I or Steph try and prevent my mother from being at the hospital? Not to mention, why is poor Zayde even being dragged into this?

I admire and respect the concern you have for your sister, and I know you want the best for her. Know that we do, too.

I've had to ask myself multiple times in recent months and years just who exactly all of you think I am, and who you think Steph is. You've known me since I was born, and I cannot understand why you would think Steph and I could be so callous and insensitive.

Even as I was becoming the family's pariah, the disloyal son, I was trying desperately to hold them close. I was trying desperately to meet my family's expectations, or at least receive their absolution for not meeting them.

Dartmouth philosopher and rape survivor Susan Brison has written about one of the conditions trauma survivors need for healing: telling their stories to understanding listeners. Was that why I craved my family's understanding so badly? Because I sensed I needed it for my own healing?

Either way, my email changed nothing. None of them replied. The family that cared so much about loyalty, it often seemed, wasn't the least bit concerned about showing any of it to me.

25

A Pattern of Instability

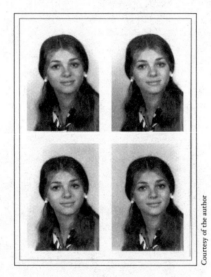

Mom as a teenager, in the late 1960s.

STEPH AND I tried to use the birth of our daughter as a fresh start with my Perecman family, inviting my mother to spend time with her new granddaughter every week, but that proved unsustainable shortly after Steph and I returned to work.

My mother seemed intent on pushing back on simple requests, like what to feed the baby or where to take her. I decided to give her a call and broached the subject gently. None of this had to be a big deal. With any of our other parents, it could've been handled in a quick conversation. Over and done with.

Instead, Mom took it all personally, hanging up on me after I started explaining the problem. Later, when the issues persisted and I raised them again—this time in person, during one of her visits—she stormed out of the apartment and slammed the door behind her.

I had other reasons to be concerned about Mom's emotional and psychological well-being. Around the time our daughter was born, Mom and I had gone out for brunch at a Brooklyn diner. On stools at the bar, we began catching up. The conversation began pleasantly enough, warmly even. After a while I began wondering, as I sometimes did during calm periods in our relationship, if despite everything we'd been through, a close relationship might be possible after all.

Then, midway through the conversation, things took a strange, dark turn. I asked about her plans for the coming years.

"Well, I was thinking I'd . . . oh, never mind," she said, cutting herself off.

"What were you going to say?" I asked.

She paused.

"I was thinking I'd spend down my savings and then, you know."

Only I, her son, *did* know. Only I *could* know.

"And then kill yourself?" I asked.

"Yes," she said, calmly.

"What are you talking about?" I said, choking up.

The memory of the visit to the psychiatric ER had scarred me, and I lived in fear of the nightmare recurring. "You need to be here. For me. For your granddaughter," I pleaded.

"Oh," she replied, "I knew I shouldn't have told you."

She was deadly serious. In a moment, my fleeting hopes for some semblance of a normal relationship were once again dashed, as I was reminded that any seemingly stable periods could, without notice, take a sudden, unexpected turn for the worse.

The birth of our daughter had created a larger space for my mother in our lives than she'd had in a long time. But the more involved she was, the greater her presence, the more disruption and conflict seemed to ensue.

One time, I'd arranged for her to meet our daughter and nanny at a Brooklyn museum. I'd given her the address and told her when to meet them, but she was running considerably behind, and had somehow gotten lost, calling and texting me repeatedly until I stepped out of a work event to call her back.

She was frazzled.

"Where are you?" I asked.

She mentioned cross streets I didn't recognize. "Where am I going?" she asked.

"I'm at a work event, Mom. I'm not in front of a computer. Can you just check your phone?" I said, suggesting she use a map app to find directions. "It's probably easier that way."

"Fuck you," she said, hanging up on me.

Such outbursts were a regular feature of our relationship, coming every two to three months, some of them precipitated by a perceived slight or offense, others seemingly out of nowhere. Each of the hang-ups, or angry emails or texts, might have been upsetting on their own. But all of them together, their frequency, was especially hard, reverberating with deeply buried emotional memories, earlier flashes of Mom's volatility, the way I'd always felt like I had to walk on eggshells as a boy, like everyone had to walk on eggshells around her, never knowing when—or why—her mood might shift.

During several weeks of calm in our relationship, I'd sometimes turn to Steph and issue a warning: "We're due for an eruption." I didn't have to explain what I meant.

Sure enough, one would soon follow. I'd try to joke about it, but every time something happened, I had a difficult time brushing it off, each of my mother's outbursts inducing a dull pain in my stomach, a tightness in my chest, and a clamping up in my back, distracting me for hours, days, at a time.

I'd sometimes find myself staring blankly out a window at work, reminding myself to snap out of it before a colleague noticed. In my limited time with Steph and our daughter before or after work—precious moments for a young family—the conversation would often be overtaken by what Mom had said or done this time. I'd go to sleep, hoping for a respite, only to wake up in the middle of the night, my mind racing, worried about what new and utterly unforeseeable outrage would derail the coming week.

During one visit to Perecman Jewelers, when our daughter was about eighteen months old, the last time Zayde would see her, my grandfather pulled me aside and started asking, once again, what was going on between my mother and me. Steph and Shushie, just a few feet away, heard what he was saying and joined the conversation.

"I think it's really disgusting how you're treating your mother," Shushie said. "She was always such a good mother to you"—a phrase her siblings repeated again and again. Was my behavior, they were saying, any way to repay her?

"Weren't *you* the one who asked your mom about all the stuff with your dad in the first place?" Shushie had asked during the one conversation we'd ever had on the subject. As if my decision to seek the truth somehow meant I shouldn't be so upset about what I discovered.

Shushie knew what my mother had done. She knew my mother had lied to me. And she also knew how difficult my mother could be. But as far as she and the rest of the family were concerned, my mom was my mom, and that was all there was to it. Nothing else mattered.

"Why do we even go up to Connecticut?" I'd sometimes ask Steph. "It's just an opportunity for them to berate us."

For my own sake and our family's, I began spacing out my mother's visits. Unsurprisingly, that only created more tension, more pushback, which my mother blamed squarely on Steph. "Why are you doing this to me?" she titled one email.

I told you even before your daughter was born that I could tell Stephanie wanted nothing to do with me and that I expected she would keep the baby from me too. You said that was not true.

And now you see it is true and I have to accept that. In fact, you have seen for yourself that Stephanie objected to having in your apartment anything that had been in mine! First, those beautiful framed nursery rhyme illustrations, then the painting of the wine bottles that had hung in our hallway for so many years. It has even been my fear that you gave away your electronic keyboard because it reminded Stephanie too much of your life with your mother.

She sent many other such emails and texts, all of them bewildering and exhausting Steph and me, neither of us able to comprehend the bizarre psychological alchemy that could convert banal home decor decisions into a campaign to erase my mother from our lives.

In a cruel irony, Mom's accusations were pushing Steph farther away, creating the distance between them that Mom's imagination had conjured from the beginning.

I'd try and assure Steph that my mother was not saying any of this out of malice, that none of her actions were out of malice. "She simply can't control herself," I'd say.

All my mother wanted, I knew, was a close relationship with me, with us. So did I. Even after everything that had happened, she was still my mom. I loved her, cared about her, and wanted her in my life, in our family's life.

I thought about how my family saw things, their belief, spoken and unspoken, that I should just move on, that, as Linda put it, I only had one mom, and that was all that mattered. But I often felt like her behavior was forcing me to choose between her and Steph, between her and our daughter, between her happiness and my own.

Sometimes, I'd think of that nightmare I'd had as a kid. About being trapped in Mom's apartment, unable to leave. With all the outbursts, the way they consumed me for hours, days at a time, had the nightmare come true? Was I still somehow trapped? Had I never managed to escape?

And then, during the calm, stable periods, I'd find myself doubting my own experience. She could be so convincing, so persuasive, that I sometimes wondered, What if she's right? What if I'm crazy? What if she's the one acting normally, and I'm horribly, inexplicably mistreating her?

Then, as predictably as one of Zayde's watches, some new outrage would occur, dragging out over days, or even weeks, and I'd remember once again the lesson I'd learned as that little boy peering into the keyhole of my mother's bedroom, wondering why she wasn't coming out: that I could never be certain which version of my mother to expect, that I shouldn't take the good periods for granted, and that I should always be prepared for things to change abruptly.

AS THE YEARS elapsed and I began opening up about my mother to friends, acquaintances, and medical professionals, people would often respond in much the same way. Not with amusement or indifference, but something approaching concern, sympathy, or even alarm. They'd tell me that what I was describing sounded an awful lot like borderline personality disorder (BPD), perhaps most widely known as the diagnosis of SNL's Pete Davidson and Winona Ryder's character in 1999's *Girl, Interrupted*.

According to the *Diagnostic and Statistical Manual of Mental Disorders*, fifth edition (DSM-5), the standard classification of disorders for mental health professionals in the United States, BPD is defined as "a pervasive pattern of instability of interpersonal relationships, self-image, and affects, and marked impulsivity." As I read the criteria for diagnosing the disorder, I could immediately identify, simply from memories readily available, incidents from the recent or distant past that seemed to corroborate every one of them.

"Recurrent suicidality," I read, "is often the reason that these individuals present for help. These self-destructive acts are usually precipitated by threats of separation or rejection."

Immediately, I thought of the breakup with her Columbia professor that had precipitated Mom's suicide attempt decades earlier.

I thought of what had led Mendel and me to rush her to the ER: a breakup and me refusing to speak to her.

I read this: "Individuals with this disorder frequently express inappropriate, intense anger and have difficulty controlling their anger. . . . They may display extreme sarcasm, enduring bitterness, or verbal outbursts. The anger is often elicited when a caregiver or lover is seen as neglectful, withholding, uncaring, or abandoning."

And this: "Symptoms tend to be transient, lasting minutes or hours. The real or perceived return of the caregiver's nurturance may result in a remission of symptoms."

I felt like I was reading a description of my relationship with my mom.

Then I read another criterion of BPD: "During periods of extreme stress, transient paranoid ideation or dissociative symptoms . . . may occur." I thought of Mom's email claiming that our decision not to hang up nursery illustrations or a painting of wine bottles was evidence that Steph was trying to cut her out of our lives.

Another, older memory also surfaced. In the immediate aftermath of Mom's departure from the think tank in the early 2000s, she had a tough time finding another job and claimed it was because the leadership of the organization—including the friend who had recruited her in the first place—was blackballing her, making it impossible to find work elsewhere.

At the time I'd believed her wholeheartedly, adopting her sense of injustice as my own, outraged by the coordinated campaign to deny my mother employment.

Now I know the think tank had done no such thing.

What else had I missed, growing up? Were there signs I hadn't had the tools to recognize?

The revelation about my identity had opened my eyes to the realities, the gravity, of Mom's mental illness, and how it had played itself out in her life and my own, in ways I'd previously managed to ignore.

Many of the books on BPD have evocative titles, eerily resonant with my own experience: *I Hate You, Don't Leave Me* by Hal Straus and Jerold J. Kreisman, MD; *Stop Walking on Eggshells: Taking Your Life Back When Someone You Care About Has Borderline Personality Disorder* by Paul Mason, MS, and Randi Kreger; *Understanding the Borderline Mother: Helping Her Children Transcend the Intense, Unpredictable, and Volatile Relationship* by Christine Ann Lawson.

I stayed up all night reading that last one. I've never devoured a book so quickly, my eyes racing, leaping across the paragraphs and pages, so recognizable was the portrait it painted, so gratifying the glimpse of a medical explanation behind behavior that could seem so exhaustingly incomprehensible.

One particular passage felt like Lawson was speaking directly to me: "One of the most devastating experiences for children of borderlines is 'the Turn.' The Turn is a sudden attack, the abrupt withdrawal of love and affection, and razor-sharp words that can pierce the heart as painfully as an arrow. . . . Children who live with a predatory mother become unconsciously preoccupied with reading their mother's moods. A fleeting glance, a furtive gesture, deceleration, and a shift of direction are signals of an approaching Turn."

Lawson enumerates a list of messages borderline mothers send their children. First on the list is "You'd be better off without me," a phrase my mom, during one of her depressive spells, once uttered, word for word.

Perhaps, I thought, after reading the book, my mother was not as responsible for some of her behavior as I'd assumed. Perhaps, as she'd written in that email, she really *was* unable to fight against some of the choices she'd made. Perhaps this disorder helped explain why things had unfolded the way they did.

During one conversation, after reciting a litany of what she perceived to be indefensible slights, Mom told me, "I don't even recognize you anymore."

"I *finally* recognize you," I answered, words I could, after more than thirty years, speak for the first time.

Later, I typed "Holocaust" and "borderline" into Google to see if I'd find any link. The first hit was an item in the US Holocaust Memorial Museum's catalog: *Borderline Phenomena in Children of Holocaust Survivors*, a 1989 PhD dissertation by Esther Karson, now a practicing clinical psychologist near Seattle.

I tracked down a copy. The theoretical literature on children of Holocaust survivors, writes Karson, discusses parents who were "emotionally depleted and unavailable, yet paradoxically, overidentified with and overinvested in their children." The empirical literature, she writes, "reports a whole array of seemingly unrelated symptomatology including apathy, depression, regulation of aggression, alienation, and problems in separation-individuation." Karson's hypothesis was that "the concept of borderline phenomena" could serve as a "unifying principle" for reconciling all of these different findings.

"The basis hypothesis of the research," Karson explained, "was that children of survivors, when contrasted with children of American-born parents, would exhibit more borderline phenomena."

"The research," Karson told me when I reached her by phone, "definitely bore that out."

Was this just another way that Bubbie and Zayde had passed on their trauma?

Of course, I am not a therapist. I cannot diagnose borderline personality disorder or any other disorder. "Why do we even call any of these things a 'disorder'?" trauma researcher Yael Danieli once asked me. "It's basically all of us doing our best to cope with life."

And yet, after reading DSM-5's entry on BPD and Christine Lawson's book, I found myself almost wishing my mom were borderline. Not because I wanted her to own the label, but because I wanted to believe that if I could just identify the cause of all the trouble, maybe I could fix it and heal her. Maybe I could make everything all right.

I couldn't, of course, and the outbursts continued. One of them followed a trip Steph and I took back to Bermuda. Steph was six months pregnant with our second child, and we'd decided to escape for a few days before the baby came, returning to New York City on what happened to be Mother's Day. Before we left, I'd ordered flowers to be sent to my mother's apartment and mailed a card. As soon as we landed in New York City, I gave her a call. Flowers, a card, a call—what else could I possibly do?

The conversation went sideways immediately.

"Was Soraya with you?" she asked, referencing our daughter.

"No," I replied as our taxi crawled through traffic on our way back from JFK, knowing where this was going.

"Well, who watched her?"

"Steph's mom," I said.

The call ended abruptly. A flurry of angry texts followed. They were so upsetting, I deleted our entire text history, going back years.

After that, I decided to tell Mom about my suspicions that she was borderline. Some therapists are wary of telling patients about the diagnosis, recognizing it may not help and may, in fact, make matters worse. But her repeated outbursts were exhausting me, and I felt I had little to lose.

So I sent her a text, telling her about my suspicion and suggesting Lawson's book. I told her I didn't want to wade into all the issues covered in the book, but thought she might find it a helpful read. Her initial response indicated that she thought borderline personality disorder was a form of schizophrenia (it is not), and she initially balked at my suggestion. After I cleared things up, she agreed to take a look at the book and ordered it online.

Some days later, I got an email from her. The subject: "I've read some of the book & I see your point." "I've read enough to see why you saw me in this book and am now very interested in reading the whole book," she wrote. She then proceeded to recite some of what she'd learned about the disorder, offering her own analysis of which criteria did and did not apply to her and asking my thoughts.

I replied that I was glad she was reading the book, but I also tried to lay down some boundaries. She was wearing me out with her repeated outbursts, and I told her I didn't have the emotional bandwidth to engage in a conversation about all of this anymore.

"I can't believe you are choosing to cut me out of your life like this," she wrote back. "I can only hope there will come a time when you recognize the mistake you are making."

I sighed as I read her email. I thought we'd settled into a good routine. Her visits had seemed to be going reasonably well, all things considered.

Cutting her out of my life?

I'd simply said I didn't want to engage in a conversation about her mental health. "Pls give me some space," I pleaded in my reply.

Minutes later, she texted. I ignored it. She texted again. I ignored it again. Then she called. I was driving home from work and decided to answer. Speaking to her in the morning or during the day could be too risky. If the conversation went off the rails, I could be thrown off for hours. So I tried to do any calls with her on my drive home.

"Mom," I said, finally losing it. "I need a break. I need a fucking break. Two weeks off. No emails, texts, or calls. Please."

Exactly fourteen days later, she texted again. "Need more time?"

I did, and waited another day before calling her on another drive home. She started by telling me she'd read the whole book and repeated that she understood why I saw her in it.

"I see myself in it, too," she said.

I told her I lived my life expecting that at some point, in the coming hours or days or weeks or years, I'd get a call about her trying to kill herself.

"I know you do," she said. Then, she brought up an episode I barely remembered, even after she described it. Sometime in 2006, she had called me up and begged me to come over. She was expecting dinner guests and wasn't "feeling well," her phrase for being depressed.

"Do you remember when you arrived?" she asked.

I did not. She proceeded to tell me that when I walked in, she was crouching behind the door, afraid to show her face. "I didn't know how I was going to get through the dinner," she said. "But because you were there, I was able to hold myself together."

Even now, I have only the most cursory memory of it. As if I've blocked out the entire experience.

The point, she told me, was that she wasn't like that anymore. I asked when she felt she had changed. She couldn't cite a specific moment. One minute, she said it was five years earlier. When I reminded her of our brunch where she told me she was thinking of killing herself, she said the change must have occurred after that, perhaps two years earlier.

I didn't know what to say.

"Being in touch with you all the time," I finally responded, "with all of the volatility that's involved, I just can't do it, Mom. It's too exhausting. Too distracting. I can't focus on my job, on my family."

"I *am* your family," she protested.

The whole thing was heartbreaking. Both of us wished for a different relationship. She wished she had a son she could be close to. I wished I had a mom I could be close to.

"I can see how I damaged you," she said, returning to the subject of Lawson's book.

I bristled at the phrasing. I certainly didn't think of myself as "damaged."

I felt lucky—still do. I had an extraordinarily privileged upbringing, full of every blessing a child could ask for. Every blessing, I now recognize, except one: a healthy, stable mother.

In other families, the impact of a troubled mother might be mitigated by the presence of a husband or multiple children to form a sort of support group, leaning on one another as a way of managing whatever storms blow through. I had neither. In that apartment, it was just Mom and I, from the time I was a boy until I left for college. And even after I left home, I remained her emotional anchor.

"All of you only interact with Mom in short bursts," I once told one of her cousins in an effort to defend myself against the family's accusations. "You can always hang up the phone or get in the car and drive away. I'm her son—it's nonstop."

For much of my life, I'd seen only the good in my mother's

parenting—the sense of compassion, empathy, she had cultivated in me, the trips around the world, the arts education. Now I was coming to terms with everything else.

When I first started seeking help, my therapist, an expert in child and family psychology, immediately recognized, she later told me, that my emotional development had been stunted. At one of our earliest sessions, she took out a cardboard wheel printed with words like *disappointment*, *happiness*, and *sadness*, the kind that helps kids name their emotions.

It was a revelation. Talking about emotions so openly, distinguishing between them, was not something I'd ever done before or knew how to do.

My formative years had been spent with a mother at the mercy of emotions that controlled her. So I grew up fearing them, distrusting them—a rather unhelpful attribute in many aspects of life, particularly romantic relationships, virtually every one of which I ended at even a fleeting sign of doubt or uncertainty, as I did with Steph before she took me back.

Mom had taught me so much. But she could not teach me how to sit with emotions, how to work through them. These things, I needed to teach myself.

The more I reflected on my upbringing and read about borderline personality disorder, the more connections I saw.

I read about what's called parentification, defined as "a disturbance in the generational boundaries, such that evidence indicates a functional and/or emotional role reversal in which the child sacrifices his or her own needs for attention, comfort, and guidance in order to accommodate and care for the logistical and emotional needs of a parent and/or sibling."

I thought about the incident my mother had recounted to Steph over lunch, when I'd stayed home from an awards ceremony in high school to care for her. I thought about how Mom would tell me that when I was a baby, she couldn't wait until I got old enough to be a companion.

Had I been a parentified child?

Did that help explain why I've always been so serious, so adult-like, so self-consciously responsible, even as a kid? I thought back to my senior yearbook in high school, where, in a satirical class roundup, my friends gave my first book the title: "How to Act 40 Years Older Than You Really Are."

Other traces of Mom's behavior, it seemed, had also left a mark. "Children of borderlines expect incongruent behavior from others," Lawson writes in *Understanding the Borderline Mother*. "They learn to hide their real feelings, to express their needs indirectly, or not to need anything at all."

That felt familiar. "Don't be bashful," Zayde would always tell me as a boy, "say what you want." Steph herself had once told me, "It takes a lot of effort sometimes to get out of you what you really want to do."

I was not only seeing Mom in Lawson's pages. I was seeing myself too.

Reading the book at a coffee shop one day, as Steph sat across the table doing work, I paused when I got to one section about what Lawson calls the "all-good child," reading it aloud:

All-good children become successful adults, but are not necessarily happy. A preoccupation with doing the right thing can suffocate the real and creative self . . . meeting the expectations of others is more important than their own happiness. They may have plenty of fame, wealth, or success, but rarely have fun.

All-good children continue to function in a parentified role in adult relationships and tend to be conscientious overachievers. They are often overcommitted and emotionally preoccupied because they fear disappointing others. They simply cannot say no.

Steph looked at me, downcast. "It makes me sad," she said. "That sounds like you."

I was less sad than concerned.

In DSM-5, I'd read that BPD is about five times more common among first-degree relatives of individuals with the disorder than in the general population. I tried to think critically about my own behavior, experiencing the fear of perhaps every child of depressed or troubled parents: Had I inherited anything of my mother's illness?

It was a fear I'd known before. Growing up, I'd assumed that at some point Mom's demons would visit me too. Depression, after all, runs in families, and every time I felt down about something, I worried that it was an early sign of mental illness.

In the wake of the September 11 attacks, I walked around Princeton's campus distracted, on the verge of tears, a tightness in my chest. One night, I met my dad for dinner at Grand Central Station and told him I was considering dropping out. He just listened, held my hand, and said he'd support me, no matter what.

After a couple of months, the feelings passed. But now, I wonder: Was my experience like the experience of those grandchildren of Japanese living in Hiroshima and Nagasaki after the 2011 Fukushima disaster? Did Bubbie and Zayde's Holocaust experience make me more vulnerable to such a pronounced response to September 11? Had the trauma of the Holocaust passed from my grandparents to my mom to me?

The more closely I examined myself, the more clearly I saw how the history Bubbie and Zayde had lived continued to play itself out, how the trauma they had endured during the Holocaust continued to reverberate through the generations.

The thought steeled my resolve to heal myself, to stanch the psychic bleeding, for my own sake, yes, but also for my marriage's. My children's. I refused to let the trauma cross over to them, to make its way to the fourth generation.

"The trauma stops with me," I said to Steph, defiantly.

It was as much a conviction as a prayer.

26

Secret Baby

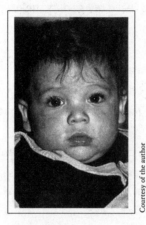

Courtesy of the author

Even as a baby, I would learn, I was
the spitting image of my biological father.

IN MARCH 2014, shortly before my thirty-third birthday, I decided it was time to reach out to Jason directly. For many years
I had not even contemplated the idea. Contacting him made the
whole thing seem real in a way I had long wanted to deny. Also,
what would I possibly have to say to him?

But after all the pain, all the disruption, the revelation had
caused, I wanted to eliminate the possibility that it had all been for
naught. I needed to know if all the heartache was warranted. If I
was, in fact, his biological son.

"I'm not sure how much my mother has told you," my email
began,

but several years ago, she told me that she believes you are my biological father.

As you can imagine, this was a stunning thing to hear, and I am still grappling with its repercussions. As part of my process of grappling, it is very important to me to know—with certainty— whether what my mother told me is true. Also, I recently got married and want to learn my genetic history as we think about having children.

For these reasons, I am writing to ask if you will consider taking a paternity test. If the results show that you are my biological father, I will ask you for a family medical history.

I recognize this email must seem like it's coming somewhat out of the blue, but I'd be grateful for your consideration and support on this.

I have no idea if my email was, in fact, out of the blue. It seems entirely possible, even likely, that my mother had kept Jason apprised of everything. But if he was aware of the ordeal I'd been going through since Mom disclosed the truth, he gave no indication of it when he replied the following morning.

"Dear Adam," he wrote, "I have no objection to a DNA test, if you would like to organize it and have someone set up an appointment to come to my apartment for a swab or blood test." His note ended on an almost philosophical note: "I am quite sure you will have a positive result with the DNA, so perhaps you should decide whether you want to live in the safety of uncertainty rather than the burden of definitive knowledge."

I was surprised, but not convinced, by his confidence. I'd also experienced firsthand the burden of uncertainty, and I decided I'd prefer to try the safety of definitive knowledge.

I bought an Identigene paternity test kit at a Duane Reade pharmacy in Times Square, choosing the legally binding option that required a third-party witness to be sure neither I, nor anyone else, could under some unforeseeable circumstance question the results.

In that first email exchange, Jason had suggested meeting at his office and then heading to his personal physician, who had agreed to do the swab. He also suggested Steph join us for lunch afterward at the Carlyle, the Art Deco hotel on the Upper East Side that exudes Old New York luxury.

I nervously approached the door to his office, Steph beside me. When he opened the door, I was startled. We looked exactly alike. Even dressed alike, with V-neck sweaters and fitted pants.

How had I not put this together sooner? I wondered. How had I not recognized what Laura had recognized when she met Jason at that Hanukkah party years earlier?

Jason noticed my surprise. "The irony," he said, "is you look more like me than any of my other children."

Even the doctor performing the paternity test did a double take as we entered his office. *Not sure you guys really need this*, said his expression, *but happy to oblige*.

I had known what Jason looked like, of course, but we hadn't seen each other in many years. What is, I gather, so ordinary for most people was surreal to me: a father who resembled an older version of myself. The glimpse into my future was unnerving.

I also had an even more unnerving experience. After our daughter was born, people would often tell me how much she resembled me, which also meant, of course, that she resembled Jason.

I saw it, too. Sometimes I'd look into her face and not only feel joy or love but also think, *This man has not only robbed my dad of a biological son, not only usurped my identity. He has hijacked generations of my family. He has supplanted the entire genetic line for all eternity.*

What was apparent to my eyes was verified by my saliva: the

results of the paternity test came back a 99.9 percent match. Science writer Carl Zimmer cited evidence in a 2016 *New York Times* article that only 1 percent of births result from what "scientists politely call 'extra-pair paternity.'" I am among that 1 percent.

All I recall from that initial lunch at the Carlyle is Steph, already assuming Jason was my biological father even before the paternity test was back, running through a battery of questions about his family medical history—and the way Jason talked about his daughter, the one I'd stayed with at the Democratic National Convention in 2000. Coldly, without a trace of sadness over what seemed to be an estranged relationship.

Upon leaving, Steph's verdict was swift and terse. "Sociopath," she said.

After that lunch, Jason and I met occasionally, several times a year, always for lunch, almost always at the Carlyle in the cozy Gallery, inspired by the sultan's dining room in Istanbul's Topkapi Palace, with hand-painted floral wallpaper, red velvet chairs, and banquettes covered in antique Turkish kilim. Jason was a familiar presence there; the waiters called him "Mr. Black," and knew his regular order.

"Maybe he really *is* my father," I joked to Steph, who had always teased me about my champagne tastes.

These lunches usually unfolded in much the same way, with Jason reflecting on his life and career, as if my presence caused him to take a measure of it all, the successes and failures. Triumphs and mistakes. Roads not taken, like the Harvard faculty appointment he said he had turned down.

"I think I've done about as much as I could've done with the strengths and limitations I was born with," he said more than once.

"How are you spending your days?" I asked at one of our first lunches. I knew he'd been a professor, but my mother had told me he'd retired years earlier.

He told me he split his time between New York City, where he ran a privately owned business, and his home in the South of France, where Marie lived much of the year.

"We don't see each other for long stretches," Jason told me. Marie herself, an elegant French woman, split the year between France and India, where, according to Jason, she traveled in "fashionable circles." Their gifts after the birth of our daughter included an embroidered children's sari.

In one of our only conversations at the small pied-à-terre Jason owned not far from his clinic—his book-filled office decorated with human skulls and nineteenth-century porcelain phrenology busts—Jason gave me an ornate blue woven folio containing several sheets of loose calligraphy pages with a history he'd written about his family.

"My paternal grandparents came to New York in the late 1800s from Odessa," he wrote, "he an opera loving communist, one of two in a family of 14 to survive the brutal winters and febrile illnesses in childhood, an intellectual who fomented revolution in a Danbury Stetson hat factory, she, a seamstress, older than he, said by my mother to be sweet, orderly and a terrible nag."

His own father, Roger, Jason wrote, "the oldest of three, was said to not so much visibly grieve the death of his father as to dutifully mourn, burying his parents along with his hopes of giving them a better life. Not a religious man in the usual sense, he walked his father's empty shoes around the block to liberate his soul." Roger, my biological grandfather, had started out in life as a chiropractor, Jason told me, before making a career switch and opening a lingerie business in Los Angeles. As a boy, Jason said, he'd fawned over the beautiful models who worked for his father.

Jason told me he was particularly close to his younger brother David, also a longtime professor, who had been plagued all his life by debilitating allergies. As a boy, I got weekly allergy shots, and grew up with doctors asking about my family's history of allergies. I'd been unable to name a single relation with anything more than hay fever.

Mom had known David, and she knew all about his allergies. Had she withheld my medical history from me and my pediatrician to protect the lie?

I remember Mom letting me know about David's death in 2003, and how upset Jason had been about it.

Why had she done that? I now wondered.

It also raised a larger question: Why would she keep in touch with Jason at all?

She still spoke to him regularly, even developing something that seemed, at least from afar, like an independent friendship with Marie. She spent weeks every summer at their home in the South of France, sometimes with Marie alone, while Jason was in New York City. Mom would even occasionally invite one of Marie's daughters from a previous marriage to dinner parties at her apartment, updating me on the girl's life until I asked her to stop.

"If you want to keep in touch with them, that's fine," I told her. "But I don't want to know about it."

Mom had always claimed she'd never wanted, never expected, me to find out about Jason. But if that were true, wouldn't it have made more sense to sever ties with him and his family altogether? Didn't she realize that having him around made it much more likely I'd eventually connect the dots?

"Why would you have connected the dots?" she replied when I asked her about it. "Did you ever think you were the son of any of the other men I dated?"

It was one of those answers that confounded me.

I didn't look like any of Mom's other boyfriends. None of her other boyfriends gave me expensive gifts over the years or came to my birthday parties or piano recitals. There were, in short, no other dots to connect with anyone else.

"Who knows about me?" I asked Jason at one of our first lunches. "Did your wife at the time know?"

He shook his head—no.

"How about any of your other children?"

"Jacob does," he said.

"What about Roxanne? Daniel?" I asked.

"No—and I'd prefer to keep it that way."

I nodded but didn't feel any obligation to honor his request. They were, after all, my family, too. And I felt I had a right to contact them if I wished. But I also felt no imminent need to reach out to them, so I didn't press it.

The whole saga was making me appreciate, in a way I hadn't before, my cosmically good luck. Of all of the families out there, of all the infinite combinations of genetics, circumstance, and twists of fate, I, a product of illicit and tragic circumstances, had landed in the life of the Frankels, a family with an unbounded supply of love to give, a family that could help ground and guide me, and whose support envelops me to this day. "Better to be lucky than good," Pa himself would always say.

At another early lunch, I'd asked Jason a question that had been nagging at me: Did I have any other half siblings besides Jacob and the ones I knew about? Mom, of course, was not Jason's only student. Had he had other affairs with students? Other children with them?

He was sitting across from me in the Gallery at the Carlyle, leaning back against the plush banquette. He smiled when I asked the question, as if I were complimenting his sexual prowess. He answered obliquely, going on about all the women—"Some of them quite beautiful"—who had wanted him to father their children over the years.

"You know," I told him, "this whole thing really messed with my sense of identity."

"In a way," he replied, "that's pretty interesting. That's something you're going to have to work through."

No shit, I thought.

"I don't think it would have bothered me that much if I'd learned I wasn't my father's biological son," he said. "I wanted to be different from him. I think if I were in your position, I'd want to know what I inherited from *my* side of the family."

The whole subject made me uncomfortable, as if merely considering the question of what I'd inherited from Jason were an act of betrayal against my dad.

But I did wonder.

Jason had written or edited over a dozen books, hundreds of articles. He had been a professor, as had his brother. Had I inherited something of my interest in writing or history, in the life of the mind, from him?

I also wondered about my personality.

I am not imperturbable, as these pages have proved. But I am fairly even-tempered and not prone to effusive displays of emotion. Steph, in occasional moments of loving exasperation, has called me "an emotional tundra."

Jason seemed similar. "A psychologist friend once said I mooch affect off of women," he told me, describing his seemingly clinical, unemotional demeanor. (Men, in Jason's telling, had no such affects to mooch.) I thought of Steph's comment—"Sociopath"—about Jason's chilly description of his daughter.

I couldn't imagine being so cold toward my own child, but I also couldn't help thinking, had I inherited something of Jason's temperament?

During one conversation, Jason told me that in the early 1980s, he and his then wife had hosted a party at their Bronxville home. The gathering was held shortly after I was born, and Jason had invited my mom and dad, who brought along little me.

Jason's mother had picked us up at the train station, and rode back in the car with me in her lap. The minute she returned, Jason told me, she pulled him into a room and closed the door.

"Don't even try to tell me that isn't your son," she told him. "It was *you* I was holding in my arms."

Apparently, even as an infant, I was the man's spitting image.

At last I realized why Jason's mother had been so kind to me all those years ago, when my mother and I had stayed in her guest apartment in LA.

She had known I was her grandson all along.

Was the reason I remembered our meeting so well because, somehow, I knew it, too?

My lunches with Jason felt at once intimately familiar and chillingly distant, many of them passing with him doing much of the talking as I listened, trying to process what I made of him, of us sitting there together, of the whole situation. I was not quite sure what I thought of him, what kind of relationship, if any, I wanted. But I felt like I needed these lunches, this contact, to figure that out.

Jason, as best I could tell, seemed to want as much of a relationship as I was willing to offer. He started signing emails "Love, Jason." Once, he called himself "Dad." Another time, he signed an email, "bad dad." "You're not my dad," I told him.

I was surprised he'd used the term. During one of our earliest conversations, he'd told me he didn't consider himself my dad. "I've always thought a dad is the person who raises you," he'd said, an acknowledgment I'd appreciated at the time. Then he added, "That's why I never wanted to interfere when you were young."

Jason could sense my wariness about a relationship, telling my mom, "Adam doesn't check in with me like the rest of my children." But he kept trying.

Every so often, he'd send an email offering tickets to some play or concert. And he'd sometimes email me papers he'd written or bring one of his books to lunch. Such gifts, it seemed, were an attempt to help me understand his work and life, to deepen our relationship.

Learning from my mother that I was in the market for a piano, he offered to buy one for me. "Consider it a housewarming gift," he said, knowing Steph and I were moving into a new apartment in Brooklyn.

"This is the kind of free that comes with strings," warned Steph.

"If he wants to buy me a piano," I replied, "it's the least he can do."

I was not above exploiting his feelings—whatever they were—for my own advantage. What was it Frederick the Great said of

Maria Theresa, the eighteenth-century Habsburg ruler? "She wept, but she took."

He also gave me another gift. During one lunch he brought a blue cloth bag, embroidered with silver. In it were a tallit, yarmulke, and prayer book. It had belonged to his father, he explained.

"None of my other kids care about any of this stuff," he told me. "I thought you might want it."

When I returned home, I tossed the bag in the back of a closet, not quite sure what to do with it, never expecting I'd ever want to retrieve it, never thinking I'd ever wear any of them to a service.

And yet months later, on Yom Kippur, I found myself rummaging through the closet in search of it. Something about it called to me.

Standing in the pews of a Brooklyn synagogue, I was surprised to feel a sense of calm, of connection, wrapping myself in the musty prayer shawl of the grandfather I had never known.

"You know," Jason said during one visit as we walked to the Carlyle, "you were not an accident."

He said it casually, an offhand remark.

I looked at him blankly, confused.

"What do you mean?" I asked.

"You were *wanted*."

An odd word, *wanted*. Did he think that would make me feel better? That the distance between us was because I'd felt like I'd been an accident?

Perhaps, but I was less relieved than bewildered: Mom and Jason had *planned* to have me?

During the same walk, Jason told me he and my mother had even discussed what to name me. I'd thought Mom and Dad had selected my name because they didn't like nicknames and "Adam" didn't have one, and because, as Dad had told me, the name reminded him of Robert Kennedy's speechwriter Adam Walinsky. Now even my first name seemed tainted by this whole saga.

A short time later, I told Mom about my conversation with

Jason and asked if what he'd said was true, if she had *wanted* to have me.

"Well," she replied, "I wouldn't say it was *my* decision."

I was silent as I absorbed the shock of that statement. Not *her* decision? I was *his* idea?

How is this my life? I thought, not for the first time. It was as if I'd been living one life for my first twenty-five years, and then suddenly dropped into another one I was still struggling to comprehend.

An accident, I could understand. That kind of thing happens. But *this*?

The next time I met Jason for lunch at the Carlyle, I shared what my mother had said, that I had not been *her* idea. That I had been *his* idea. I had one question for him: Why?

"Well," he replied coolly, "the idea of having a secret baby appealed to my sense of mystery and the erotic."

Seriously? I thought. What the fuck is wrong with this guy?

All of this, all the pain Jason and Mom had caused, all the havoc they were willing to risk in Dad's life, the Frankels' lives, their own lives—my life—was the result of some weird narcissistic fantasy?

I suddenly remembered my mother's abortion—or miscarriage— the one she'd had when I was a boy. Whatever it was, Mom and Dad seemed to agree it had been Jason's. My mind began racing: were Mom and Jason trying to deceive my dad into raising a brood of Jason's children? Not only a secret baby, but secret siblings? A secret family?

After that lunch, I wondered why I'd been so relentlessly chasing the truth. I had wanted to believe that if I could understand my mother, understand Jason, understand what had happened, it would bring me peace.

And yet the harder I pushed, the more I learned, the more sordid the whole saga seemed, the less I could wrap my head around it.

How could I even be sure Mom or Jason remembered exactly what they were thinking back then? It was, after all, more than thirty years before. How could I be sure they were telling me the whole story? At a certain point, what difference did any of it make?

It is written in the book of John, "And ye shall know the truth, and the truth shall make you free." I found, however, that the pursuit of truth sometimes seemed to shackle me, mire me in the ethical swamp of my mother's past, of Jason's past.

Had I made some terrible mistake? I wondered. Would I have been better off if I'd never started asking questions in the first place?

Was Shushie right? Was it my fault, in a way? Had I brought all of this upon myself?

Over the course of our lunches, a picture began to emerge of what exactly Jason thought about my mother and their relationship. At one point, he complained that she hadn't been "faithful" to him because she'd had other affairs. Another time, he expressed regret that my mother hadn't become, as he put it, "a fully realized version of herself."

"Good thing you didn't get her personality," he said during one lunch. "That sort of personality on a man would really be something."

What was that supposed to mean? Was insecurity, mental illness, a better look on a woman?

"In those days," he told me, "I was attracted to broken women, and they were attracted to me."

I wasn't quite sure how to respond, and I told my mom about it.

"Oh my God," she said, laughing nervously. "That's sick."

We were standing in her kitchen—a small, narrow kitchen with olive wallpaper and dried flowers hanging over the sink. I'd gone over to her apartment for dinner, telling her I wanted to ask about Jason, to try to get to the bottom of a few things.

"How did the affair begin?" I asked. I knew Jason had been one of her professors when she was getting her PhD. But I didn't know any more than that.

"I don't want to talk about it," she said, a pained expression on her face.

I kept asking. She finally answered.

Jason had an office on the East Side, she said, and asked her to come by. "I thought it was to talk about the work. But he wanted more and made that very clear."

"Meaning?"

She sighed and put her hand on the counter, steadying herself.

"What did you do?" I asked.

"I just remember being very shocked this was happening. I had no idea what was on his mind when I arrived that day."

Silence.

"I'm sorry we have to talk about all this," she said. "It's all"—she searched for the right word, biting her lip—"ugly."

"I don't know what to say," I replied, trying to hold back tears. "It kind of takes my breath away."

"Which part?" she asked.

"All of it." I was quiet for a moment. "How do you go from *that* to having feelings for this person?" I finally asked.

"I don't know," she said. "He's nice to you. Buys you presents. Takes you to dinner. And all the while, he's a very accomplished person who has the respect of a lot of people. It's flattering for someone who has no self-respect. It gives you respect to be associated with him."

Around the same time as we were having that conversation, the *New York Times* and *New Yorker* were breaking stories on Harvey Weinstein's sexual harassment and assault, and the #metoo movement was gaining traction. I couldn't help seeing certain parallels.

My mother had lied to me all my life about my identity. She had distorted facts about our relationship to extract sympathy from her family. So I had to acknowledge she had a difficult history with the truth. But I believed her.

I *also* know this: my mom was, as Jason himself had called her, "a broken woman" when their affair began, only a couple of years after a suicide attempt that had nearly killed her. Jason was also her professor, in a position of influence over her career.

Whatever happened between them was inappropriate. And my mom deserved better. Of that, I am certain.

Of course, my mother was not a passive participant in the long affair. "There has always been the European in Ellen," her friend Beth told me, trying to help me understand my mother's thinking at the time, "this notion of men having mistresses that everyone is sort of aware of. Men had always done it, so why couldn't women?"

Was that a part of it too? Was the affair, in some sense, an expression of independence, even empowerment? Perhaps, but after that conversation in her kitchen, I couldn't help seeing my mother as she often saw herself. As a victim.

I thought of that fight years earlier, where I'd mocked her sense of victimhood. "Poor you," I'd said, "my heart breaks."

Now, my heart *did* break. She *was* a victim—and a survivor. Of so many things. The cruelty of mental illness. Intergenerational trauma. Jason. Her Columbia professor Bob. How many others?

I thought of my mom so desperate, so vulnerable, she had made a plan to take her own life. I wish I could've been there. I wish I could've told her how special she was, how much she had to give, how wasteful and tragic such an act would have been.

During my next lunch with Jason at the Carlyle, I decided to raise what my mother had shared with me. I didn't tell him exactly what Mom had said, but I didn't have to. He understood immediately what I was asking.

"I never pushed myself on her. I never exploited her," he told me. "I don't want you to think that."

I asked what he thought of Weinstein, and the controversy surrounding Alabama judge Roy Moore, a credibly accused child molester then running for the US Senate.

"If you ask me," he replied, "I think the whole thing seems a little overblown."

I looked at him, an old man of nearly eighty now, roughly the same age that Pa had been when he passed away. And yet so vastly different from Pa, from Dad. I'd once asked my dad what he considered the proudest accomplishment of his career. "Writing one of the first sexual harassment policies at the UN," he told me.

Those were my dad's values, *my* values. Had I been raised by Jason, would I have absorbed *his* values?

Jason told me a story about some friends of his in France—a man who'd had an affair with his own stepdaughter. The man's wife, Jason said, "was fine with it." Then he added, "This sort of thing happens in families." I remembered Beth's comment about "the European" in my mother.

"This sort of thing seems to happen a bit more frequently in your family," I replied, alluding to a rumor that my mother had once shared about another secret baby in Jason's family tree. It was one of the few times I let my anger and bitterness slip out during our lunches.

"Oh, Adam," he replied, "you've traveled the world, but you haven't seen it."

I tried not to let his condescension get to me, but it did. I also wondered, Was he right? Was I just being naive? Do lots of people have stories like mine, stories of sordid family secrets? Probably, I had to concede.

My conversations with Jason were clarifying. Over the years, I've heard various versions of the question: Doesn't everything that happened—the cheating, the secret baby—somehow reflect poorly on your dad? I know where the question comes from. Dad had been cuckolded, and in some eyes, that makes him seem weak, like less of a man.

Dad certainly doesn't look like a tough guy. He is rather slim, mild-mannered, and earnestly curious about people and the world, and as a boy, there were times I wanted him to display some of the more conventional attributes of toughness and strength.

During a trip to Cooperstown we met up with a friend of mine, who was there with his own father to visit the Baseball Hall of Fame, and we challenged each other to a friendly game of pool, one father-son pair against the other. I was certain Dad and I would win. Grandma and Pa had a pool table in their basement, and I'd grown up admiring my dad's game—a gentle game of subtle angles and soft pushes.

My friend's father, by contrast, was a former college athlete, and practically snapped the cue in half with every shot, the crack resounding across the pool hall. We got our asses kicked.

Such conventional notions of strength and weakness, of manhood, seem entirely inapt, however, for understanding Jason's and my dad's respective roles in the whole saga. And it raises all the age-old questions about what constitutes strength and weakness, and what it means to be a man.

Jason had an inappropriate relationship with a vulnerable, less powerful woman. Does that reflect strength? Is that what a *real* man does?

Dad was faithful to my mom, vowing to help her heal and repair her relationships with Bubbie and Zayde. Does that reflect weakness? Are we comfortable saying that's not what a *man* should do?

During that same lunch with Jason where I'd asked about Harvey Weinstein, I reminded him I was writing a book about all of this.

"What are you going to say about *me*?" he asked.

"I don't know," I replied. "I haven't written that part yet."

When I'd first reached out to Jason, I hadn't wanted much. Just a paternity test and some answers about his family's medical history. I hadn't even considered the larger question of what kind of role I wanted him to play in my life.

As I got to know him better—and learned more from him and my mom about what had happened—the answer emerged: none.

I felt an unmistakable sense of familiarity, kinship, with Jason. At certain points during our conversations, I'd find myself forgetting my anger and anguish, and actually enjoying our time together, even laughing at his jokes.

And yet I've also had to ask myself a few questions: If I believe, as I do, that he abused his position of power in a relationship with my mother, and abused it at a particularly vulnerable time in her life; and if I believe, as I do, that he committed an unforgivable moral crime against my dad and his family; and if I believe, as I do, that his decisions are at the root of untold heartache, how can I choose, *why* would I choose, to have any relationship with him?

The bonds of blood, I now realize, are not sufficiently strong a reason. My conversations with Jason helped illuminate the differences between the bonds of blood and the bonds of love, helped illuminate what I inherited from him, my mom, the Frankels—and what *I* contributed, what is simply *me*.

Even a revelation as traumatic as mine, I've come to see, cannot change the people I love or who love me. It cannot change the person I choose to become or the meaning I choose to give my life. It may obscure but cannot silence the sound of my inner voice. Much of that—the grist of my destiny—is in *my* control. It belongs to *me*. Everything is heritable, Jason taught me despite himself, except some of the things that matter most.

I also learned something else from Jason. He helped me understand my story in a new way, and understand how to integrate the revelation into the narrative I'd constructed about my life. I'd grown up proud of my family's story, of Bubbie and Zayde's story, of my Frankel and Minow family's story.

But now, I understand, I'm not only the product of stories that make me proud. I'm also the product of stories that disappoint me. Stories that break my heart. The beautiful, the ugly, the heroic, the tragic, the noble, the shameful—my identity has expanded to accommodate them all.

"The ancient Chinese had a practice," writes author Anne Lamott in *Hallelujah Anyway*, "of embellishing the cracked parts of valued possessions with gold leaf, which says: We dishonor it if we pretend that it hadn't gotten broken."

Many jagged edges run across my shattered identity. But as I've pieced it back together, shard by shard, I no longer try to hide the broken places. Now, I adorn them with gold.

27

The Phases of Forgiveness

With Mom on the Upper West Side in 1981.

IN 2018, TWELVE years after I suggested, during that first conversation with my mother, talking to our rabbi about forgiveness,
I finally reached out to that rabbi: Roly Matalon of B'nai Jeshurun
on the Upper West Side.

I had known Roly since I was a boy; he had presided over my
bar mitzvah. But I hadn't seen him in many years when I walked
into his office at the B'nai Jeshurun Community House on West
Eighty-Ninth Street.

He knew the reason for my visit from the email I'd sent requesting a meeting. So, after some small talk, he turned to the subject
at hand.

"That is quite a revelation you've had to deal with," he said.

After holding on to my anger for so long, I knew forgiveness would not come on its own. Time, I'd learned, does *not* heal all wounds. Some wounds require attention, work, to heal.

"I have a very selfish reason for wanting to forgive my mom," I explained. "I'm tired of carrying around this anger. I want to forgive her, not for *her* sake, but *mine*," I said, citing research linking forgiveness to reduced anxiety, fewer physical health symptoms, and lower mortality rates.

I'd come across a forgiveness model, I told Roly, developed by University of Wisconsin–Madison psychologist Dr. Bob Enright, with four phases: the Uncovering Phase—identifying the harm that's been done; the Decision Phase—choosing to forgive; the Work Phase—finding compassion for the offender; and the Deepening Phase—discovering greater meaning in the pain.

I was somewhere around phase two or three. I had decided to forgive my mother, but I was having difficulty.

"Have you ever read *The Sunflower?*" he asked.

I had not. Simon Wiesenthal, the Holocaust survivor and Nazi hunter, had written an account—apocryphal, some say—of being assigned to clean waste at a hospital during the war, where he had met a dying Nazi soldier, a member of the SS, who begged his forgiveness.

"I know that what I am asking is almost too much for you," pleaded the Nazi after confessing his crimes, "but without your answer I cannot die in peace."

Wiesenthal wrote that he left the room silently, sharing what had happened with some friends, who offered their perspectives on whether the Nazi should have been granted his dying wish of forgiveness.

"You would have had no right to do this in the name of people who had not authorized you to do so," one friend told him. "What people have done to you yourself, you can, if you like, forgive and forget. That is your own affair. But it would have been a terrible sin to burden your conscience with other people's sufferings."

After reading Wiesenthal's book, I realized that my mom had

committed two injuries, two offenses for which apologies were due: the first was the affair with Jason; the second, lying to me about my identity.

The first injury, however—the affair—was not against me. And, as Wiesenthal's friend had told him, I had "no right" to offer forgiveness for it. Only my dad could do that. Besides, my forgiveness would, in some sense, be an acknowledgment that she had been wrong to have me. Did I really think that?

One of the people my twenty-seven-year-old mom confided in about the secret baby she was carrying was her therapist at the time. "I stopped seeing him," she once told me, "after he said I was making a terrible mistake having you."

It's a strange thing to hear your mother say something like that—and agree with the therapist. But of course, he was right—it *was* a terrible mistake. She should not have deliberately had a child with Jason, and lied to everyone about it.

And yet how can I wish away my own existence? How can I reject certain behavior as appalling and yet credit my life with it?

One of the qualities clinicians attribute to people with borderline personality disorder is an all-or-nothing, black-and-white way of looking at the world. Borderlines have trouble seeing gray.

And yet what is the fact of my conception but a shade of gray? What are the circumstances of my birth but some impossibly tangled web of good and bad, right and wrong?

I had a different perspective on the second injury my mother had committed: the lying. I had a right to know who my father was, and she had an obligation to tell me.

I was, however, willing to acknowledge that I wasn't so sure *when* my mother should have come out with the truth. If she'd done it before I was born, Dad might have insisted on her getting an abortion, as he said he'd done with the other child—my only full sibling. If she'd done it when I was a baby, Dad and my whole Frankel family might have simply walked away, refusing—quite understandably—to raise another man's child.

So I understood, perhaps even endorsed, withholding the truth when I was a child. But why not tell me when I was older, after I'd formed my own relationships with the Frankels, after my mom could be more confident that they wouldn't abandon me? Why not in middle school? Or high school? Or when I left for college? Or when I graduated from college? Or when I left for graduate school?

One could make an argument for delaying the disclosure, in the belief that I might have been better equipped to withstand the chaos of it when I was older. But that wasn't Mom's argument; she'd never intended to tell me at all.

She preferred to have everyone think I was my dad's son. Later, I'd learn she'd actually discussed all of this with some of her closest friends at the time. "She would talk about it a lot," her friend Beth told me. "She was worried your dad would find out. She didn't know whose son you were until you were born. But with your physical appearance, she feared a connection would be made. She didn't think Jason would make a good father. And she was glad you had a relationship with her husband and he took you as his son."

When I reached out to Isabel, the friend who'd saved my mom's life after the suicide attempt—the first time we'd connected in more than a decade—it was as if she'd been waiting for the call. "I've thought of you often over the years. You know," she told me, "you had three people loving you when you were growing up—some people don't even have two.

"Over the years, I've wondered if your mother would tell you," she continued. "It just wasn't my place to say anything when you were young, so I never did. I'm sorry." I told her she had nothing to apologize for, but her words were a reminder of the ways secrets can haunt even those not directly affected.

I thought back to what Mom herself had told me when I asked if she'd ever intended to tell me: "Maybe on my deathbed."

"How can I forgive *that*?" I asked Roly.

He paused for a moment.

"Yom Kippur," he said, referring to the holiest of Jewish Holy

Days, "is about atoning for sins against God. Even God," he said, "only forgives sins against Himself. He does not forgive sins committed against others. Only people can do that. Has your mother ever asked for forgiveness?"

She had, many times over the years, said the words "I'm sorry." She had expressed regret. She had seen the pain she had caused, and I believe she genuinely felt bad about it.

And yet only after Roly asked the question did I realize she had never said the words "Will you forgive me?" And her apologies had always been general, all-encompassing. She'd never explicitly apologized for the lies.

So I decided to give her the chance. A few days later, I called her on one of my drives home from work, and told her I was writing about forgiveness. I was reflecting on it, I said, because I wanted to forgive her. I was trying to forgive her.

I told her it was a lot easier to empathize with the twentysomething who started the affair with Jason, the one who'd attempted suicide a couple of years earlier, than the woman she was in her thirties, forties, and fifties when she continued to lie to me about who I was.

"I never *lied* to you," she replied. "I never said he *was* your father."

I was at a loss. Even after all the staggering things I'd heard, my capacity to be staggered was somehow never exhausted.

"Are you *really* trying to tell me that because you never uttered the words, 'Stephen Baskin Frankel is your biological father,' you never lied to me?" My voice was growing louder. I could feel myself getting worked up as I drove down the Brooklyn-Queens Expressway.

"Well, when you put it *that* way," she replied. She told me she just didn't think about it. "Maybe," she continued, "I just didn't *want* to think about it. Maybe it was too much of a burden. And I didn't want to hurt you or your dad, and didn't see the need to rock the boat."

I didn't buy that. Sure, I thought, part of the reason might be that she didn't want to hurt us. But I also thought what she had done was incredibly selfish, and I told her so. "I think you were ashamed and embarrassed of what you had done—and afraid of Bubbie and Zayde and everybody finding out. I think that's a big part of it, too."

"You're probably right," she acknowledged.

All I wanted, I said, was for her to own up to everything, fully and unreservedly. "I just want you to say, 'I know what I did was wrong. I know it would've been a painful conversation whenever it happened, but you had a right to know, and I'm sorry.' I just wish you'd said that, Mom."

I wished, I told her, *I* hadn't been the one to figure it out, that *she'd* been the one to tell me. Something about having to extract it all from her, her unwillingness to come clean, made the whole thing that much harder to forgive. If only she'd taken the initiative to tell me, I was convinced, I would have been more understanding. I would have respected the way she'd handled it with me, perhaps even found some courage in it.

"I see that now," she said softly.

It was not the apology I wanted. Not the one I needed. But it was all she was capable of giving. "We forgive," said the eighteenth-century French woman of letters Madame de Staël, "what we really understand." I've finally come to understand my mother, at least well enough. And I forgive her.

28

Reborn

Giving my Dad a hug shortly
before my wedding ceremony.

I T'S FUNNY, THE things that change your life. I couldn't fathom telling my father the truth or even consider the idea without physically recoiling.

Then I saw Sarah Polley's 2012 film *Stories We Tell*, about her own family's story.

Sarah is the product of an affair between her mother, Diane, and a Canadian producer, Harry. No one in her family knew Harry was her biological father. Not Sarah. Not her siblings. And not Michael, the man who raised her. Sarah herself learned the truth when she was twenty-seven—roughly the same age I was—more than a decade after her mother passed away from cancer.

Sarah and her family are well known in Canada. And after learning that the Canadian press was preparing to run a story saying she was not Michael's biological daughter, she made the difficult decision to tell him herself.

I did not know what the film was about when, in 2014, Steph and I selected it on Netflix; the trailer appropriately left out some of the more salient details. I watched it warily, the subject a little too close to the bone.

For me, however, its most stunning revelation was not the truth of Sarah's parentage, but how Michael responded to it. With love, compassion. The truth had not created distance between them. It had brought them closer together.

Until I saw Sarah's film, I hadn't considered that possibility. If someone had told me it might happen, I wouldn't have believed them. The only thing that could've persuaded me was seeing it myself.

That is the gift Sarah Polley gave me.

Sarah's film opened my eyes to what a relationship with my dad might look like on the other side of all this, a relationship founded on honesty, acceptance, not as he *thought* I was, but as I *was*, as I *am*.

I didn't know if I would find such acceptance. But the pain of going without it, of the secret, was taking so heavy a toll that, after more than a decade, I decided I was willing to gamble on my dad's love.

During one of my early conversations with my mother in 2006, she had offered to tell him herself.

Now you're willing to tell him? I thought.

That was still how I felt. My parents no longer had an independent, ongoing relationship. The only times they saw each other were occasions, celebrations, where I invited them both.

If anyone were going to tell him at this point, I decided, it was going to be me.

So I called him up. "I'd like to come see you tomorrow," I said. "I want to talk to you about something."

"What is it?" he asked.

How do you tell your father that you're not his son?

"I'd rather not get into it on the phone," I said. "I want to talk about it in person."

"Okay," he said, "now you're making me worried."

I took the train up to Hastings-on-Hudson the following morning.

The trip seemed to last forever. I stared out the window—at the Hudson, the Palisades, the little villages along the way, my heart beating faster at every stop.

Spuyten Duyvil . . .

Yonkers . . .

Greystone . . .

When the conductor announced Hastings, I took a deep breath.

Dad was sitting in his gray Prius and greeted me with a smile. I tried to make small talk. I didn't want to get into it in the car. My voice cracked more than once. He looked over, and put his hand on my knee.

I started the conversation as soon as we got to his brown clapboard home. We were sitting on couches in his living room, surrounded by books on virtually every wall. Helen was out—giving us some time alone, I assumed.

Over the previous days, I'd rehearsed what I wanted to say, sometimes silently, sometimes aloud in front of a mirror, always with trepidation.

Here we go, I thought, bracing myself.

"You may remember a number of years ago when I told you I had to take Mom to the ER," I began.

"Yes," he said. He remembered.

"What I didn't tell you was that the reason she had a breakdown was because I hadn't spoken to her in months."

I continued slowly, cautiously.

"And the reason I hadn't spoken to her in months," I said, "is because she told me . . ."

I paused, gathered myself. Tears streamed down my face. I couldn't get the words out. They were trapped inside.

". . . that I am Jason Black's biological son."

I couldn't bring myself to look at him. I was too scared of what I might see—his eyes changing, the loving look gone, a sadness falling over him.

"Uh-huh," he said. "Uh-huh."

Brief pause.

"Yeah . . . I know . . . I know."

"You know?" I eked out through the tears.

"Yes," he replied calmly. "I've always known it was *possible*."

"You *have*?" I said, incredulous. More tears.

"Yes . . . yes," he said. "And I made a decision a long time ago that it doesn't matter one way or another. You're my son, Adam. And you always will be."

Even now, I cannot write—or read—those words without tearing up. Such simple words. Yet so full of love. So full of grace. Words I had never dared imagine him saying.

I walked over to him, and wept in his arms.

"I thought you wouldn't love me as much," I said, heaving.

I clung to him tight. All my life, I have never hugged anyone as hard or as long as I hugged my dad in that moment.

Then we sat down.

"Is that *all*?" he joked. "Well, at least now I know not to come to you for a blood transfusion."

I still couldn't believe it. All this time, I had dreaded telling him. All this time, he had known, or at least suspected it. No sea monsters lay lurking in the deep.

Some of the reasons for his suspicions, he told me, had been the same as mine: the lack of a physical resemblance; the expensive gifts Jason would buy me. He told me Jason had sort of hovered around during my childhood, that Dad didn't want him at my bris, school performances, and birthdays, but my mom would always invite him anyway. He was always interfering, Dad said, refuting Jason's claims to the contrary.

Later, I'd hear that my parents had been traveling in Milan when they learned, after my mother came down with what seemed like a nasty stomach bug, that she was pregnant. The mother of her friend Isabel lived in Milan and accompanied them to the doctor, later telling Isabel that she wondered about the state of my parents' marriage after witnessing Dad's reaction to the news of his wife's pregnancy: shock.

He and my mother no longer had a physical relationship by then, Dad later told me—with one exception, during the summer of 1980, which is why he could say, as we walked down Broadway the day this saga first began, that he remembered the night of my conception.

Was that night, I now wonder, part of Mom and Jason's plan? An intentional act of misdirection aimed at sowing doubt about who my father was, at persuading Dad there was a chance I was his biological son?

Over the years, Dad had confided his suspicions to a few people. Helen knew, he said. So did a former colleague, whom Dad had tried to lift up during a difficult time in the man's life.

He had even asked Mom about it when I was a baby.

"How can you ask such a question about a child as sweet as Adam?" she had replied.

During my parents' lawsuit, he'd briefly considered a paternity test, but decided he didn't want the results, didn't need them. By then I was his son—and he was my dad.

A couple years later, my stepbrother Greg had his own conversation with Dad, coming out to him and his mother Helen about being gay.

"What did you say?" I asked Dad.

"I told him it changed nothing," he said. "That I loved him just the same."

I was struck by the similarities between Greg's conversation with Dad and my own, both of us knowing a truth about ourselves—some fundamental aspect of our identities—but keeping it a secret, wondering, to varying degrees, if we'd be accepted. And Dad, accepting us, loving us—both of us, his *real* sons—for who we are.

Now I understood, as I hadn't before, as I couldn't before, just how expansive Dad's character was. Just how good a man, just how strong a man, he was. Dad's strength, I realized, was his goodness; his goodness, his strength.

This, I thought, is what it means to love unconditionally. *This* is what it means to be a father. *This* is what it means to be a man.

Psychologist Eduardo Duran tells a story of holding therapy sessions with members of a Native American community when a strange thing started happening. Duran started sensing someone was in the room with him, someone—or some *thing*—besides Duran and his patients.

One day a local healer came to see him, and Duran told him about it. The healer understood immediately.

"The reason you're having that experience," he told Duran, "is because they're there."

"Who's there?" asked Duran.

"The ancestors."

The healer explained that, according to natural law, everything we do affects seven generations. But not just seven generations *forward*. Seven generations *back*, too.

As Duran's patients were being healed, explained the healer, their ancestors were showing up to be healed in the realm where they had been wounded. And the unborn ones were being healed alongside them. The healing, according to tradition, was unfolding across fourteen generations.

I am not a mystical person. And yet I can feel the truth of Duran's experience, the way peace in one generation can bring peace in another, the transmission of intergenerational healing. I felt it in Dad's home that day.

During my conversation with Rabbi Roly Matalon, he'd used a phrase that stuck with me. After I'd shared all the details of the revelation and its aftermath, Roly had said, "In a way, you were reborn."

Rachel Yehuda of Mount Sinai had said something similar. I'd taken a moment during our conversation to ask for her professional advice. Here, after all, was one of the world's leading trauma experts. Surely, she could help me.

"How," I asked, "will I know I'm healed?"

She couldn't answer that question. The state of being *healed* lay too far beyond her ken. She could, however, tell me how I'd know I was *healing*.

"You'll know you're healing," said Yehuda, "when you look back on this event as the beginning of a new you."

She was, I suspect, referring to the whole experience—the disclosure itself and the years of grappling with it. But her words were also true of a particular event, a specific moment: that conversation in Dad's living room.

That conversation, of course, did not mark the end of my journey. The difficulties in my relationship with my Perecman family would continue for some time. The challenges of being close to my mom continue to this day. And my wounded identity was not fully healed, I was not miraculously made whole again, in a single afternoon. I still had tears to shed, pain to ease, and questions to answer. I suspect I always will.

But that conversation is what liberated me to begin opening up about what had happened to the rest of my family. To my friends. To myself. That simple expression of a father's love—*my* father's love—is where my healing began.

EPILOGUE

I N AUGUST 2017 I decided to make a trip to Connecticut. It had been a couple months since I'd seen Zayde, even longer since he'd seen our little daughter. So I called him up at The Store and let him know Steph and I were planning to come see him a few days later, on Saturday, timing our arrival for the morning to accommodate the baby's nap schedule.

I had assumed my ninety-three-year-old grandfather's weekend plans—to the extent he had any—could be adjusted on relatively short notice to allow for the visit. I was wrong. That particular Saturday morning, he informed me, was reserved for Peter, the professional watchmaker who occasionally came over for lessons.

I called Zayde back a little later to see if he'd mind asking Peter to come another time. Shushie picked up and yelled the question across The Store. I could hear Zayde yell his reply back.

"No," he shouted. "I'm sorry."

He had given Peter his word, and that was that.

So the following Saturday, I drove up to see Zayde. Not in the morning, with Steph and the baby. But in the afternoon, alone.

I could hear the shuffle of Zayde's walker as he answered the door. His body displayed the ravages of time and illness, the right side of his face drooping, disfigured after the removal of a cancerous growth around his jaw. Every few months, it seemed, I'd get a call about one health scare or another.

The sun was out, and Zayde suggested we sit on the back porch, accessible through the kitchen. On our way outside, I noticed a couple of decades-old Yellow Pages stacked on the kitchen table, watch parts meticulously arranged on top of them, beneath a rusty lamp—Zayde's makeshift bench at home, where he'd no doubt return to work after I left.

On the back porch, Zayde asked how I was doing, how Steph and the baby were doing. Then, his voice growing louder, less from anger, I thought, than poor hearing, he asked, once again, about the tension between my mother and me. He told me, once again, I was not being as supportive, as loyal, a son as he had always hoped, as he had always expected.

I could feel my heart rate picking up, my breath quickening.

Calm down, I told myself. This could be the last time you see him. Don't say anything you'll regret. Whenever I visited Zayde in those years, I always knew it could be the last time.

I told him I was sorry he felt that way, and expressed my own sadness for the way things had turned out. He told me he loved me. Then he added, almost apologetically, that he was just looking out for my mom, just looking out for his daughter.

"I know," I replied, the sun beating down on us. "And I love you, too. I respect you and admire you so much, Zayde. You're my hero," I added, tearing up, the words carrying the weight of all that had passed between us, all of the emotions I felt toward him—reverence, love, sadness, frustration, regret.

We moved inside, and he asked if I ever wanted to get involved in politics again.

"I don't know," I said, standing by the kitchen table. "Maybe one day."

"You want to be a big man," he said.

I couldn't tell if it was a question or a statement.

"I'll never be as big a man as you," I replied.

As I pulled out of the cul-de-sac, I looked back. Zayde was still standing in the doorway, hands on his walker, watching me drive off. I wondered, once again, if it was the last time I'd see him standing there.

It was. Several weeks later, he was drifting in and out of consciousness at Yale New Haven Hospital after a catastrophic stroke. Every few minutes he'd open his eyes, tightening his grip or tilting his body. At one point, he seemed to try to get out of bed. One of the doctors, displaying somewhat less bedside manner than we'd expected, told us this was the end.

I asked if I could have a few minutes alone with him, as I'd done with Pa so many years earlier. Only Mom and Shushie were in the room—the rest of their siblings either in the hall or on their way— and they graciously agreed. I leaned over Zayde's ear so he could hear me clearly. I told him, as I had on the back porch, that he was my hero, and that I loved him. And I told him he didn't need to worry about my mom, that I'd take care of her. That all of us would take care of her. That she'd be okay.

I thought I could detect the faintest trace of a smile.

Then I kissed his forehead—cool, damp beneath my lips—and said goodbye.

Even then, incapacitated, his body no longer fully responding to the impulses of his mind, I could see in his eyes the life force, the will to live, undiminished, undaunted. "One of God's preselected," I thought, remembering the words of the surgeon who'd performed a miracle on his spine years earlier.

He passed away after sundown on the first night of Rosh Hashanah, the Jewish New Year, a few months after Grandma herself at age ninety-five. I was struck by the coincidence of Pa and Bubbie, Grandma and Zayde, dying within months of one another, eighteen years apart—a symmetry that felt meaningful, as if the families were bound together in some mysterious way.

According to Jewish tradition, on the morning of Rosh Hashanah, a prayer called the Unetanneh Tokef is recited, setting out, as it is written—and as Leonard Cohen sings—"Who will live and who will die . . . who by water and who by fire."

At Zayde's memorial service, the rabbi explained that he had died after sundown and before morning services, after the prior year's deaths had been carried out and before the upcoming year's deaths had been appointed. Zayde, he said, had therefore departed not according to anyone else's schedule—not even the Angel of Death's—but at a time of his own choosing, dying, as he had lived, in command of his own destiny.

Then the rabbi said a few words in Yiddish. The words stirred something in me—their sound, their intonation, if not their meaning, so familiar. I thought of Zayde's childhood, of Michalishek, of the extraordinary life of the man we mourned, as out of place and anachronistic in his final years as the lost language of Yiddish in twenty-first-century America. A man who'd always seemed to straddle two worlds, the Old and the New, like the street address of The Store—896 1/2 Whalley Avenue.

I was one of the pallbearers, and after the service, I walked ahead to help lift the casket into the hearse. Then we joined the procession of cars, navigating a series of narrow residential streets to an Orthodox cemetery in a blue-collar New Haven suburb, where Zayde would be buried beside Bubbie, their gravestones bearing for all eternity their assumed names—Abraham and Lea Perecman—just a few feet from the gravestones of Zayde's father, Abram Gubersky, and his sisters, Frumke and Blumke. All of them reunited once more.

According to Jewish tradition, it is a blessing to help fill the grave of a loved one, and a mound of dirt sat beside the open hole in the earth, plunged with two shovels for that purpose. Each of us tossed some dirt onto the casket, and handed the shovel off. When Mom's turn came, she grabbed the shovel and tossed a heap of dirt onto the casket. And then another. And another. And another. Caring for her father in death as she had cared for him in life.

One by one, family members and friends kept walking past her, handing off the other shovel and giving someone else a chance to honor Zayde, while Mom kept at it, digging and tossing, digging and tossing, digging and tossing, until she started breaking a sweat in the crisp fall air. The assembled mourners started shooting her looks—just like that service years earlier when Mom had refused to sit down.

"Chayke, it's enough," her sisters began whispering loudly.

Mendel, seated a few chairs away from me, leaned over. "Go tell your mother to give the shovel to someone else," he said.

I walked up to my mom and took the shovel from her hands. She let go and leaned on me, weeping as we walked out of the cemetery.

From there, we headed back to Zayde's home at the end of the cul-de-sac. The house, always so sleepy on my visits, was now packed with mourners. Standing around talking with some of my cousins, I finally told them the truth about my identity. Zayde was no longer alive. Neither was Grandma. And Dad knew the truth. There was no longer any reason to hide it.

One of my cousins told his mother, Linda, about our conversation, apparently expressing in a way I had never managed to convey the heartache of what I'd experienced. My aunt came up to me as I was standing with Steph.

"I just wanted to apologize to you," she said. "I never saw things from your perspective."

"Thank you, Linda," I said, choking back tears. "That means a lot."

Mom saw the exchange. She couldn't hear what was being said, but she sensed it was about her.

"What was that about?" she asked when Linda walked away.

"Linda was apologizing for the way she'd acted toward me in recent years. For not appreciating how hard the whole situation with you was."

Mom bit her lip and nodded.

I sought out Mendel a little while later.

"I just want you to know," I said, "that I took it on the chin for years. For *years*," I repeated. I could feel myself getting worked up and restrained myself, remembering where I was. "Zayde knew nothing about what happened, and I was protecting Mom's relationship with him even as she was shitting on me."

He seemed surprised.

"I knew you would never say anything to him," he told me. "It never even occurred to me you *might* say something to him."

Such were the expectations of loyalty in our family.

Mom seemed different after Zayde's passing. She had called me up, shortly afterward, weeping uncontrollably. I just listened. "Did he know I loved him?" she asked through the tears. "Did he love me?" "Was I a good daughter?"

"Yes, of course," I said, trying to soothe her, even as I knew the only person whose answer mattered could no longer give it.

The tears, I could sense, were as much an act of grieving as a catharsis, a purging—like this book has been for me. I was too scarred, too exhausted by the past, to get my hopes up too much, to think any of the spells she'd battled all her life, all of the swings, had been banished for good.

And yet I did notice *something*. She seemed more at peace, like she'd been liberated somehow. From what? A portion of her own darkness? A burden of her own inheritance?

On a call with my dad a couple of months later, he asked if my mother had mentioned the email she'd sent him. "No," I replied, asking him to forward it. He'd be happy to, he said, if my mother didn't object. Even then, he was still willing to grant her that small courtesy.

The subject of the email was "a belated apology." "Dear Stephen," it began.

> I know this is very late in coming. But I wanted to apologize to you for being unfaithful during our marriage.
>
> Why now? I have no idea. It may be because I am now parentless and feel the need to really be an adult, which means taking responsibility for my actions. I will not try to make any excuses,

and I don't expect you to forgive me. I do want you to know how deeply I appreciate your kindness to me since my deceit was revealed.

You continue to be a wonderful father to Adam. He has always adored you and still does. But I'm sure you already know that.

Very sincerely,
Ellen

When Dad first told me about Mom's email, I'd gotten choked up. Her apology may have been almost forty years overdue, but sometimes the right thing to do is just the right thing to do—no matter when it happens. And I told her so.

"I thought you might feel that way," she replied. "I'm glad I sent it too."

She'd written the note, I could tell, as much for me as for Dad, knowing I felt she owed it to him. And she was right. I did feel she owed it to him. But that email was also a part of my own healing, a binding-up of a still-open wound, a making right of a wrong that had bent me up so painfully.

More than a decade earlier, I'd been thrust unwittingly onto this journey of self-discovery, deciding, after years of hiding from the truth, to confront it head-on in the hopes of quieting the upheaval inside. Now, finally, after all of the heartache, all of the wrestling, that quiet had begun to return. I'd begun to hear my own inner voice, clear and unmistakable, whispering to me once again.

Standing with Steph as we put our daughter to sleep in her crib one night, smiling as I thought about our son on the way, I felt something I'd never known before: the sense of stability, of peace, that comes with being part of a close, loving, intact family. *My* family.

I was now free in my own right, I thought. To be the kind of husband I wanted to be, the kind of father I wanted to be, the kind of person I wanted to be. I could now see the revelation and all of the chaos that had ensued as Rachel Yehuda had assured me I would one day see it—as the beginning of a new me.

I thought back to Zayde's funeral, as I sat in the first row, a few feet from the casket, Steph on my right, Mom on my left, clutching my hand. Sitting there, I couldn't help thinking that Zayde's loss was not only *my* loss, not only the Perecmans' loss, but also *our* loss, humanity's loss, the loss of yet another member of the generation that had waged, won, and survived history's bloodiest conflict.

Soon, I thought, they'll all be gone. I was saddened by the thought. And yet I also felt a sense of comfort, a certain strength, knowing that something of Bubbie and Zayde—and something of Grandma and Pa, too—would remain with me, knowing that something of that generation remains with all of us, inside us, a part of who we are.

They had not only passed on their scars and sorrow, I understood at last. They had also passed on their sense of hope—defiant and unbounded. They had not only passed on their trauma. They had also passed on something else. Resilience.

POSTSCRIPT

WHEN I FINISHED writing this book in early 2019, the only people on my Frankel side besides my Dad who knew about the revelation were a couple of Minow cousins. With Dad's permission, I'd told them, deferring to him on when—or even whether—to inform anyone else in his family, including his siblings Nancy and Tom.

I suspect Dad knew that at some point before this book came out, he'd need to tell his siblings, but he wasn't in any rush. It was only after a description of the book was about to be posted online that Dad decided it was time. It was best, he felt, that his siblings hear the truth directly from him rather than from some friend who'd stumbled across it on the internet.

Dad talked to his sister first and emailed me afterwards. "Spoke to Nancy yesterday," he wrote. "Went very well—some things came out of it to share with you."

I called him the next day on my way to pick up my daughter at preschool. "I had a good conversation with Nancy," he began, "and then the strangest thing happened." He told me Nancy had called him back a few hours after they'd spoken. The initial conversation had caught her off guard, she told him, but after she'd had some time to process it, a long-buried memory returned to her.

When I was about four or five—around the time of my parents' separation—Nancy had a conversation with Pa. He'd recently returned from one of our trips to Bermuda, and it was just the two of them talking. Nancy was asking why my parents were separating with a little child to raise, and Pa told her about the affair, information I never knew he possessed.

Then Pa said something that had stunned Nancy, only to recede in her consciousness over the ensuing three decades until Dad's call that day brought it back to the surface.

"You know," Pa told her, "it's *possible* Adam is not Steve's son."

I listened as Dad relayed Pa's words, scarcely believing what I was hearing. He'd not only suspected it? He'd vocalized it? Confided his suspicions to Dad's sister without ever saying anything about them to Dad himself?

"And you know what?" Pa continued. "It doesn't matter. He's my grandson. He's my other child. I adore every step he takes—and I always will."

As Dad repeated Pa's words—words so similar to the ones Dad himself had used when I told him my truth—I nearly lost my balance, putting my hand on a car to steady myself, as I sobbed on a Brooklyn street.

It was an answer to a question that had torn at me since that first conversation with my Mom more than a decade earlier, one I'd long ago accepted I'd never receive, a piece of healing I never imagined would be open to me.

The story immediately dispelled all of the concerns, all of the doubts, I'd had about how Pa would have acted if he'd known the truth. It immediately validated all of my experiences with him, all of the love he'd ever shown me. He—and, I now believe, Grandma, too—knew the truth all along, and loved me anyway.

Acknowledgments

WHEN I TOLD a friend what this book is about, she remarked, "This has clearly become more than a book—it really sounds like an emotional journey." She is right. And I'm deeply grateful to all the many, many people who helped on the book—and the journey.

To help find documentation of my grandparents' stories, I relied, most of all, on the US Holocaust Memorial Museum. Its archives are extraordinary, and so is its staff. I'm particularly grateful to Sara Bloomfield, Neal Guthrie, Steven Vitto, Vincent Slatt, and Martin Dean. I am also grateful to Lital Beer and everyone at Yad Vashem who helped shed light on my family's story.

Tal Goren not only connected me with Yad Vashem, but also helped track down the one true Abraham Peretzman in Israel. And my cousin Dovid Katz introduced me to the works of his father Menke and the rich world of Lithuanian Jewry.

Historian Edith Raim patiently answered my questions on Kaufering and generously reviewed a portion of the manuscript. So did Daniel Uziel, a scholar of the German aviation industry during World War II, who carefully reviewed several chapters and provided valuable feedback. Danuta Drywa at the Stutthof Museum responded to every question about my family's experience at the camp and reviewed portions of the book for accuracy. Dachau archivist Albert Knoll and historian Sabine Schalm helped me understand Zayde's experience at the camp. Rachel Yehuda and Yael Danieli were gracious with their time, helping me understand their research on intergenerational trauma and how to situate my own experience within it.

Others helped in different ways. Doris Kearns Goodwin and

the late Dick Goodwin, one of America's great speechwriters, gave me the idea of opening the book with Zayde in the present day, and shared their wisdom and insights on writing history. Family law expert Naomi Cahn of the George Washington University Law School opened my eyes to the ways my experience bore similarities to the experiences of some adoptees and donor-conceived children. Kevin Leonard, archivist at Northwestern, where Pa's papers are held, helped me understand my grandfather's student activism and public service. Jack Schlossberg helped research Pa's service in World War II. Ben Stark secured some hard-to-access papers and books on intergenerational trauma. Kristen Bartoloni and Alex Platkin helped fact-check the book.

Needless to say, any errors are mine alone.

My agents David McCormick and Pilar Queen, who is also one of my oldest friends, believed in this project, in its various forms, from the beginning. I feel incredibly fortunate to have had Jonathan Jao as my editor. Jonathan has been a patient, thoughtful partner, helping tease out the story I had inside me and needed to tell. Without his careful editing and support, this book never would have been written. I am also grateful to Tim Duggan for acquiring the book in the first place.

Considering the intensely personal subject of these pages, I also want to thank Pilar and the other friends who have supported me— from the time I learned my secret up to the present day: Drew Warshaw, who has always been there to talk or listen; Charlotte Warshaw; Andrew Bellas; Brian DeLeeuw; Sarah Shepard; and Dana Warren. Brian, a gifted writer and editor, reviewed an early draft of the manuscript, and his insights helped shape the way the book evolved.

I also want to thank Fran Schwartz. Without her wisdom and guidance, neither this book, nor my healing, would have been possible.

From the beginning, my mother and father have been wary about this book for different and entirely understandable reasons.

At no point, however, has either of them asked me *not* to publish it. Their reservations have never vanished, but each of them has come to understand this book's importance to my healing. And they have supported me.

For that, and many other things, they have my gratitude and admiration. I particularly admire my dad's candor in sharing uncomfortable personal details about his life, and my mom's courage in speaking so openly about certain aspects of her past, including her depression and mental health. I hope that sharing her story will help, in some small way, dispel the stigma that has done her, and so many others, so much harm. My mother and my stepmother, Helen, also translated many of the Yiddish, German, and Russian documents that illuminate so much of our family's story. I'm also grateful to Helen for the love and support she has always shown my dad. In addition, I want to thank my entire Frankel and Minow family; as well as Steph's mother, Eileen Medvey, and family; and Pearl Wexler and some of my Perecman cousins for the support they've shown since my secret was disclosed. I am particularly grateful to my cousin Nell Minow and sister-in-law Jen Psaki, who reviewed a draft of the book and provided invaluable feedback.

Above all, I want to thank my wife. Throughout this ordeal, Steph has been my rock. She urged me to confront my secret head-on and patiently supported me through all the turbulence that ensued, even as it created disruption and difficulty in her life and our life together. As I began writing about everything, she never wavered in her support of me or the project, even when I was not as present, emotionally or physically, as I should have been. "Do you want to read what I've written about you and us?" I'd occasionally ask. "Sure, but I'm not going to veto anything," she'd always say. "You need to write your truth as honestly as you can." I have continually been awed by the strength of her character and am certain I would not have had the courage to grapple with everything, much less write about it, without her.

About the Author

ADAM P. FRANKEL is an advisor to Emerson Collective, a social change organization. He was a senior speechwriter for President Barack Obama from the 2008 presidential campaign through Obama's first term in the White House. Frankel is a graduate of Princeton University and the London School of Economics, where he was a Fulbright Scholar. He lives in New York City with his wife and two children.